THE PRACTICAL
GARDEN OF EDEN

*Beautiful Landscaping with
Fruits and Vegetables*

THE PRACTICAL
GARDEN
OF
EDEN

Beautiful Landscaping with Fruits and Vegetables

FRED HAGY

Illustrated by Clare McCanna

The Overlook Press
Woodstock, New York

This book is dedicated to the plant scientists whose efforts have made this landscaping concept possible for the average homeowner—especially to Elwyn Meader for his lifetime of contributions.

First published in 1990 by

The Overlook Press
Lewis Hollow Road
Woodstock, New York 12498

Library of Congress Cataloging-in-Publication Data

Hagy, Fred.
The Practical Garden of Eden

Bibliography: p.
Includes index.
I. Landscape gardening.   2. Fruit-culture.   3. Fruit. 4. Nuts.
5. Food crops.   I. Title.
SB473.H27   635   87-7623

ISBN 0-87951-208-3

Printed in Hong Kong by South China Printing Company

Designed by Suzanne Haldane

Contents

THE PRACTICAL
GARDEN OF EDEN

Beautiful Landscaping with
Fruits and Vegetables

Introduction

*T*here is nothing new about landscaping with food-producing plants. If we take the long view historically, the food producing plants were never separated from the purely ornamental ones until Renaissance times. The "dooryard garden" was a common feature during the Colonial era. Thomas Jefferson's Monticello is a beautiful example of the concept on a larger scale. During the nineteenth century many landscape architects fostered the idea. Probably the most prominent among them was Andrew Jackson Downing, who practiced in the Hudson Valley. However, major new landscape design currents during the nineteenth century were created by changes in home architecture. The Victorian style was becoming popular, and one of its characteristics was a raised floor level, leaving a large exposed foundation wall for the landscaper to screen from view with masses of shrubs. New fine-textured lawn grass varieties were developed to replace the coarse-textured meadow grasses of earlier times. With the advent of mechanical mowing, as well as the new grass varieties, came the ability to stretch a green carpet from the front door to the street to provide more "foreground." Landscaping was thought of in terms of providing an appropriate setting for these grand homes. Behind the houses there were semiformal or formal gardens affording the family privacy. Even now it is the predominant style of residential landscape in the United States. With this book I'd like to change this tradition of landscape design.

The average European, seeing so many homes set in their pretty landscape of willows, evergreens, and petunias, might be surprised that people willing to make the tremendous financial commitment that home ownership involves would expect so little from their lots. Europeans not only use their own land more practically but collect every useful scrap to be found along the railways and highways. Like homeowners in Europe and many other parts of the world, Americans need to be more aware that we cannot continue to waste our resources indefinitely—neither personal nor national. But we are accustomed to thinking that in America there will always be more—more good soil, good water, good weather. And what about those farm surpluses that are reported year after year? The farm gluts and giveaways that we hear about in the media do exist—in grain and dairy farming. The situation with the foods we would be likely to grow as a part of a home landscape, fruits, vegetables, nuts, and so on, is quite different. Every year we lose three million acres of farmland to erosion, and another three million to development. We have toxified the soils of thousands of acres of prime California production areas with runoff from desert irrigation projects. Already short of water, we buy billions of gallons a day from Canada. In some cases we could sink deeper and deeper wells and lower the water table even more, but that's not economically feasible given today's price structure for food. The truth is that our domestic farming system is in serious trouble. Our production curve for produce is flat and our population curve rising. More and more, we import cheaply produced fruits and vegetables from Third World countries. In some situations it makes sense, particularly in regard to South America, where the seasons are reversed and mesh nicely with our harvest schedules. But it also means that fruit and vegetable prices are held hostage to the cost of oil and to the political stability of countries not known for political stability. This dependence in turn weakens our own agricultural system. No matter how you look at it, the days of cheap food are nearly over. So, there are some very practical reasons for creating what's coming to be known as an edible landscape.

On the brighter side, there are other good reasons for landscaping with food-producing plants. We Americans tend to be extremely visually oriented and prefer to buy the vegetable and fruit varieties that look the nicest and stay looking the nicest longest. The farmers, who have always been economically squeezed, must plant varieties that give the most production in the least amount of acreage and that hold up well in the picking, storing, and shipping process. To enhance these qualities the product must be picked before it's really ripe. The end result is that out of the literally thousands of fruit, nut, and vegetable varieties available, we find only the few dozen on our market shelves that best meet the above needs. Every backyard gardener knows the difference between store-bought and tree- and vine-ripened produce. What I am interested in personally is flavor, nutritional value, and the absence of pesticide residues.

Many Americans are already involved in edible landscaping. One has only to look at the covers of *Organic Gardening* to see the trend. But that particular emphasis and the one I propose in this book are a little different. Here, we will be more concerned with the permanent plantings that compose the edible landscape—the shrubs, trees and vines.

One of the first things a young landscape architect in training is taught is that the objective of landscaping is "maximum beauty, maximum utility." By maximum beauty my teachers meant not only choosing beautiful plants and arranging them as attractively as possible, but ensuring that the landscape would remain attractive for as long as possible with the seasonal changes. From a landscape architect's point of view, then, a landscape based heavily on plants that die back to the ground each year is a one-season landscape whether they come up again the next year or not. By "maximum utility" my teachers meant using the space available as efficiently as possible and arranging the different areas in the most logical way. Edibility just wasn't considered important. The flowering shrubs, trees, and ground covers in the world of horticulture were not the same as the fruits, nuts, berries, and so on in the world of agriculture. This insistence on separating the two areas is one of the reasons why edible landscaping is not more popular today. The very people who could promote an alternative style are not familiar with the pallette of materials available. The division is so severe that I had to go to agriculture experiment stations and botanic gardens myself to observe some of these plants in order to complete the information the reader will find later in this book.

Another reason for the lack of popularity of edible landscaping is that an adequate range of plant varieties suitable for home use has not been available. They're available now, but the average landscape nursery doesn't stock them. Over the years, plant scientists have been developing the bush fruits, and the semidwarf and dwarf tree fruits that are so useful in the residential landscape.

They have also greatly extended the climatic ranges, improved the disease resistances, and in some cases, extended the harvest period. The scientists who made these contributions did so out of love for amateur home gardening while working in a field dominated by commercial interests. Ironically, it's just those commercial interests that have accounted for the recent explosion in plants useful for the home landscape. This has come about because the yield is higher per acre with the new semidwarf, dwarf, and bush fruits, making them more commercially viable than the ''standard'' or original size plants.

The reader will find many useful features in this guide to landscaping with food plants. There is a step-by-step process to follow in order to create a beautiful landscape. Accompanying that process is direction on a simple but accurate drawing technique that will enable anyone to translate their ideas into a personally designed landscape.

Another contribution this book will make is the guidance it gives the reader on coping with nursery catalogs. These catalogs often contain a wealth of valuable information, but they are also sales tools. The information provided here will help the reader make an independent judgment.

Hardiness—how much cold a given plant can take—is a major issue with food-producing plants. Hardiness maps have been developed over the years that break down the country into zones of relative coldness. The plants are rated according to which zones they can survive in. Yet when it comes to books or nursery catalogs the maps tend to be so small or drawn so inaccurately that many people cannot be sure which zone they live in. In this book, the reader is provided with full-size double-page maps that include many reference points to aid in locating themselves in a zone.

The reader should find the plant information sheets extremely useful. Identical to sheets used in horticulture, they provide all the information needed for the homeowner to make solid design decisions. The reader will also be able to comfortably mix horticulture and agricultural plants because the terminology and format of the information is the same as found in horticulture reference books. There is also a set of appendices that contain any information needed to make important decisions.

A weakness of much literature on the food plants is the relative sparseness of listed varieties in books for general readers. The home owner might choose, say, a semidwarf apple for its place and shape in the garden, but the ultimate success of the garden will depend on how well the chosen variety performs. There are many factors that affect this and an adequate breadth of choice must be offered. In addition, those knowledgeable about the varieties often bring a commercial bias with them when they advise the homeowner. The book addresses this issue in a realistic way.

After the discussions on the design process and the selection of plants, the book takes the reader through the installation and maintenance of the garden. Here again I think it has something special to offer. It seems to me that whenever the subject of pest and disease control comes up, whoever is speaking has an axe to grind. I have given the reader of this book an opportunity to pick from among different philosophies and methods, choosing those that best reflect their own needs and interests.

The process involved in producing a beautiful personal landscape is simple. This book is only a beginning.

1
Making a
Beginning

*S*ome homeowners feel overwhelmed at the thought of designing their own landscape. They can't see how they'll be able to put together all the things they want and need and still make it attractive. Add to that the differing plant needs—and in our case the pollination requirements of the food plants— and it seems even more confusing.

Actually, it's easy with a method landscape architects use: they break the job down into parts that are understandable, deal with these one at a time, then finally fit the pieces together to form the whole design. So the first few sections are a step-by-step "how to" for an edible landscape. If you intend to use this book as a tool to develop your own property, you're probably better off reading the first five steps through first. After the overview go back to the beginning again and follow the step-by-step procedure.

The design process can be broken down into seven steps. Each one is an important concept by itself, even though some take only a few words to describe and others the better part of a chapter. These steps are: (1) collecting pictures and ideas; (2) becoming knowledgeable

about your lot; (3) deciding what you need; (4) establishing priorities and use area relationships; (5) developing the plan; (6) taking the practical and well-ordered and making it beautiful; and (7) choosing the individual plants. Notice that choosing the individual plants came last. This is the essential difference between a designer and a collector.

Each of these steps will be discussed with enough detail to enable you to produce a landscape that's both practical and truly beautiful —and to produce it solely with the material presented here.

Step 1
Collecting Pictures and Ideas

The beginning of any design process is a mental pumping up. The best way to do this is to make a collection of favorite pictures from landscape-oriented magazines and books. Don't be concerned if the books and magazines you look at have no food-bearing plants in the pictures; there's enough variety now available among the food bearers that a plant of similar size and shape can be found in Chapter 5. *House and Garden* and *Garden Design* are good magazine sources, as are *Western Living* and *Southern Living*. *Better Homes and Gardens* and others often do a special landscaping issue in the spring. The Ortho Chemical Company and Lane Publishing (the *Sunset* magazine group) both produce a series of excellent 8½ x 11 trade paperbacks.

Another exercise might include visits to public and good private gardens and taking pictures of appealing subjects. Public gardens are more conscious of edible landscaping today and many have demonstration gardens. One of the most attractive can be found at Longwood Gardens near Philadelphia.

You'll find that once your picture collection is together, you can see a thread of similarity running through it; a consistent character, naturally with a few oddballs thrown in. Having this personal vision in your mind is what will enable you to take fuzzy ideas and turn them into a consistent project that's you. The pictures will also be invaluable if you need the assistance of a carpenter or mason when you're building your garden. You'll be able to show them exactly what you want if you need some construction help beyond your own abilities.

Step 2
Becoming Knowledgeable About Your Lot

Most homeowners feel they *are* knowledgeable about their lot, at least until the landscape contractor's truck disappears into the septic tank. Professional landscape designers begin a project by trying to fully understand the "problem" before they think about the solution to the "problem." So in Step 2 you'll compile information about existing features, features that are man-made, like the driveway and walks, and those that are truly natural, like drainage, soil type, and existing trees and shrubs. The features will need to be located on a drawing, one that's an accurate scale representation of the lot. For the sake of economy of effort that drawing will become the base sheet for the design. Inaccuracies in measuring the lot or getting those measurements on paper could mean the nice parking spot you designed will land in your neighbor's yard, or that you'll have a horseshoe court only big enough for a six-year-old to enjoy.

Your drawing will be much easier to do than those of professional designers; they have to look like pros and produce nice drafting. You'll start your project by getting some cheap

Too far left: you can see the side wall

Too far right

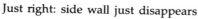

Just right: side wall just disappears

yellow tracing paper to use for overlays, and some graph paper. Get the kind that has ten blocks per inch and is 17" x 22" (C size.) Get a larger size paper if your lot is bigger than 150' x 200'; but stick to the ten blocks per inch.

First, measure your lot. Take a couple of 100' or 200' measuring tapes and drive a stake at any corner of the house. Put a nail in to hook your tape on. Then, back off and sight down the building wall, moving back and forth until the side wall just disappears from your eye-view. Only then will the tape line be the accurate extension of the building wall you need for measuring. Stretch the tape out as far as you can. If you run out of tape before you run out of lot, drive another stake and continue. This is called establishing a base line and it has to be done well; later measurements depend on it and you'll use it to locate your house on the lot.

When you're ready to record your measurements on the graph paper, let one foot in reality be represented by one small block on the graph paper. That will give you a scale drawing where 1" on the paper represents 10' on the lot. Locate the street in front of your house along the bottom of the graph paper. It will make the drawing more understandable. A full set of base lines would look like this:

You will be able to measure off of those base lines to locate accurately anything of importance to you on the lot by kneeling or standing squarely facing the base line tape and measuring with the other tape at a right angle to it. If your eye is not so great use a roofer's square. These lines are called offset lines.

What you should end up with is a series of right angles and distances that enable you to locate everything on your lot with surprising accuracy.

Once that's finished you're ready to go more deeply into the qualities of your lot. For an edible landscape, one of the more important considerations is sunlight. Most of the plants will need a minimum of six hours direct sunlight a day. More is better, but don't worry about it; you're not a commercial operation and you don't have to maximize production. Go out on your lot and look carefully at where you have sun and shadow throughout each part of the day. The sun's position changes considerably during the procession of the growing season, so to come up with a good design you need a method of reasonably predicting where it will be over a much longer period of time. The technique used is drawing a "sun diagram" directly on the house. Use a

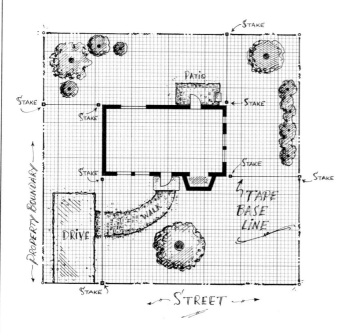

Offset Line Sighting   The zero end of the tape base line is at the corner of the house. Sight along the second tape to the existing landscape feature—in this case, an existing tree. Move back and forth along the tape base line until you have a right angle. Then record the distance from the house corner and the offset distance to the landscape feature in your notes.

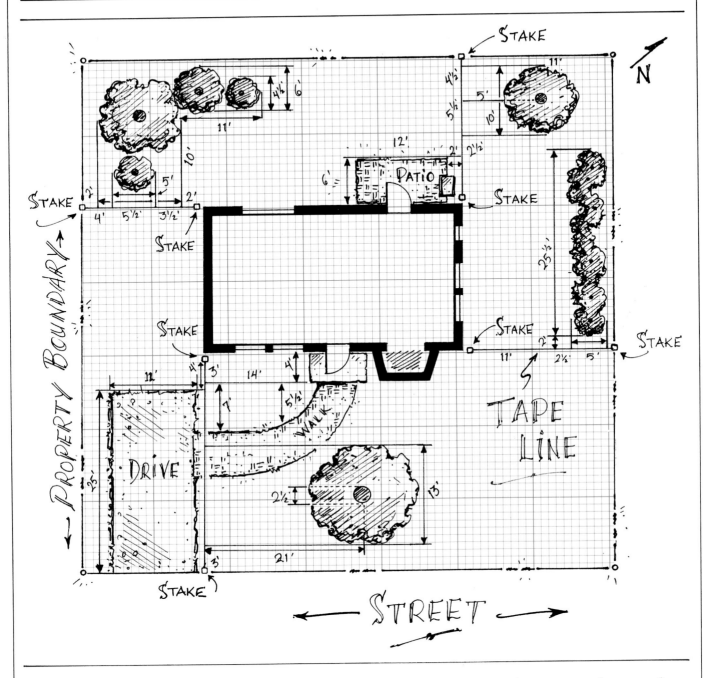

piece of the tracing paper to cover your graph paper base sheet. Take a compass out on your lot and locate north. Then draw a north/ south line across the center of your house about 4" long. Next do an east/west line. You have made a compass rose. Next draw a line from the center of the compass rose toward the margin a bit less than 1/3 of the way from east toward north. This will give you the approximate sunrise for the longest day in summer. Do the same on the west for the summer sunset. Repeat the procedure for the

winter. The angle is the same, only toward the south. It should look something like this when you're through:

On the first day of spring and fall, the sun rises due east and sets due west. The sun is much higher in the sky in summer than in winter; almost straight up at noon in the summer, and only a little more than halfway up at midday early and late in the season.

Look at the sun diagram and imagine the sun's rise and set throughout the seasons. Then go back to your lot and imagine how the shadows will evolve and change throughout the season.

With the sun diagram completed go back to the overlay sheet and plot any wet areas you have. Standing water is a problem for most plants and it's a particularly serious one for most food plants. A ''wet area'' is defined as any area that takes more than six days to dry out after a heavy spring rain. Next, plot the drainage patterns. Watch which way the water flows just after a rain; then put arrows on the plan that show which way the water runs off. In Appendix E you'll find some ways to solve wetness problems if they're unavoidable. They'll all cost money, so if you can eventually come up with a plan that meets all your needs *and* avoids wet areas, it will be more economical.

Next in your lot study, notice such attractive landscape features as nice shade trees, handsome landforms, rocks, good views. These don't necessarily have to be *on* your lot, just visually connected to it. Be sure to include your *potential* good views as well. Look at what might be attractive if something in the way was removed. Then be sure to mark the *bad* views: you'll want to get rid of them. Note noise or air pollution sources and the breezes that might carry them in. In the Northeast, for example, the winter winds generally come from the

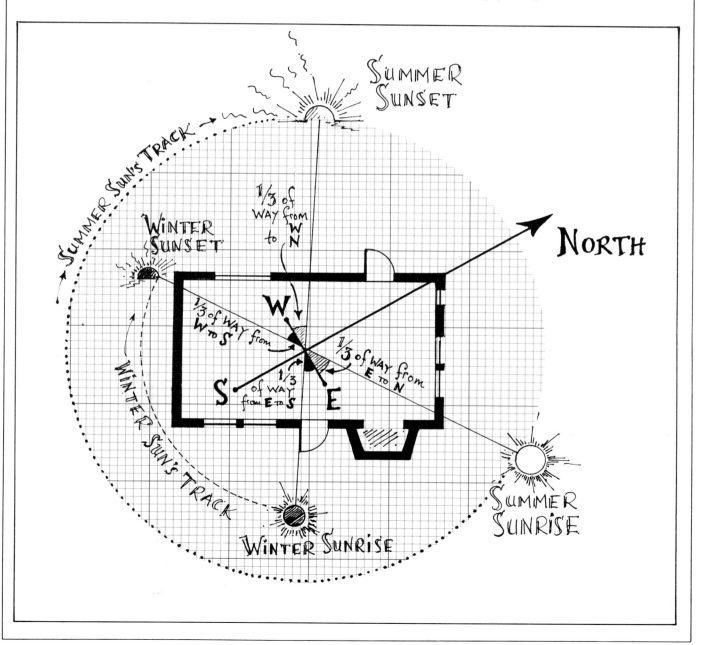

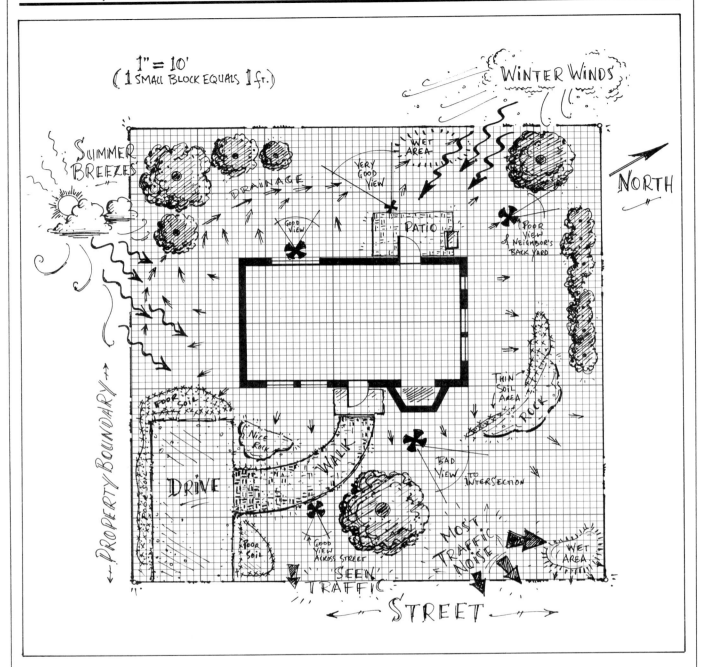

1" = 10'
(1 small block equals 1 ft.)

WINTER WINDS

SUMMER BREEZES

NORTH

DRAINAGE

VERY GOOD VIEW

WET AREA

GOOD VIEW

PATIO

POOR VIEW OF NEIGHBOR'S BACK YARD

PROPERTY BOUNDARY

POOR SOIL

NICE ROCK

WALK

THIN SOIL AREA

ROCK

BAD VIEW TO INTERSECTION

DRIVE

POOR SOIL

GOOD VIEW ACROSS STREET

MOST TRAFFIC NOISE

WET AREA

SEEN TRAFFIC

STREET

Northwest, and the howling storms from the northeast. You may want some protection from these for some of the plants. During a northeast summer the breezes are variable, southwest to southeast—a blessing on hot days and in some situations not to be blocked. Find out where these winds come from in your area and plot them on your overlay.

Last, become familiar with your soils. Almost every area has a county agent who can help you for free, or who can steer you to another agency that will do the same. Most counties have mapped all the soils in their jurisdiction.

These maps have a description of the soil and how it behaves with respect to drainage, fertility, and more. They'll also tell you about the sizes of the particles that make up the soil. This is an important issue to plants as some have preferences. If the soils have mostly fine particles they are called clayey or tight soils and are inclined to drain slowly and poorly and have limited air space. A good soil is one-quarter air. If the particles are mostly large, the soils are called sandy, open, or coarse soils. These are generally good for food plants except for the fact that water drains too well, sometimes taking with it basic materials the plant needs to make food. The middle ground is called a loamy soil, or silt loam if it leans toward the fine particles.

There's a simple test you can do yourself for determining soil type. After a rain, but not while the soil is soaked, dig up a ball of soil the size of a Ping-Pong ball and squeeze it in the palm of your hand. If you can see your hand print in the ball it's a clay soil; if it won't make up into a ball it's a sandy soil. The rest fall somewhere in the middle.

One last issue with soils is their fertility—how much decayed plant material they have. Dig a hole and observe how far down the soil looks dark. You'll find there seems to be a fairly well-defined band of darker soil on top of a lighter one. That darker band is the topsoil. If there are areas on your property with little or none of it, the extent of these should be marked on your tracing paper overlay.

The process of understanding the lot that you have just finished is what designers call a site analysis. It forms a strong base from which to begin the design. The scale drawing is necessary to form the structure for placing your needs on the lot. Before that can be done, of course, you'll need to figure out just what they are.

Step 3
Deciding What You Need

In planning a home landscape, absolute necessities are usually easier to figure out than those features that may be merely useful or desirable. In both cases, however, it is not soul searching or technical knowledge that's required, just a complete checklist; it is usually impossible to be aware of all the possibilities without one.

The following list is one the author has used in his business and found to be successful. It's thirty-five items long and might best be skimmed over at first reading. When the time comes to use the list in your own project, sit down with everyone involved and make thorough notes. Handling it that way gives you the most value for your time and effort.

If you make a strong beginning with the picture collection, site inventory, and needs analysis you'll find the project flows freely from then on. All the common blockages to the flow of creative juices will be gone.

NEEDS CHECKLIST

1. Make sure visitors can see and get to the door you want them to enter. If they can't, do something with the design to focus attention on that spot.

2. If you're starting with an existing property, make sure the front walk is wide enough for two people to walk side by side, at least 4½ feet.

3. Make sure you have what *you* feel is enough off-street parking. Put it where it's convenient without cutting down on your ability to provide an attractive setting or foreground for your house.

4. Look at what kind of outdoor entertaining you do. Be aware of how many people you feel should be comfortably accommodated for both lounging and dining. You'll need to know later when you size things.

5. If you like to barbecue or grill outdoors, the facilities shouldn't be too far from the kitchen unless you are deliberately seeking a ''picnic'' feeling. In that case, place the grill as far from the house as possible and surround it with greenery. Consider whether you would enjoy a portable grill or a permanent barbecue. If at all possible, include some storage or work surface. Don't reject the idea of adding another door or sliding doors to your house if it makes a good connection between indoor and outdoor eating and living. It's often a less expensive job than people realize.

6. Examine the ways and places you use electricity outside. Locate additional outlets if necessary.

7. Provide outside lighting for the front walk and front door. You can also create a beautiful landscape feature with lighting: use bullet lights mounted on spears. They will give you location and light level flexibility to get just the look you want because you can move them around even after the outlets are in place and you can experiment with different wattage and color bulbs. (Get two or three price estimates for outdoor wiring and have work done before major planting.)

8. Think about irrigation; even if it's not absolutely necessary you might want it for convenience. (Get two or three price estimates and have work done before shrubs are in and the lawn seeded.)

9. If you like to be outside in all kinds of weather, consider overhead protection against both sun and rain. Sometimes big umbrellas are sufficient.

10. Locate a specific play area for young children. An activity site outside should bear the same relationship to the patio that the family room bears to the inside living room. It should be visible from the kitchen.

11. If you expect to keep the house for awhile, plan play areas and equipment for the children as they get older.

12. Don't forget play areas for adults, too. There are plenty of inexpensive good games around like horseshoes, volleyball, and badminton. (Size requirements are in a later table.)

13. If you want a swimming pool now or later, it will be a major element in your design. If it's to be above ground, screen it with plantings or fencing or both. Consider safety: many jurisdictions require a fence. Put the equipment (filter/pump) where it's least intrusive—pool contractors often don't. A changing room or toilet is a convenience but really runs the cost up. If you're not planning on a pool until later, design in such a way that plantings that go in now will not be destroyed by the heavy equipment needed for installation. Be sure to consider access to the worksite for that equipment.

14. Examine carefully how much maintenance time you are willing to spend or pay for. The food plants that remain above ground all year (trees, shrubs, and so on) will require modest amounts, but reward you accordingly. Vegetable areas along with perennials and annuals will require more time, although some perennials require much less maintenance than others.

15. If you are a flower gardener you'll find many flowers are edible. Herbs can be beautifully integrated into the landscape and some vegetables as well, especially if you consider growing in containers. Think about a separate small service garden close to the kitchen area; they can be very attractive.

16. If you plan a compost pile, check out wind direction and place it downwind.

17. Do you want a greenhouse? If so, a location facing south should be reserved, particularly in northern climates.

18. Plan for adequate storage space for such outside items as garden equipment, mowers, hoses, outdoor furniture during the winter, garbage cans, trailers, boats, and campers. Provide a dry, secure, locked place for such garden supplies as fertilizers and insecticides.

19. If you dry your laundry outdoors you will want to keep it out of plain view.

20. Remember that pets can be destructive to the landscape, especially dogs on chains. Provide them with their own area.

21. Don't be shy about providing plenty of privacy. If you plan to put up tall property line fences, tell your neighbors beforehand; it's a courtesy you'll thank yourself for later.

22. Do you want a quiet space to read or just be alone with your thoughts? It can be anything from a sunny/shady corner to a private courtyard—perhaps off the master bedroom.

23. If you have a hilly lot with slopes steeper than 3 to 1 (3 feet horizontal distance for each vertical rise of 1 foot), think about a shrub mass or ground cover. Slopes more than 3:1 can be dangerous to mow.

24. Where there are steep spots that might need a retaining wall, study them to see if regrading is possible. It can usually be done in situations as steep as 2 feet horizontal distance for 1 foot of vertical rise. Beyond 2:1 you'll have to have a retaining wall. The expense of retaining walls can encourage a lot of study. Railroad ties or "landscape timbers" are the cheapest. Hide them with plantings if they're not in character with your house and landscape design.

25. Don't plant shrubs that will interfere with your line of sight when pulling out of the driveway.

26. If you live in a snow area, consider where the snow must be pushed when plowing the driveway.

27. Locate all the utilities: gas, water, electric, phone and cable. If the electric lines are buried, the power company will locate them for you. When you're digging near buried lines, be careful. If they're overhead, and you plant something large underneath, you can be sure either the phone or power company will eventually cut them.

28. Find out if you have an individual septic system on your lot or if you're hooked into the city sewer. Locate your septic tank and drainfield. It's amazing to see what happens when a contractor drives over and smashes either the tank or tile lines.

29. If winter winds are severe on your lot, you should plant a windscreen on the winterward side of the house, somewhere between the house and lot line. The best natural windscreens are 25' thick and evergreen. Most commonly they include both trees and shrubs and are effective downwind for ten times the height of the planting. They also help to block drifting snow.

30. If your summers are mostly still and hot, find the breezes you do have around the lot and locate the outdoor living space where the breezes are. If the breeze comes from a direction that requires screening for privacy, think about a fence design that lets the air through. You can also funnel what breeze you have to outside living areas with plantings or fencing.

31. Deciduous shade trees (i.e., those that shed their leaves in winter) are nature's air conditioners. They provide shade in summer and allow the sun to filter through in the winter. Look for a spot to the south or west that could accommodate one.

32. If car headlights, street lights, or sun glare affect the enjoyment of your lot, block the light source with a natural screen.

33. Buildings, especially masonry ones, and all pavings absorb a lot of heat in summer. Place a natural screen between them and the sun, or between you and the surfaces; it can reduce the temperature between five and ten degrees.

34. If you live in a city or industrial area, you may be subject to air and noise pollution. This can be controlled by a dense planting of deciduous and evergreen materials 25' thick and full to the ground. Use all evergreen material if you need good control in winter; deciduous material cannot help without its leaves. In fairness, it must be said that plants alone (even in a 25' to 50' thick mass) cannot eliminate all pollution; but they certainly can make a substantial difference.

35. Screen out constant motion, as with a lot of traffic or the activity in a business yard or parking lot.

If you have gone through the checklist item by item you now understand why even professional designers don't work without one. It is very comforting to know that all the bases are covered and you're ready to begin the most enjoyable part of the project.

Make your own list from the preceding one. Include both the things you know you *will* do and the ones you *might* consider as you work. Put this list next to your site analysis and you will be ready to begin the next step.

2

Putting the Plan Together

*T*he project can go forward now that you know the kinds of things that could be done with the landscape in terms of uses and the problems that need to be solved. The next step is taking those use areas and establishing logical relationships among them. To do that you must know how much space the various uses take. Once you know how much space an activity takes up, you have to be able to sketch it in scale on the lot drawing. In that way you can determine what will fit and how.

Step 4
Establishing Use Area Relationships and Priorities

There are standard sizes for just about everything you might want to do in the landscape. A second checklist follows. When priorities are spoken of at this point in the process, it is really more in the sense of what will fit rather than budget considerations. Budget considerations in landscaping, particularly in

do-it-yourself landscaping, are often more a question of how much of an instant landscape you want (that is, how big will the plants be in the first place). Particularly where there's little or no construction involved, the same plan might cost double or quadruple, depending on the size of plants chosen.

Where game sizes are given, they are the official sizes established by the regulating body of the sport involved. These sizes should not be respected as gospel for home use. They are often squeezed down in size within reason rather than forcing a choice between having the activity or not.

Stay flexible at this point. For example, you wouldn't know at this point in the process whether a seating spot for 6 should be 10' x 14' (rectangular table) or 11' in diameter (round table). You will probably come back to the list again later for sizing the smaller details like walk paths in the beds so you can harvest the fruits of your edible ornamental plants.

STANDARD SIZES

Site Features	Size
Front walk width	4½' minimum
Parking space (per car)	9' x 18' minimum
Driveway width	12' minimum
Automobile turning radius	15'–17'
Pedestrian turning radius	5' minimum
Garden path width	3' minimum
Work path within wide beds for edible planting	1' square or round stepping stones best
Planting bed width for food-bearing plants (without central path, access from one side only)	3' maximum
Planting bed width for food-bearing plants (access from both sides)	6' minimum
Standard shrub bed	3' minimum, any maximum
Espalier/trellis bed	2' minimum
Vegetable garden	100 square feet per family member*
Patio/deck	12' x 15' minimum or 45 square feet per person (count family members plus number of people usually entertained)
Patio/deck bench or sitting rail	2' minimum length per person
Formal outdoor dining area (including table and "pushback" space for chairs)	
For 2 persons	5' x 10' average
For 4 persons	10' x 10' average
For 6 persons (rectangular table)	14' x 10' average
For 6 persons (circular table)	11' diameter
Chaise longue or chair with footstool	2' x 6'
Individual chairs	2½' x 2½'
Outdoor steps (no minimum or maximum, sized by formula)	2R + T = 26" (Twice the riser height plus the tread width equals 26")

*Rough average. Does not consider low-space efficiency crops like corn.

Game Courts*	Size
(Sizes are actual court size and include 'walk around' space where needed)	
Basketball ½ court	42'L x 50' W 10' rim height
Badminton	20' x 44' 5' net height
Volleyball	50' x 60' minimum 6' behind each back line 7'6" net height
Tennis	36' x 78' minimum 21' behind each back line, minimum 12' at sides, 3' net height
Deck (platform) tennis	20' x 44' minimum 4' behind each back line, minimum 2' at sides, 4'6" net height
Tetherball	10' diameter
Horseshoes	10' x 50' Poles 40' apart (men's) 6' x 6' pitcher's box
Quoits	25' x 80' Poles 54' apart
Boccie (Bowls)	18' + − x 62' + − wooden surround
British croquet	84' x 105'
Croquet	40' + − x 75' + −
Ping-Pong	5' x 9' 4' side clearance; 7' rear clearance
Archery	20' x 60' - 100 yards 60' minimum clearance behind target
Shuffleboard	6' x 52'
Swimming pools	According to budget; but 14' x 32' considered minimum for serious swimming. 3' minimum walkaround 3' minimum behind diving board
Pump and filter space (for pool)	6' x 6' minimum
Changing/shower room (for pool)	6' x 8' minimum
Changing only	3' x 3½' minimum (4' x 4' better)
Children's swing	Twice the chain length plus 21'

*For complete layout and exact dimensions of these and more games, see *Architectural Graphic Standards* Ramsey, Sleeper et al. (New York: John Wiley & Sons, 1970)

Once the items on your own checklist are sized, they can be drawn to scale on the base sheet. Now take your graph paper base sheet, overlay it with the site analysis, and put a fresh piece of tracing paper on top. Begin to lay out the various features of your project. Start by cutting out undefined shapes of paper the size of each of the various features you want in your design. Size the features by counting blocks on the graph paper; one small block equals a foot in reality. Slide these shapes around on the tracing paper to get a sense of where you will want them to be on your landscape. It's important to be loose at this stage. Most professional designers are extremely careful to make nondescript shapes for their areas and features at this stage of development. Working with pencil and paper rather than directly on the land has its drawbacks as well as its advantages. For example, if you make a rectangular shape for a patio, every time you look at the paper the subtle message will be "make it a rectangle" even though in actuality an oval might make more sense.

Keep sliding your sized loose shapes around on the tracing paper overlay until the arrangement makes sense to you. You'll want an "outdoor living room" to relate to the one indoors. How close the "active" recreation area is to the patio/terrace/deck is a matter of lifestyle and personal preference, but don't get it too close. If space is limited, at least think about partial walls between spaces that are used for different purposes like the wall between a living room and a family room. Make long, lineal, amorphous shapes for circulation spaces and appropriate ones for parking and trash cans.

While you're sliding the shapes around, keep looking at the site analysis underneath so you can reconcile your areas with it.

Arrange things in such a way that while you're establishing good functional relationships you're also finding sun for the food plants. Draw in a big dash-outlined zone for the sunny area of your lot. Avoid placing plant masses in wet or thin-soiled areas. Think about how to accentuate the positive and eliminate the negative views, particularly as you locate your shade trees. Remember to study the shadow locations and to make sure you use the trees sparingly on your plan. Too many can make a planting look crowded in a hurry. You'll need two trees to frame the house the way a picture frame contains a painting; may-

be one or two toward the south or southwest for cooling shade in summer for the outdoor living room or the house itself. That's all you need except for a mass of evergreen winter wind protection.

This process forms a very solid base for the design because it blends together the influences and specific advantages of your site with your personal requirements while also dealing with your site's disadvantages. Once you are satisfied with your arrangement, trace off the shapes onto the tracing paper overlay; it's called a use relationship schematic drawing. When finished it should look something like this:

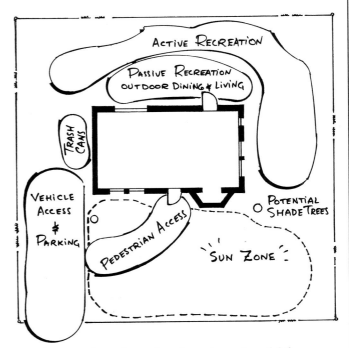

Remember that the drawing should have a dashed-in zone for the sunny areas of the lot. The importance and influence of this cannot be overstated when you're dealing with an edible landscape, since so many of the prospective plants need sun.

Step 5
Developing the Plan

The development of the plan from this point depends on more depth of knowledge about the implications of the sun zones, as we call these sunny areas on the lot. As you go through this next step, you'll find that the suggestions are not a fanatical approach to edible landscaping, but a practical one. Exclusively food-bearing plants are located in the sunnier areas only, and a mix of edible with standard landscaping in the shadier areas. There's much less choice available among the shade-tolerant food plants.

If you got a chance to see how the sun fell on everybody's lots you'd find the situations could be categorized into three basic patterns: where the bulk of the sunny spots are in the front yard; where they are in the rear yard; and where they are to one side or the other.

This is an oversimplification, of course, but it is useful to study the basic situations. Many homeowners will have combinations of the patterns. The sunnier areas that occur outside

of the main ones are referred to in the drawing as secondary sun zones.

Basically, there are three landscape situations: 1. a front area/public space, where the front of the house faces southerly to the street; 2. a private area/rear yard space where the back of the house faces southerly; and 3. a walking garden/circulation space where either side of the house faces southerly. The word southerly is used very purposefully rather than south because a southwest or southeast orientation will still get the minimum six hours direct sunlight you need as long as you watch your shadow areas.

Before you complete your use relationship schematic it will be useful to look at the three

SUN ZONES

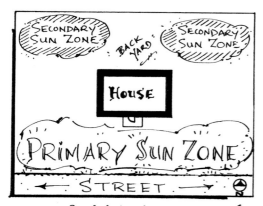

South-facing front yard

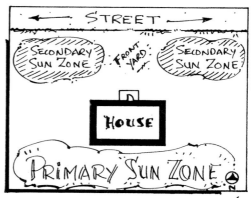

North-facing front yard

East-facing front yard

West-facing front yard

different basic landscape situations to see what they have in common and how they differ and to examine in detail your own situation. We'll look at the similarities first.

Similarities Among Sun Zones

For most lots, large mass plantings are necessary to take full advantage of sunny areas, maximize food production, and provide privacy. In addition, providing a sense of place is one of the most important tasks of a landscape designer. A poor landscape situation occurs when a large number of plants are placed here and there indiscriminately. It not only creates a maintenance problem, but it is unsightly as well. You also don't want to fall into the trap of thinking the only way to arrange your plants is the way a commercial producer does, in tightly packed rows. In an orchard-type arrangement each plant gets an equal amount of sun, but an orchard is what we call a monoculture, that is, each plant is the same. Good perhaps for a grower who has no other need than maximum profit, but it increases pest control problems. A home edible landscape should use a wide variety of fruits, nuts, berries, vegetables, herbs, and miscellaneous other edibles whose maturity is spread throughout the growing season. In mass planting, variety is called polyculture.

The shape of those mass plantings, what is called the composite form, has tremendous influence on the number of food plants that can be grown. Since they are mostly sun loving, only half (the southern half) of the whole area may be utilized depending on its shape. If, for example, you planted tall plants in the middle they would shade out the ones to the north.

When you plant the tallest plants in the middle of a mass planting with medium size and smaller plants on either side, it's called mound form. How much the taller plants will shade out the smaller plants to the north will depend on their relative heights. Remember, the sun rises high in the sky during summer, the producing months. These mound form mass plantings imitate the form of the earth; they are also usually the most pleasant aesthetically. They can be placed more or less anywhere and look attractive. The exception is mountainous, rocky, or hilly areas, which call for more vertical plant masses.

When the tallest plantings are at the back (north side) with medium, then small ones in the front, the entire zone is usable for sun-loving plants. This is known as transition form. Transition type plantings can be expected to look attractive where they make or seem to make transitions from horizontal to vertical lines. This is a subtle and little understood point. Many landscape designers don't fully understand that a strong vertical line meeting a strong horizontal one does not result in a structure that appears natural to its setting. They do know from experience that softening the juncture with some kind of transition planting is one of the most important things they can do to make the structure fit into the landscape. In a way they operate like an engineer who is pragmatic enough to use electricity without fully understanding its

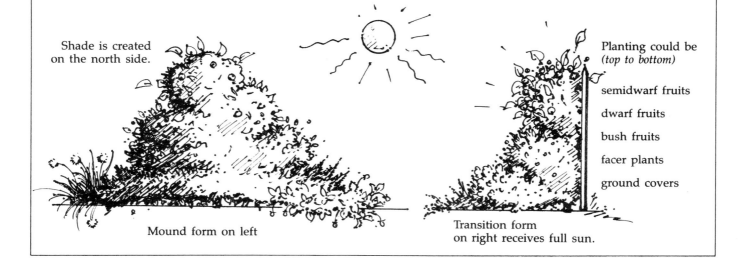

Shade is created on the north side.

Mound form on left

Planting could be (*top to bottom*)

semidwarf fruits

dwarf fruits

bush fruits

facer plants

ground covers

Transition form on right receives full sun.

nature. You can do the same. The most common form of transition form is the foundation planting.

Planting provides transition from horizontal line of ground to vertical lines of building.

One of the reasons foundation plantings remain such a popular style of planting is they still perform the aesthetic function of making a transition from building to ground even though the huge foundations of Victorian architecture that needed to be hidden are gone. Transition forms are also very helpful in providing a setting for a house, another important function.

No landscape scene exists in a vacuum. We view it from someplace—a point of view—and there always seems to be a background. It could be another house, some trees, or a mixed planting of some kind. If that background is higher than the transition planting, then at least from the point of view the transition planting works. The following sketch is a good example. The planting is successful because it makes the transition from horizon-

tal to vertical even though what it's related to is the house next door.

If the design is such that someone will also have a point of view to the end of the planting, you can always put smaller plants on the end so you have a transition in both directions.

The other characteristic the sun zones have in common is that spaces will be formed by the mass plantings within them. This is obvious, but what's not obvious is the incredible significance of the comment. What you should really be doing in any kind of landscaping is using the plant masses to form pleasant and attractive spaces for humans to be in. You use the plants the way architects use walls to form a living room. It's the quality of the space they most focus on, and you have to think the same way. The flower colors, for instance, are like decorations on the wall. In addition, it is important in basic human terms to create what we might call a territory. We're the products of millions of years of evolution but we're still territorial in that we want a place of our own. Since our visual sense is so dominant, we have a need to define this territory visually. We talk about privacy, but creating a territory or a space to be in really goes much deeper. In addition, professional designers consciously create, when they can, a sense of place. Most of us wouldn't feel much at home in the middle of the desert or the middle of an Iowa cornfield. Having a wall to lean against would help some, but not much. You need to create a finite space to feel really at home. The smaller your lot, the more you have to think in these terms and the more the

Bird's-eye view of site

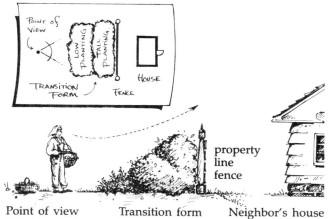

Property Line Transitions In this site plan, the view is toward property line fence and neighbor's house. Planting of fence is the transition form.

Bird's-eye view of site

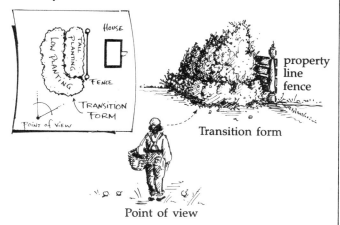

Handling End Views Check points of view to see if transition form should be finished off with low plantings.

open front lawn so common in most American neighborhoods becomes a luxury that's not sensible in basic human terms.

The actual shape of the space you form depends a lot on its use. What follows is a zeroing-in process on each of the individual sun zones and the landscape situations involved with them. If you're developing your own plan as you follow along, you should probably read through the three situations first and then reread the section that's most like your own lot. It's at this point the use area relationship diagram begins to develop into a more concrete form. Each of the following sun zone locations has its own advantages and disadvantages. The major difference is the way in which the space can most practically be used.

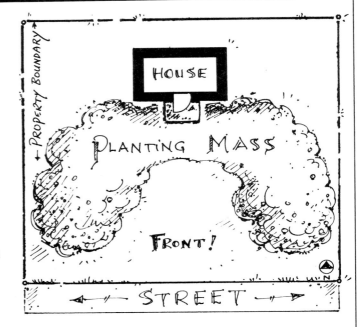

Differences Among Sun Zones

1. A Front Yard Facing South

A planting area that takes full advantage of the sun and still gives a sense of place might look something like the drawing at the top of this page.

If you wanted to form some private space you could put the mass planting along the street. Handling the space like the drawing kills two birds with one stone. It provides an attractive setting for the home with food-producing plants and it protects your crops from passers-by. Either way you'll have less lawn, but you can live without it. Nobody in the world is as devoted to grass as Americans, despite the fact that the time involved in maintaining it accounts for an overwhelming percentage of the time spent on a home landscape; certainly far more than the modest amount required for the maintenance of dozens of semidwarf or dwarf fruit and nut trees. Developing the concept into more concrete form might look like the following, especially if you're like most people and don't want your light and views blocked by large plantings in front of the windows.

The tall plantings could just as easily be a

This is a hard-edge, more architectural approach for south-facing front entry, with low and tall plantings on both sides. Fence encloses lower planting area.

much wider and more complex plant grouping, but the drawing illustrates the basic principle. This approach allows for a transition planting next to the building and still uses the sun zone effectively. If the drawing is starting to look suspiciously familiar to you, you're right. Espe-cially if you've seen Williamsburg or historic New England houses. It's just an entry garden like those found in both Colonial and later period houses. In fact, entry gardens were the predominant landscape style from medieval until Victorian times.

**WHIPPLE HOUSE
SALEM, MASSACHUSETTS**

WILLIAMSBURG HOUSE

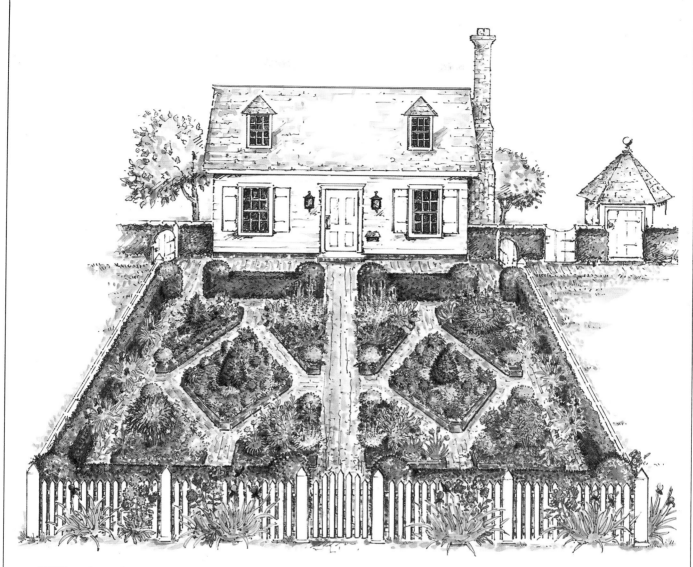

Williamsburg house (with artistic license showing a more typical Colonial arrangement with the main walk centered on the front door). The actual garden of this house is much off center to the right.

A modern entry garden that included a herbaceous planting area wouldn't be very different from its predecessors; the feeling or character would be the same although the plants would be different. The Colonial front garden was dominated by herbs for culinary use, teas, and plants for aromatic sachets and for medicinal purposes. Certainly the culinary herbs would be included in a modern garden, but since we depend on modern medicine for health care, and our scents and deodorants come out of a bottle, the bulk of the garden can be turned over to growing vegetables. There were some vegetables in the older gardens, but today we have a much wider selection available and, handled correctly from the design viewpoint, almost any can be used in your landscape. In addition, there have been many new varieties created for high yields in limited spaces. They are just the thing for these kinds of areas as well as for container planting. A listing of some of the more successful ones can be found in Appendix F.

If you're thinking of using herbaceous

material in the front area, you'll need a protective enclosure to keep small animals out. That's what all those Colonial picket fences were for—and especially why they had pointy tops. You might as well start thinking about how to place an enclosure fence at this point in the design process; specifics can be worked out later, once the Aesthetic Design section has been read.

You should devise a plan for the herbaceous front entry garden that allows for crop rotation, essential for pest control, while providing variety. Some people prefer raising the elevation of the planting beds above the walkway level. This has both ease of working and additional pest control advantages.

Here are two traditional plans of differing sizes that have been common since medieval times. They both provide an attractive framework that provides the skeleton of the garden while allowing you plenty of flexibility for fleshing out your garden.

Both of these plans are rather formal and geometric, certainly not the only way of handling things. Notice though that both of them allow for lots of color around the edge of the garden. Many garden flowers come back year after year as do many herbs; some have parts that are edible. These perennials should form the backbone of the frame and there

are more than most people realize that are virtually maintenance free. For variety from year to year you can always pick up some annuals. Even though these plants only live one year, they're often in bloom for the entire growing season and provide a nice splash of color all summer. The perennials usually only bloom for a few weeks.

That's as far as the south-facing front yard can be developed without considering the influence of aesthetic design. For now the south-facing rear and side yards will be developed to the same point.

Perennial edging—including standard and edible flowers, herbs, and perennial vegetables—surround rotating annual crops, especially ornamental vegetables.

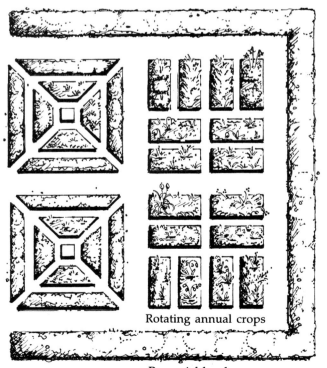

Rotating annual crops

Perennial border

2. Rear Yard Facing South

Where the back of the house faces a southerly direction, the main food landscape is the private area of the lot to the rear of the house. It's the situation that calls for the greatest variety in design; the kinds of things that are raised in the backyard can vary from family to family. However, there are some common threads in all of the situations. The sun zone is essentially this:

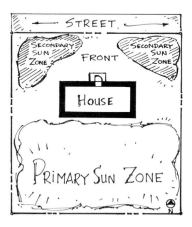

If you again shape the mass planting area with the aim of forming a space to be in, it might look something like this:

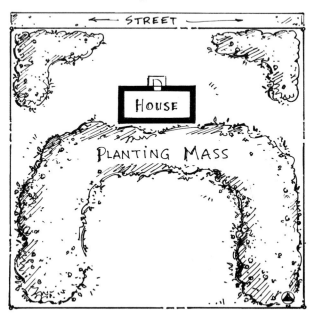

If the lot is large there's no problem with this kind of solution, but in backyards it's important to maximize the space usage for the various family activities. A large-scale plant mass to enclose space may be fine for a big lot but

a good approach for a smaller one might look more like this:

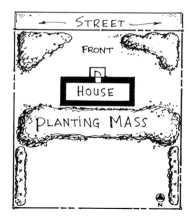

This kind of solution employs both large plant masses and lines to enclose space. The lines could be fences, a line of semidwarf fruit trees or a line of espaliered dwarf fruit trees, that is, trees trained flat against a wire or fence.

Grapes or trailing type berries could be trained on a trellis. Obviously there are lots of possibilities. The lines don't have to be straight either. Another excellent solution is softening them by putting them in a planting bed to allow for a small transitional planting. If you plan on creating outdoor rooms for different use areas, you'll be using even more lines as partition walls. These lines all need to have a similar character—think theme and variation—or you'll wind up with a hodgepodge. Take things a step further and your plan might look like this:

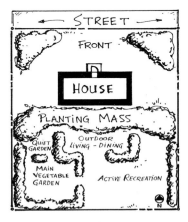

Keep the sun orientation of the lines in mind; it's just as important there as it is for the larger plant masses. If you are planning hedges it won't matter; but if you want an espalier or a line of plants along a fence, you will handle it differently if the fence is to run north–south than if it runs east–west; the need to maximize sunlight has to be taken into account.

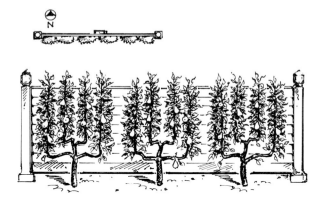

Top, a fence oriented north to south could be a solid type, providing complete privacy. Plants located on the south side would get plenty of sun.

Bottom, a fence oriented east to west should be open enough to allow sunlight on both sides.

Espaliered dwarf fruit trees are particularly good line solutions anywhere limited space is a problem in a sun zone. This is especially true in the southerly rear yard because the main objective is to maximize utility of space.

Another issue to be resolved is the location of the outdoor living room in a southerly rear yard. If it's near the house, which makes sense functionally, it will take up space in the valuable sun zone. The outdoor living room is a perfect place to do container growing, since you'll be trying to utilize the space as best you can for food plants. Use everything from small pots for herbs and flowers to large tubs for those trees classified as "garden dwarf."

A terrace should be placed at least slightly away from the house, whether you're using food plants there or not. This distancing gives you the opportunity to make a transition planting between the outdoor living space and the building and to get some green up against the building wall. You are looking for outdoor living space, and there is nothing outdoorsy or charming about staring at the joints in the siding. In a backyard facing south you must resolve the conflict of wanting sun in the sun zone for food plants and some shade so you don't get baked in your outdoor living room in the summer. One good way to do this is to plant a shade tree 10' to 15' from the house; it will shade your house and still leave plenty of sunny backyard space for your plants. This is closer than those large trees are normally planted, so you'll eventually have to prune its limbs next to the house. We don't see this placement much anymore but it's not because it's not feasible—it's just that it's not a *convenient* situation for a builder to have during construction, so the oldest and most beautiful trees get bulldozed. What's most important is that you have a strong-wood tree that will pose no threat to your house. A sugar maple would do the job, but there are lots of other strong-wood and nut trees.

A second way to provide some shade for your south side outdoor living/dining area near the house is to use a trellis with deciduous vines on top. This solution gives shade in summer, and sun in winter. And if you plant grapes or some other food vine you will get a crop besides. Not exactly a novel or original idea to Europeans but a solution used rarely in the United States. Both the close shade tree and trellis solutions can also be used for a south-facing entry garden. The trellis concept will provide shade much more quickly than a maturing shade tree.

The third way to get shade near the house in back is to do it structurally, with umbrella tables or some kind of awning. You can spend a lot of money on a awning that can be raised up and down for climate control, or you can do it with a simple galvanized pipe frame with a canvas cover.

Another possibility for the area near the house is a kitchen garden, a small variation on the herbaceous entry garden. Since a rear yard facing south could have sun throughout the day, the shape and location of even a major vegetable garden is arbitrary. It can be fitted in after you locate your recreation and service areas. If you're the type who wants a vegetable garden but sees it as strictly a service function, it can always be screened off from the rest of the yard.

3. Side Yard Facing South

In American-style landscaping, a side yard is used merely to get from the front to the back of the house—a nice way to say wasted space. Obviously, it's available land that's usable, and in most other countries this land is used as efficiently as the rest of the lot. The south-facing front yard is a complex design job because of having to think about creating a setting as well as framing the house. The rear yard has all the functional needs and relationships. With a south-facing side garden you can focus on the view from the inside and create a beautiful circulation space from front to rear: a walking garden.

The first technique to use in developing this area is a carefully studied transition planting along the south building wall. The windows

Not this

but this

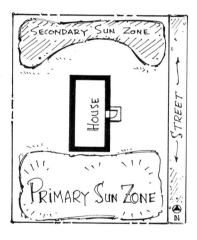

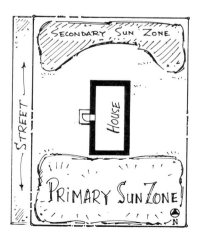

can't be blocked. If you line plants up like soldiers along the wall it won't be attractive because there'll be odd gaps. A more informal approach is best.

Since you'll want to use the sun zone as efficiently as possible, it makes a lot of sense to put a walkway adjacent to the transition planting and then add another transition planting on the other side, like this:

Now you're walking *in* a garden instead of next to one. It goes back again to that sense of place. Be careful about the relative heights of the plants so they each get as much sun as possible. The nicest walking garden is one that's balanced, that is, that has the same amount of planting on each side. It's best if the forms are similar too. This may mean you'll have to use shrub and dwarf fruits that will take some shade on the north side of the taller plants in the grouping. See the list of shade-tolerant food-bearing plants in Appendix I in addition to the individual ornamental information sheets. The way you arrange the plants and other landscape features in the front and back yards will determine the precise location of the entrance to the walking garden. Running a straight line down the side of a building is probably the least interesting way to connect the front and back entrance. The subliminal message of the straight line is to push on without stopping to enjoy. In addition, it draws the eye quickly through the space and makes the viewer focus on the opposite end of the walk. One way of making it more interesting is to put in something worth looking at; a focal point, like a nice entry gate or arch.

The focal point could be a piece of sculpture or a specimen plant. It could be something larger, a garden structure like a gazebo, for example. To further develop the space you could wind the walk around enough so the viewer isn't so aware of the whole length from one point of view. This will force the walker to look at the plants—not just the end of a tunnel.

Or, if you have enough side yard width, you can position the focal point in the middle, which will make it seem even less like a corridor.

Or, you could close off the long narrow space and make it into smaller, better proportioned ones. Do it with architecture, fences and walls, for example. Walls coming out from the building are especially effective because they help the building make a transition into the landscape.

No matter what sun orientation your house has or how small your lot, there's always going to be at least one sun zone to work with. Be alert to other smaller areas too: if you have a sunny side yard (house facing east or west) and your lot is large enough, you can also have large open sections with direct backyard sun from noon to 6:00 p.m. That would provide the critical minimum of six sun hours.

It will add a lot of edible landscaping space, even though these patches are not usually enough to base your design on.

Now that you've found your sun zones and have considered their implications along with some new design ideas, you're ready to go back to the graph paper and continue the design process. Check the use area locations with the sun zones firmly in mind. Then complete the scheme. Pencil in planting areas. You'll determine the exact sizes of these areas later when the various plants are chosen. Now is a good time to locate more specific things like fences, drives, walkways, and structures. Don't be concerned with the materials to be used for them or exactly what they'll look like. That will be determined at the next step in the design process. When you've brought your drawing up to date, it should look something like the drawing below.

Readers who have been working along on their own projects should now have the following: 1) a picture in their mind of the general character of the garden they want to create; 2) a firm idea of the activities they want to take place on the lot; 3) a realistic view of what will physically fit on the property; 4) a general idea of how to form the spaces in which

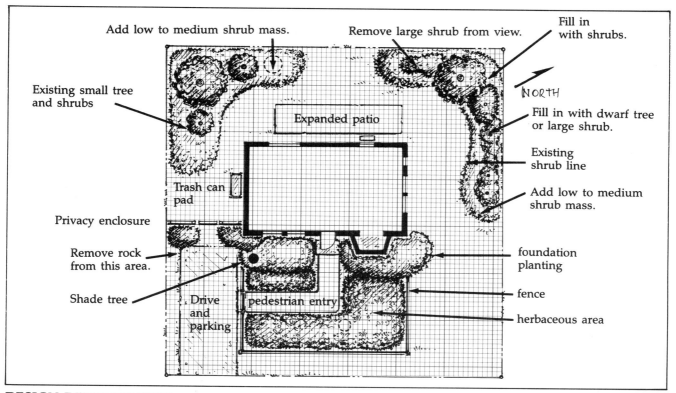

DESIGN DEVELOPMENT

Scale: 1″ = 10′; 1 small block equals 1′

the activities will exist; 5) an arrangement for the plan that takes into account the ecological strengths and weaknesses of the lot; 6) a plan that plays up the existing lot's aesthetic strengths and eliminates its aesthetic weaknesses; and 7) the ability to record the decisions made at the correct scale on the graph paper plan so it can be translated accurately onto the lot.

3
Giving
the Arrangement
Final Form

*T*his section contains the instructions for taking the plan in its present stage and giving it finite form. More precisely, it fills in the pieces of the design puzzle which enable you to take a scheme that's already practical and well-ordered and turn it into your personal Garden of Eden. It is also during this stage of the process that most of the budget decisions will be made. From this point on, the focus of attention will be on knitting things together to create a harmonious whole. Aesthetic change made for financial (or other) reasons obviously will affect the result as a whole. Like a chess game, a change in one place usually has many implications in another. For example, suppose the fence you want to enclose the patio has brick posts with stained wood fence boards to help tie a brick patio together with some wooden elements on the project. However, you discover that a custom fence like that will cost about twenty dollars per foot while the material cost of one-year-old hedge plants would be about a dollar per foot. Extended out, then, here's a decision with tremendous financial implications. Conceivably, though, it could have

few or no aesthetic ones, *if* the financial decision was made in concert with the aesthetic one. You could tie the elements together differently; for example, you could divide the brick patio into sections by using wood bands. Or you could use a wooden frame around the brick. You might introduce planting pockets within the patio to knit it to the softer, greener character of the hedge. That's the kind of chess game the design process becomes at this point.

Step 6
Taking the Practical and Well-Ordered and Making It Beautiful

As for creating beauty itself, it's simply a matter of arranging so-called elements of design according to so-called principles of design. The design process is just a question of breaking down the whole into parts that are understandable, then looking at them one at a time. In this case it is a visual scene that's broken down into its component parts. Those parts being: 1) the shapes of the objects in the scene; 2) the color of the objects; 3) the perceived surface texture of the objects; and 4) the lines that run throughout the scene and give it structure. Included are obvious lines like sidewalks and tree lines, and such not so obvious ones as the lines created where the lawn meets a planting bed, or a tree line meets the sky. The lines that seem subtle at first are the very ones we pick out to represent the scene in a pencil or ink sketch. That an artist can represent an entire scene with just lines is testimony to their importance.

These components of the scene, or elements of design, will now be discussed individually. They will be followed by the concepts or techniques for arranging them together, that is, the principles of design.

Element 1: Form

"Form" is a term used more commonly than "shape" in design jargon, but the essential meaning is the same. We see the shapes of things like patios or pools more clearly than those of plants; but plants too have quite specific natural shapes. Landscape designers take a keen interest in these shapes because some combine much more attractively together than others. To help them in their study, they categorize plant forms into the specific geometric shapes shown below:

These plant shapes are then further defined in horticultural literature with the adverbs "narrowly," "broadly," and "loosely." Since most designers have a picture in their mind's eye of the overall composition they want to create, they adjust the spacing between plants according to whether they choose a narrowly oval tree or a broadly oval one. "Loosely" has two meanings. First, it means the plant is not a rigid geometrical form, that it is more "naturalistic." Second, it means there are commonly gaps in the form. So where an "oval tree" might be used for complete screening, a "loosely oval" one would be better as a foil; it would not block completely. Occasionally a plant shape will defy being categorized and is termed "irregular," but I am not aware of any of these among the edible landscaping plants.

Since most of us have to live with the deciduous plants without their mantle of leaves for a few months, branching patterns are also broken down according to their forms, shown at right.

When individual forms are put together we end up with a composite form, that is, a form for the group in total. A composite form is looked at in the same way as an individual form: the total form of a group of plants is arranged according to the same design principles that an individual form would be. If you've ever seen a flower bed or shrub mass with plants sticking out in every direction, you know that whoever planted it wasn't thinking in terms of

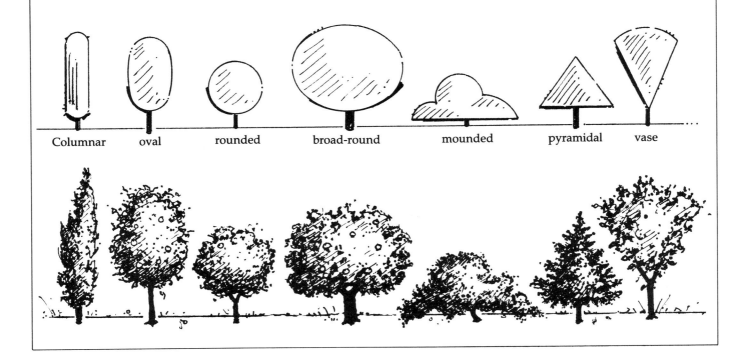

Columnar   oval   rounded   broad-round   mounded   pyramidal   vase

BRANCHING PATTERNS

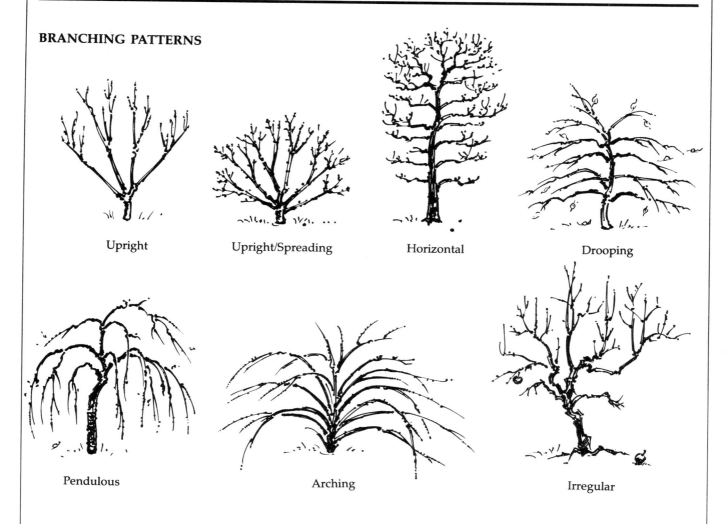

Upright

Upright/Spreading

Horizontal

Drooping

Pendulous

Arching

Irregular

composite form. Interestingly, when two or three trees are planted in the same hole (as is sometimes done with apple trees for the sake of variety or pollination requirements) they will often take the form of a single tree with multiple trunks, although somewhat wider in circumference. The group forms are categorized like the individual forms (mounded, oval, and so on) with three additional forms that do not occur naturally in individual forms. These new forms are called block, linear, and transition.

COMPOSITE FORMS

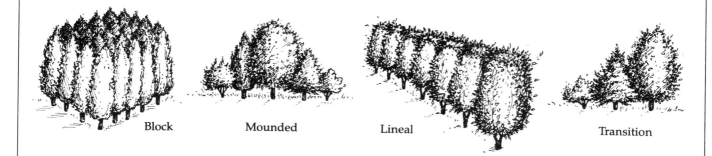

Block

Mounded

Lineal

Transition

Composite forms must be considered carefully. An unsightly situation occurs when individual plants are spaced so far apart that the intended composite form cannot be recognized. The landscape starts to look spotty and jarring to the eye. Be sure to provide "breathing" space around both individual plants and composite groups, enabling them to establish their own sphere of influence.

Nonplant shapes like driveways, walkways, or decks are reduced to their geometric form to study. Patios, for example, become squares, rectangles, or whatever. Geometric forms, in turn, have a habit of always wanting to complete themselves: a square wants to be a full square, a circle a full circle. So when you're designing a patio or forming the shape of a lawn area with a shrub border it is important to use the whole form. If the form has to be broken for functional reasons (not having enough room or needing some steps) it likes to be broken in a strong way rather than a weak one: don't lop off little corners here and there. With circles, if you have to take out a piece, use a half or a third of a circle. The result will look much better than an odd piece apart or combined with other forms.

Element 2: Line

In visual designing the line is used to connect two points. Lines of course are also used in combination to create forms. However, in a landscape design we generally consider them as being used to make two-dimensional patterns. Sometimes, for example, we end up with a lot of paving in proportion to the plantings, particularly if the lot is small. By the time there are sidewalks, entry walks, a driveway, and some kind of patio or deck, a fair amount of paved space is accumulated, which means lots of lines. Such a situation can be made more attractive and interesting if some kind of pattern is created. The Europeans are experts at this: you never see merely a slab of concrete or asphalt; instead, some kind of pattern has been created to make it more pleasant to live with. Lines are also created when there's a change of materials. Their purpose is to attract the eye by being aesthetically pleasing. If you've ever seen a yard that seemed as though it should have been beautiful but instead looked sloppy and awkward, take a good look at the walk and driveway edges and especially the lawn edge that defines its shape. Chances are you will not be able to discern any pattern.

Lines have movement. Since the eye will follow lines, the design can be controlled by handling them carefully. Make the lines go where the eye should go; to the front door or to a pleasant view that already exists or has been created in the landscaping. Make the lines pleasing; if they're curved, like many planting bed edges are, make them flowing. Don't let them get too tight or too awkward. Use a good heavy garden hose to lay them out.

A painter controls the viewer's eye and the painting's beauty by arranging the lines so the eye travels around within it—not by arranging the lines so the eye can run off the side. The painting is also enhanced by putting a frame around it. Depending on the kind of painting there might even be a mat and a frame. Complicated frames have many lines going around the picture. In landscaping, this is called bordering or collaring if it's done on a horizontal surface, and framing if it's done for a vertical scene. Just as with the mat, more than one border can be placed around the form.

USING LINES

Unbordered   Bordered   Double Bordered

The last significant thing about lines themselves is that they can give pace or speed to a design. Straight lines draw the eye quickly and directly. The longer the line, the faster the eye's trip—not a good situation for a small garden. If intersections are added or lines going off at angles are included, the action is slowed down and has resting points—appropriate places for sitting, reflecting, or viewing. Curved lines, especially sweeping gentle ones, are slow moving, restful, and are also useful for naturalistic settings.

Element 3: Color

Color is the design element that's most subject to personal taste. Colors evoke the emotions more than the others. Color is based on three concepts: hue, value, and intensity.

Hue is the shade of color. Professional designers look at hue with the aid of a color wheel that looks like this:

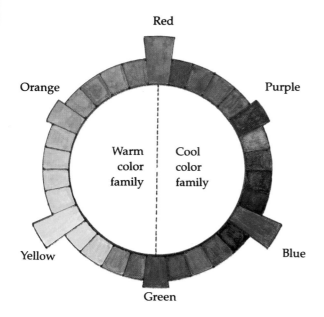

HUE WHEEL

The primary colors of red, blue, and yellow are the ones that are mixed together to form all the other hues and are spaced out evenly along the circle. At points halfway between them, the hues that have an equal amount of the two primary hues on either side are found, that is, red and yellow produce the secondary color orange; yellow and blue produce the secondary color green. All the other shades are found in between secondary points on the wheel. Mix many different hues together (or opposite ones) and you get the neutral hues: browns, beiges, and so on. Hues that are either opposite each other on the wheel (complementary colors), close together on the wheel (similar colors) or neutral colors, all look well together. As for the rest, even though most of us aren't artists or intuitive colorists, we can still have attractive color schemes; that is if we respect one rule: Don't violate hue families. When the hue wheel is divided in half, as shown, a warm family and a cool family are created. If color schemes in any given area are kept within a hue family we usually end up

with a color scheme we can live with. If you've ever seen a home landscape with blue spruce or blue-green junipers mixed together, and it looked nasty, it's because hue families were violated. Fortunately, this is not a major problem with an edible landscape since almost without exception the leaf hue of the trees, shrubs, and ground covers are in the warm family. It's the flower hues we have to be careful with. Establishing a warm color scheme and using some complementary colors from the cool family is the conservative approach.

Another quality of hues is apparent movement. Warm hues tend to come toward us and cool hues tend to recede. So when there's an area that needs emphasis, like a front door, it's better done with warm hues. Conversely, if there's a quiet shady corner somewhere, cool hues seem to work better.

The second concept involved with color is intensity. Intensity refers to how much of the actual hue there is in a given object—an apple, for example. A pure primary red apple would be the most *intense*. As more and more white is contained in the pigmentation, the hue red would become lighter and lighter pink, fading finally to a blush white. Black works the same way in darkening a hue. All the time there's only one hue, red, but a varying intensity. This matters because anything that is looked at for a long period of time, like a planting outside the kitchen window, or around the patio, should not have too much intensity. It can be very jarring, like watching a fire truck go by for eight hours a day. Highlights are preferable to intense colors.

The third color concept, value, means how much light is absorbed or reflected by an object. Intense or light colors tend to *reflect* more light, dark or low intensity ones tend to *absorb* more. Therefore, when the intensity of a prospective design is studied, keep in mind that glossy surfaces, both leaf and flower, tend to increase the apparent intensity because of their high value. There has to be compensation in the design to keep it from getting too all intense.

Element 4: Texture

Texture is the surface character or surface structure of forms. It's a good element to manipulate with the principles of design because it remains constant while the others vary. You'll watch the size and shape of your plants grow and change for years, altering the quality of the space and light, but their texture will always be the same. For design purposes, texture is divided into three categories: fine, medium, and coarse. Leaf surfaces themselves can be anything from very rough or bumpy to very smooth, or from coarse to fine texture. More commonly, when a landscape designer is talking about texture, he's talking about relative leaf size. Grass is considered to have fine texture, as are most plants with small or finely cut leaves. Other fine-textured plants include the small-leafed azaleas, sweet peas, and moss-curled parsley. Medium-textured leaves tend to be of average size like the large-leafed azaleas, apples, and Italian parsley. Peaches are considered medium-coarse plants, some of the cherries almost coarse. You'll find coarse texture is fairly uncommon among the food plants; good examples of coarse textured plants are the large-leafed rhododendrons and catalpas. It's a little hard to think of the texture of a deciduous shrub in terms of leaves it doesn't have in the winter, so when plants aren't in leaf, texture refers to branching pattern and form. A big, open, clubby tree might be coarse-textured in winter, and it might have small leaves and be classified as fine-textured the rest of the year. A final interesting aspect of texture is that it can change with the viewing distance. A coarse-textured plant viewed from far away might look fine-textured compared to plants that are closer in the same scene. So it is really *apparent* texture from the garden observer's viewpoint that you must be conscious of in design.

The Principles

Principles 1 and 2: Repetition and Variety
The first two design principles (design element arrangers) are looked at in combination because they give each other meaning. Repeating elements in a design is what pulls it together; too little repetition and the plan rapidly becomes a muddled, chaotic mess. Too much repetition results in monotony, and variety is the relief of excessive repetition. Most beginning designers err on the side of too much variety.

Since the elements and principles apply to all design, it's helpful to get perspective on the importance of repetition with an allied art form—music. In most songs there's a melody; one melody is repeated exactly the same or nearly so two or three times; then a different part (or bridge) is played; then the same melody is played again: repetition and variety. Played

with the melody are notes related to it called harmonies. Repetition with a little variety built in again. We would think it was ridiculous if a band got up on stage and each musician played a different tune, or if the backup musicians played something that had nothing to do with the melody. Yet how many landscapes are as well knit together as a piece of music? To make the situation worse, a landscape has a lot of variety already built in. Throughout the day, the sun constantly changes its position, creating different shadow patterns and light intensities. The wind changes direction and speed, changing a plant's form, giving it movement. In addition, there's a progressive, seasonal variety, especially with an edible landscape: flower blooms and light green leaves in spring; big, bright-colored fruit with darker, fuller foliage in summer; then bright fall colors; and finally the branching patterns of winter, sometimes emphasized by snow and ice. It's true that the amount of repetition in relation to variety is largely a matter of personal taste. But in general it's better to err on the side of too much repetition. You can always add bedding plants or something extra here and there for variety.

Saying the design elements must be repeated is not the same thing as saying you must have a lot of the same plants or nonplant forms. Similar plants with forms that have many of the same elements within them can be used.

There's another kind of repetition that helps knit things together: sequence. Here you set up change a little bit at a time. Let plants in a mass become a little less upright and a little more rounded as they go from middle to end, or bigger to smaller, or the spaces between them become larger and larger. The implication of sequence is that at least one element is changing, and it's changing with some kind of orderly progression. If too many elements are changing or the changes are disorderly, it's not sequence; it's just change. Sequences are good when leading up to a door or major center of interest like a pool or patio. They're also good for relating an open space (lawn) to a closed space (woods.)

Once you firmly establish a theme by having the various repetitions, you're in a position to set up the most emphatic form of variety: contrast. Like counterpoint or backbeat in music, contrast achieves its effect from freshness or shock.

Principle 3: Emphasis

As we have noted, contrast is one kind of emphasis. The principle of emphasis says that something in the design has to be stressed. Like the climax of a symphony or the center of interest in a painting, something, some focal point, catches and holds attention. In our case, it's placed where you want the eye to go—to the front door, for example. Too much emphasis or, more exactly, too many places of emphasis and, like the boy who cried wolf, it loses its meaning. Anything you can do in one spot to make emphasis stronger is good. Spread out, emphasis becomes jarring. Strong attractive forms make the best focal points. Plants like the yucca or the weeping forms of the hemlock, cherry, and plum work well. Any plant that's particularly beautiful in itself will work to a degree. One word of caution: strongly vertical plants are very hard to use for emphasis. If you look at an individual vertical plant, its form is often not all that attractive; and if many are used they're like a paragraph where every sentence has an exclamation point. Unless you live on a mountain or have a strongly vertical house where the vertical lines can harmonize with the surroundings you're probably better off without vertical emphases.

Principle 4: Balance

The principle of balance says that if you draw an imaginary vertical line down the center of a view in the landscape, both sides should have equal visual interest. To think about balance, you have to think in terms of the point of view you're looking from, for example, from the front walk. We humans like to be the center of our own universe; we like what we see to relate to us—*especially* if it's from our own home. If what we look at is out of balance, we feel intuitively or perhaps consciously that we're looking at things the wrong way or from the wrong place. Balance is just a way of making the landscape scene we're viewing relate to us in an attractive way. Landscape designers talk about two kinds of balance: formal (or symmetrical) and informal (or asymmetrical).

Formal balance is found in that kind of landscape where one side of the imaginary line down the center of the view is exactly the same as the other; in other words, the two sides are mirror images of each other. Each element is repeated on one side as it appears on the other. Formal symmetry has been the predominant landscaping style throughout

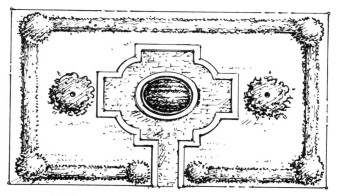
symmetrical

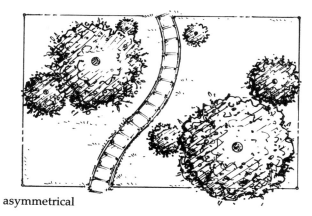
asymmetrical

history. It's only since the early 1700s that the informal style has come to be appreciated.

Balance plays a particularly strong role in providing a setting for a house. Many Colonial houses are symmetrical; the door is in the middle, one side of the front pretty much like the other. Since in an entry area you focus on the front door (the center of the landscape scene) keeping the two sides of the scene balanced is a matter of doing approximately the same thing to both sides of the house. Most

symmetrical

asymmetrical

houses of today are asymmetrical, though, with the bulk of the house to one side of the door. Here, to balance the landscape scene you're creating, you have to compensate by putting most of the landscape interest on the side of the door that has the least building mass. Handled properly this will create informal balance.

Principle 5: Proportion
The implication of proportion is that aesthetic pleasure occurs where there is not only a proper relationship among sizes of things, but also *between* the sizes of things and the space they're in. Imagine a small living room filled with big sofas and other large pieces of furniture. It would not only feel crowded, but it would look odd because the furniture is too big relative to the size of the room. Or imagine the reverse; a gigantic living room with tiny apartment-size furniture. Or perhaps worst of all, imagine a mixture of gigantic and tiny furniture. The living room would be most attractive if the sizes of the furniture were relative to each other and relative to the size of the room. Whether you're talking about pieces of furniture in a room, or plants in an edible landscape, the principle of proportion applies.

It applies to more than just the relative *sizes* of objects too. It applies to relative number or magnitude. You can't have too many of one kind of plant relative to another, or the few will just look scanty. Nor can you have an important line too tight relative to another that is too sweeping, as with sidewalks or planting bed edges.

Sometimes the relationship of sizes is referred to as scale, particularly when it's related to human size. Things are called *in* scale or *out* of scale, meaning they do or don't have a nice size relationship to humans or the scene around them. We don't want to be made to feel like a giant or an ant. Again, this is part of wanting to feel like we belong in our surroundings. For example, sitting next to a 6' high fence is more comfortable than sitting next to an 8' or 10' one. To landscape designers, indoor scale and outdoor scale are two different things. Did you ever go out and buy what you thought was the perfect size Christmas tree for your living room, only to find it too large once you placed it there? You were tricked by the difference between indoor and outdoor scale. You picked the tree relative to what designers call "outside planes of reference" for a space that was relative to what they call "inside planes of reference." The walls, floor, and ceiling inside a building are the inside planes of reference. In a house, the ceiling, 8' and up, forms the overhead plane. The walls, commonly more or less 15' apart, form the vertical plane. On the outside, however, a high tree branch, or the sky, is the overhead plane of reference. The neighbor's house, a distant view, or the horizon form the vertical reference planes. For a space outside to feel the same as one inside, it has to be bigger; and the elements in it have to be kept in proportion to that bigness. So if you were thinking of a 10' x 10' patio you can be sure it will appear to be much too small.

An understanding of the elements and principles of aesthetic design (line, form, color, texture, repetition, contrast, emphasis, balance, and proportion) will mean you'll be able to go back to the design drawing and turn a workable scheme into a beautiful finished plan. Before you do that, however, do the following three things:

(1) Write the elements and principles in a corner of the paper and everytime you make a design decision from now on, check to see how it stacks up against them.

(2) Review your collection of pictures to prime your subconscious.

(3) Review the idea sketchbook on edible landscapes in the next chapter. It will present ideas within the design framework established. It also refines the ideas already presented and offers more specific suggestions.

4

An Idea Sketchbook

*I*n plans with a more formal herbaceous area there's one thing to watch out for: since the beds are all planted with different species, you need something to pull the whole thing together visually. The best way to provide a consistent and unifying pattern for the eye is to use the same kind of edging or one kind of plant for a border around all the beds. The repetition will keep the plan from looking chaotic. If those border plants are evergreen you get the bonus of year-round interest. Naturally, the bed shapes have to be attractive to start with; so respect the rule stated earlier that geometric forms want to be whole and not broken in small or awkward ways.

If you can afford it, an informal paving material is best for the garden walks. Brick or stone laid in sand is particularly attractive. To prepare the bed for such a walk, begin with a 4" thick layer of ¾" crushed stone for drainage. Over that lay a "setting bed" of sand 1" thick; the brick or stone will be set into the sand. The drainage layer is particularly important in areas with a lot of freezing in the winter. It prevents the stones from heaving

out of place over the years. Precast concrete pavers, available from commercial and consumer sources, can be substituted for brick or stone paving. Premade forms to make your own pavers are available.* Use a ground cover in the joints between the pavers. Creeping thyme is especially effective.

For the front-entry vegetables, try to plant those with foliage that will last a long time and those whose crops are picked from the plants while the plant itself remains intact (bush beans or tomatoes, for example). Save the pole vegetables for trellises on the building or for garden pergolas or arbors that you include as a design feature. If you use plants that must be removed wholly, like head lettuce, take every other one or at least make sure the ones that are left form some kind of a pattern. When you plant vegetables, try intensive gardening spacing, or about two-thirds of the space recommended on the seed packages. This will give a more attractive character to the plantings and at the same time cut down on weeding and provide a

*Montgomery Ward Home Improvement catalog

Spring Effect Here is how the plan developed in Chapter 1 would look (without the herbaceous area) in spring with plantings of snowdrops and tulips (General Eisenhower hybrid Darwins and smaller multiheaded Praestan Von Tubergins).

Growing against the house, from left to right: South Dakota Ruby bush cherry, semidwarf Ashmeads Kernel apple, Garden Sun dwarf peach, row of three Zaiger dwarf apricots, Black Beauty bush cherry at door, crabapple, and, at far right, a Collins blueberry. Below is pine bark mulch with border of Fraises des Bois strawberries. In foreground is a Kenworthy butternut tree.

Summer Effect   And here is how it would look in summer. Fruiting along the house from left to right: bush cherry, semidwarf apple, garden dwarf peach, Zaiger dwarf apricots, bush cherry at door, and, at far right, a blueberry. With underplantings of Fraises des Bois is a bed of bush beans, left of doorstep. Butternut tree stands in foreground.

Summer Effect with Entry Garden   In this case, the butternut tree is pruned high to minimize shade. The added herbaceous entry garden includes daylilies growing at fence where the walkways end. Raised beds contain (*left to right*) in back row: celery and kale, tomatoes, carrots, compact tomatoes, leaf lettuce, two cabbages, spinach, parsley, bush limas. *Left to right*, front row: carrots, nasturtiums, ornamental peppers, ornamental eggplants, garlics, chives, salad greens, and herbs.

"living mulch" for moisture control. Notice the technique of using a bark mulch for a large area spring and fall ground cover while using bush beans, bush limas, or something similar for summer. This is an especially effective technique if you are planting a large area with these vegetables for canning or freezing. Bear in mind, though, that extra nitrogen will be needed to compensate for the bark mulch's habit of robbing nitrogen from the soil as it decomposes. For protection from the damage of small animals, picket fence sections can be bought prefabricated from fence companies. The fences can also be custom made, of course. Other good enclosure solutions include a low (3'–4') solid fence or a dense low hedge planted around a 1" mesh galvanized chickenwire fence like this:

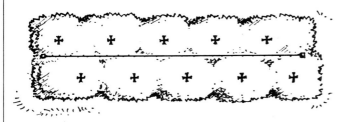

Chicken wire or other inexpensive fence in center of individual plants (note staggered spacing)

Either an evergreen or a dense deciduous plant will do for hedging; but since a foodscape tends to be overwhelmingly deciduous, the evergreen is preferable. You'll still need an attractive gate to complete your protection from small animals.

Here the horizontal lines of a ranch house are extended into the landscape with edging of railroad ties, which slightly raise the beds.

Trees, *left to right:* semidwarf Stayman-Winesap apple, dwarf Prima apple, standard Delicious apple (one each of early, midseason, and late varieties was chosen to extend picking season for three months). Some sense of enclosure is given at entry by thornless black raspberries trained on fence. Raised beds hold Top Hat blueberries edged with Caraway thyme. Taller Northland blueberries sit to the far left; Creeping thyme fills in walkway; bachelor buttons flank doorway.

Good solution for a split level: the slope is dealt with gradually. Again, the entry has some sense of enclosure. The railroad ties protect the garden from vehicles, and with the heights of the plants chosen, make a nice transition planting.

A weeping Santa Rosa plum stands above two black raspberry bushes. Lemon thyme covers the raised areas (with Creeping thyme in walkway) and daylilies are at the door. Latham red raspberries are in the raised bed by the house.

If the architecture of the house is undistinguished, one can always use a "stage set" approach to create something interesting in the front.

Here an overhead arbor, for Concord grapes, is used above a patio. Pavers and then edging stones create a transition into the lawn, while providing a sunny place for the garden dwarf peaches in tubs. Reugen Improved Alpine strawberries and balloon flowers surround pavers.

At right of sliding door grows a wineberry bush. American/European hazelnut hybrids rise from bed of New Zealand spinach surrounding patio. By steps, a dwarf plum sits over Latham red raspberries. A Fallgold raspberry occupies the back corner. Planters contain various tomatoes, impatiens, bush cukes, eggplants, and chives. Backdrop is a tall hedge of North Star and Compact Stella cherries.

A low deck is an excellent solution for a high foundation wall. In both backyard plans, the passive recreation area is separated from the more active area.

A Green cage plum and a lower beach plum grow through the deck, which is framed underneath by Snow King strawberries. A full-size Red Delicious apple tree gives shade, and a Meader American persimmon is backed by a fence of espaliered pears.

Clockwise from left of bottom step the pots hold: bush cantaloupe, garlic, ornamental peppers, peppers, Bibb lettuce, eggplants, nasturtiums; at back corners: leaf lettuce, ornamental basil, parsley, thyme, garlic chives, ornamental cauliflower, parsley, patio tomatoes, basil, impatiens, calendulas, cabbages, leaf lettuce, nasturtiums, patio tomatoes, ending with bush cukes at right of bottom step.

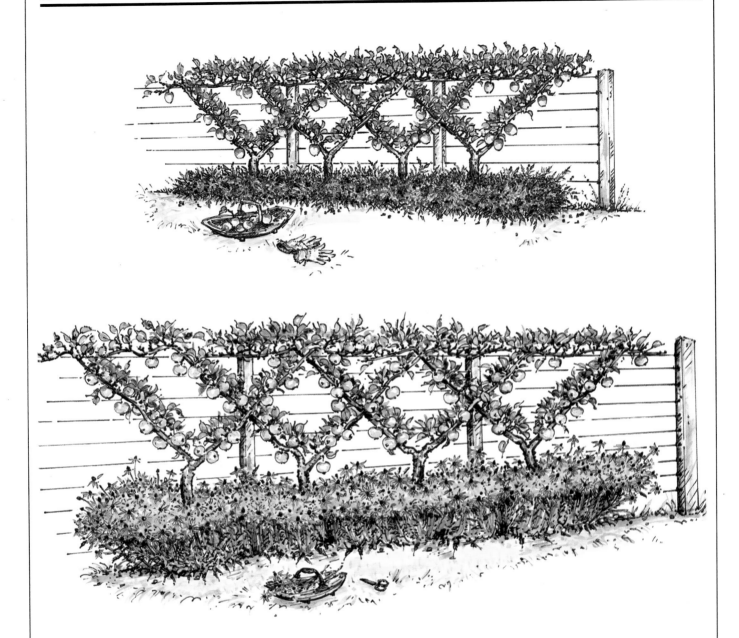

A single idea can translate into different forms depending on the character and color scheme desired. Here both plans have Belgian espaliers. In one case, dwarf Kandil Sinap apples, with their almost porcelain white and red finish, are used with compact Oregon holly grapes, which have dark, glossy, broadleaf evergreen foliage and bloomy purple grapes. In the other case, spur-type Yellow (Golden) Delicious semidwarf apples are planted with a mass of (nonedible) black-eyed susans.

The amount of knowledge and work required for training espalier varies wildly with the pattern, some taking six to eight years to accomplish; so if you want to use espaliered fruit trees, be canny in your approach. The surest way to deal with the problem is to buy trees already trained by a nurseryman. At least one source (Henry Leuthardt, East Moriches, New York) offers these. Although pretrained trees are not inexpensive, they may be a wise choice: having a large attractive focal point, a frontispiece, in the early years of your landscape will be very rewarding since a foodscape is usually installed with young, immature trees. Most of your plantings will bear in two to three years, but they will take a few years longer to become ornamentally mature.

The more economical approach is to train your own espalier, sticking to the simpler forms like horizontal cordons and Belgian espalier—these both give moderate to good privacy while letting air through. Working with the simple forms is not beyond the skill of the average homeowner, so long as you follow a guide for their training and care.* The more complicated espalier forms are not beyond the skills of an experienced gardener, but they are a bit of a labor of love. The different espalier forms are shown in Appendix H. The illustrations there will give you an idea of their relative complexity.

Some strawberries will cascade beautifully. Harvest Hang-ups are shown here in widely available wire baskets lined with sphagnum moss.

*_Espaliered Fruit Trees_, Henry Leuthardt Nurseries, Box 666, Montauk Highway, East Moriches, NY 11940

1. Ornamental cabbage
2. Edging of pot marigolds
3. Sweet woodruff
4. Marjoram
5. Daylilies
6. Facing beds of Stevens cranberry
7. Japanese iris
8. Siberian iris
9. Caraway
10. Ornamental pepper
11. Butterfly weed
12. Peppers
13. Variegated leaf sage
14. Small side paths for crop picking (edged with creeping thyme)
15. Top hat blueberry
16. Ornablue blueberry
17. Elliot blueberry
18. Bluehaven blueberry
19. Dwarf Bosc pear
20. Red Lake currants
21. Delite cherry plum
22. All-Red plum
23. Dwarf Comice pear
24. European plum
25. Dwarf apple
26. Latham and Heritage red raspberries
27. Oregon hollygrapes
28. Burlington blueberry

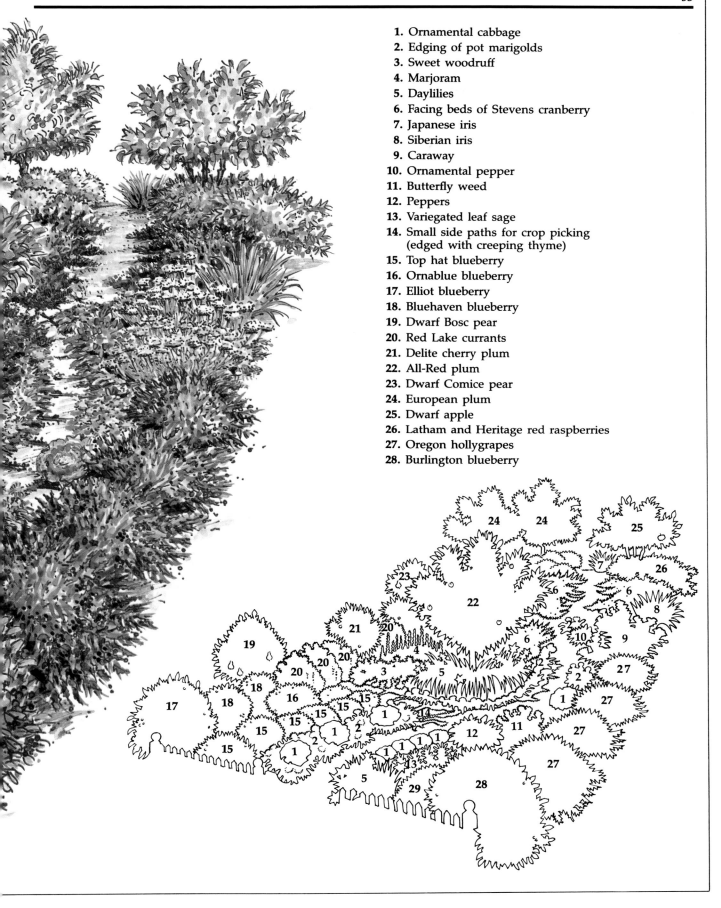

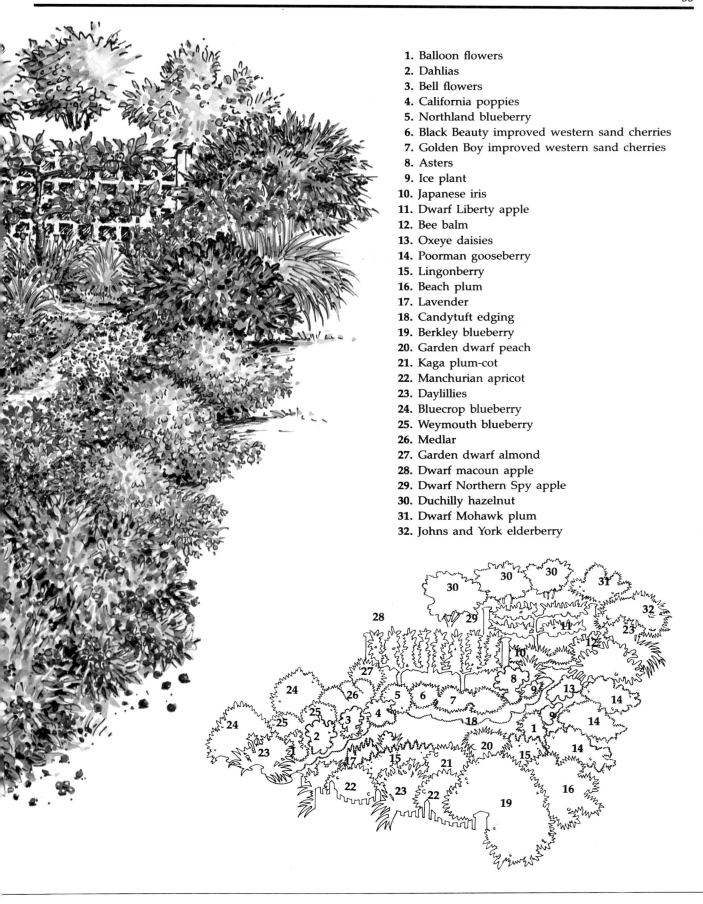

1. Balloon flowers
2. Dahlias
3. Bell flowers
4. California poppies
5. Northland blueberry
6. Black Beauty improved western sand cherries
7. Golden Boy improved western sand cherries
8. Asters
9. Ice plant
10. Japanese iris
11. Dwarf Liberty apple
12. Bee balm
13. Oxeye daisies
14. Poorman gooseberry
15. Lingonberry
16. Beach plum
17. Lavender
18. Candytuft edging
19. Berkley blueberry
20. Garden dwarf peach
21. Kaga plum-cot
22. Manchurian apricot
23. Daylillies
24. Bluecrop blueberry
25. Weymouth blueberry
26. Medlar
27. Garden dwarf almond
28. Dwarf macoun apple
29. Dwarf Northern Spy apple
30. Duchilly hazelnut
31. Dwarf Mohawk plum
32. Johns and York elderberry

If you put herbaceous plants in tubs for summer, it is nice to have tulips for spring. When it is time to plant your summer crops, bulbs can be lifted and eaten or saved for next planting. Except for the species types, most tulips last only four or five years, even with bonemeal added each year.

A summer grouping of oxeye daisies, ornamental kale with pot marigolds, and nasturtiums.

A grouping of ornamental eggplants (the blue-and-white–striped kind would work well here, too), chives, moss-curled parsley, and thyme in the medium tub, and a second planting (where summers are cool enough) of Sugar Bon peas.

Window box planting of edible Shingaku chrysanthemums, leaf lettuce, and cascading tomatoes

You're now ready to complete the design by going back to the graph paper with its overlays. Remember that the backbone of any landscape must be the woody plants: the shrubs and trees that are there all year long. In an edible landscape this means the fruits, nuts, berries, and some vines. It does not include the vegetables, flowers, and other herbaceous plants that are used to flesh out or add color to the landscape.

Where there are small sunny spots on the lot, adjust the location or configuration of the elements to accommodate them. It's a matter of details, like the orientation of a line or precise location within an area.

The use–relationship diagram at left, for example, might evolve as shown at right or at top of next page.

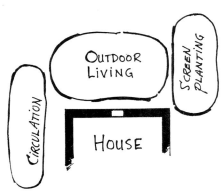

This use-relationship diagram

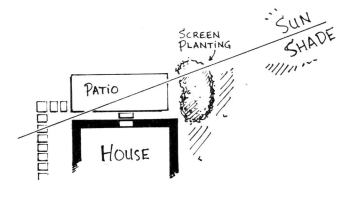

might become this

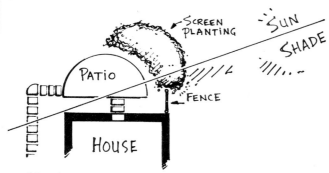

or this, if it was adjusted to take advantage of the sun.

This is the kind of refining process you'll apply to the whole plan. Pick your materials now. For example, what material do you want for a fence or terrace? How do the materials for each relate to the other? Be quite specific in your planning. If you want brick for a patio, what pattern will you use? Will you use one pattern for most of it with a different one for a "collar" around it? How will you relate it to the fence? If you can't afford a brick wall, how will you use these materials together? Can you make sequences? If the fence is wood, what about wood edging or wood area dividers in the patio? These are the kinds of decisions you have to make at this stage.

Some of your plans will only be lines on a drawing, but what they represent should be clear in your mind. Choose the individual plants at this point in the design process. You'll find the information you need in Chapter 5. First, determine what sizes are best for your needs and what shapes will be attractive together. The height is picked according to the degree of enclosure you want, the amount of privacy. Remember, if the space you're creating is small, you don't want to feel like you're living in a hole, so an enclosure height of no more than 8' should be planned for. That would mean dwarf trees or large shrubs. Mark the plants as such on the plan. If the spaces you're creating are particularly large, those enclosure plants should be about 10' to 15' (semidwarfs) to keep things in good proportion or scale. Semidwarfs might be big enough to block the view from a neighbor's second story window, too. When you're looking for some definition of space, but not total privacy, a height of between 3' and 4' works well. This would be good for the front lawn or those spots where you want to make visual use of land that lies beyond your own.

Before you pick actual plants, read through the basic information at the beginning of Chapter 5. The plants' shape and heights are listed on an ornamental information sheet for each plant. Go to the section that has the size range for your particular purpose to see what's available. Choose the larger plants first; you can pick the facer, or transition, plants later. It's the big ones that set the character and theme for the area. The "size at maturity" line on the ornamental information sheets will determine exactly how wide that planting area should be or how many plants will fit into the length of planting area you show on your plan. Don't forget to allow for those 1' square or 2' square pavers within wide edible planting beds where access is necessary. The look you want affects the total sizes and number of plants you can accommodate too. For instance, do you want a composite form like this, with individual plants, tip to tip same size;

or like this mounded composite form, with larger plants in the middle:

Or do you want a looser, more informal mix of dwarf and semidwarf sizes mixed with lower shrubs:

Draw the plants on the plan at their mature size or somewhat smaller if it is less confusing. If you draw them smaller, make sure you don't lose sight of the mature sizes when you lay things out. Most people find investing in a circle template worthwhile. They're thick plastic sheets with a variety of circle sizes cut for guides. They make it possible to draw circles quickly and easily. It is important to locate the center of each plant where you would actually plant it so you can measure off the plan when installation time comes. Keep the scale you're working at in mind.

The example below is the finished plan of the lot we've been using for study:

FINAL DESIGN

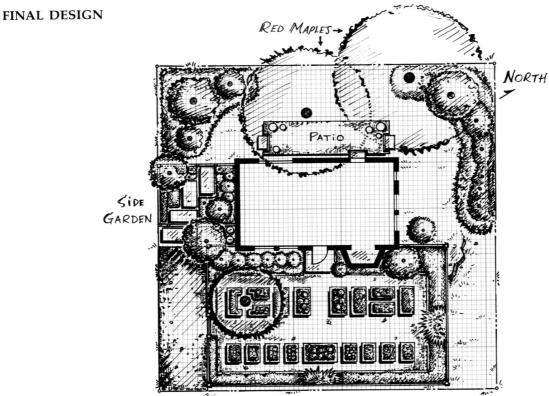

Scale 1″ = 10′, 1 small block = 1′

The front entry garden has been enlarged and redesigned with a perennial flower border including daylillies, within a picket fence and enclosing raised beds of herbs, flowers, and vegetables. A pruned hickory serves as the shade tree, and fruit trees (left to right: peach, apricot, currant, cherry) abut the front of the house. A partially-shaded side garden has been created and enclosed in solid board fencing which serves as an espalier for Wineberries and Northern Kiwi vine; a Meteor Cherry has been planted (top left) over ground cover of Well's Delight Creeping Blueberry and inedible Spiderwort beds; top to bottom along the side of the house are Northsky Blueberry, Northblue Blueberry, Compact Stella Cherry, and an Apple tree. Dwarf Oregon Hollygrape has been planted among the existing shrubs in the left corner of the backyard, and two Red Maples have been transplanted as shade trees. The right corner of the backyard has been supplemented with a low mass of Dwarf Oregon Hollygrape and filled in with Nannyberry Viburnum to match the existing shrub line.

5

Choosing the Individual Plants

Step 7 in the design process encompasses choosing the particular plants that will fill a place in the landscape design, succeed horticulturally, and put desirable produce on the table.

The information is divided into three parts: Part 1 contains some background on plants; Part 2 is an explanation of the data found on the ornamental information sheets; and Part 3 comprises the sheets themselves. You'll find these sheets to be a valuable aid in plant selection; they contain such details as shape, size, and flower color. This information is often hard to find in standard gardening and landscaping sources because the plants belong to the agricultural world. The best way to make the plant choices is to study the section in order. After absorbing all the general information, look at the specific information about each plant to decide which will fill specific places in your design.

Part 1
Background Information

Every plant listed in this book is available to the general public through mail order or local nurseries. The most important change in the edible landscape world during the last decade or so has been an explosion in the variety of plant material available to the consumer. An apple tree, for example, used to be available in one size—about a 25′ to 45′ tree depending on the individual variety of apple. It was of use in the home landscape as a small shade tree but required much time and some special spraying equipment to reach the top. Those apple trees, along with just about all the other fruits, are now available in full size, semidwarf, dwarf, and garden dwarf—the last being the new subcompact of the fruit world. These size varieties mean three things to us: first, their smallness means protection from pests can be accomplished with an ordinary garden sprayer and only a few minutes' effort per plant for each spraying. Even those who raise food organically have a wide variety of disease-resistant plants to choose from. They also have pest-control techniques that work if they don't demand all glamorous-looking fruit. The second advantage of the new sizes is the many additional design possibilities for home landscaping. There are plants available now for virtually all of the standard landscaping uses, including foundation plantings, corner plantings, shrub masses, privacy screens, and even ground covers. The third advantage of the smaller versions of the original standard-size plants is their earlier bearing. In a mobile country like ours where the average period of home ownership is five to eight years, a crop in two or three years is worlds better than one in five to ten years.

In addition to the size variety, much hybridizing has been done to improve disease resistance and to extend the geographic range of many plants. Newer varieties have been created to improve the flavor that was lost when the ranges were originally increased. It's hard to imagine a quieter revolution; there are more than two thousand varieties of fruits, nuts, and berries available at the retail level today.

Most people are unaware of it because of marketing conditions that we really create ourselves; there's a kind of vicious circle that goes on with little known but ornamentally valuable food plants: if they're not known, growers won't grow them fearing there's no market and if they are not grown, no market for them can develop.

Interpreting the Catalogs

Since most local nurseries and garden shops do not stock much edible landscape material, the best place to obtain plants is from mail-order catalogs. You'll find the following information to be very useful in dealing with their descriptions and other peculiarities.

Mail order is for you, if you can adjust to the shock when a scene like this in the catalog—

Mail-order houses sell both one- and two-year-old plants, but even two-year-old plants make a modest ornamental impact at first. The one-year-old plants are really for commercial use. Spend the few dollars more for the size and earlier bearing of the two-year-old. They're usually only 3' to 6' in height anyway. If you're ordering two-year-old plants, make sure you're getting two-year-old plants by confirming by letter or phone with the supplier—it's not always clear in the catalog. As is customary in the trade, when catalogs talk about a semidwarf or dwarf they're only speaking of it *relative* to the standard version. There are no fixed size implications at all. It makes an impossible situation for a designer who's looking for a special size and shape plant for a specific situation. The problem is compounded even further because a plant one company calls dwarf, another may call semidwarf. For example, you might find the filbert (hazelnut) called a shade tree or a

turns out to look like this when you get the plant.

dwarf. The companies that call it a dwarf are warning us that it doesn't get as big as the other nut trees it's listed with. But, as you'll see in the information sheets, it's not a dwarf by size (it's really 10' to 15' tall, but variable) or horticultural definition ("smaller than others of its kind"). There are no others; they only come in one size.

The only way a designer can deal effectively with these vagaries is to fix size ranges to the terms. So when you are choosing plants, don't accept the catalog's terminology relative to size, use the information listed on the ornamental information sheets given here. From now on in this book the size-category terms used will mean these fixed-size ranges:

Size Category	Height
shade tree	45' +
small shade tree	20'–45'
semidwarf tree	10'–20'
dwarf tree/large shrub	6'–10'
garden dwarf tree/medium shrub	3'–6'
small shrub	18"–3'
ground cover	2"–18"
vine	by length
herbaceous material	varies

By definition then the standard peach is a semidwarf size. Both the standard plum (15'–20') and the semidwarf plum (10'–12') are semidwarf sizes and will be listed accordingly in the semidwarf section of the plant sheets. The issue of the same plant being called a dwarf by one company and a semidwarf by another brings up another important ornamental issue: the question of what kind of roots the plant has, or more specifically, what kind of rootstock the plant is grafted on. It's the roots that determine the size of many food plants. This is particularly true of the fruits. What the roots *don't* determine is the size of the fruit (that's always full size). In the purely ornamental world, plants for different purposes in the landscape (shade, privacy) are different plants, sometimes close relatives. In the edible landscaping world, it's different. A Golden Delicious apple could be a 45' shade tree, a 6' hedge, or a foundation plant, depending on the roots that the plants are grafted on. To be able to choose many food plants for a given purpose in the landscape, you have to know the rootstock. That's why the rootstocks are listed on the ornamental information sheets later in this chapter. If you're choosing a dwarf over a semidwarf for design reasons, you'll know what roots it must be grafted on in order for it to achieve a given size.

Which brings us back to the catalogs. Don't believe their words; believe their rootstocks. For example, there are apples on M7 (a common rootstock) listed as both dwarf, which it's not, and semidwarf, which it is. Rootstocks have varying adaptability to different soil types and drainage and that can affect your decision too. (Check Appendix D for a brief discussion of the cultural implications.) Often you get a choice of rootstocks for the same size. Deal with nurseries that tell you what rootstocks they're using. If they don't know but they have what you want and they're in your region, you might call or write the grower and ask them what rootstocks they use. This precaution will save you from getting plants that will not thrive in your region or climatic zone.

In various catalogs you see the terms "miniature," "genetic dwarf," and "garden dwarf" used interchangeably to describe plants 4' to 6' high—the subcompacts of the tree world. Strictly speaking, the term genetic dwarf implies that the tree is not grafted onto dwarfing roots, but is naturally small—but all the terms at least refer to the same size plants. It's great to see these plants come on the market as they help fill in a formerly thin area in the size range. There are some other catalog terms that require translation: "pretty" and "reliable" for instance. "Pretty" usually means the plant has glossy foliage, which is prized in the ornamental world, or that it has attractive blooms (or both). "Reliable" usually means it bears well every year. Many food plants have a tendency to alternate between good and not-so-good years as far as both the quality of the bloom and the amount of fruit goes. Be aware that "reliable" does not mean "hardy." "Hardy" means absolutely nothing. Plants are spoken of in the catalogs as hardy, but only the growing zone designation will tell you if the plant is hardy enough for your area. In choosing your cultivars, use the hardiness zones appearing in this chapter rather than those appearing in catalogs. (Elberta peaches, for example, do not do very well on the Canadian border, as suggested by one catalog.) When referring to hardiness, some catalogs prefer the words "does best in zones so and so." This translates to "This is it, Charlie, forget about taking your chances." Expect the plant to do well *only* in those zones. Occasionally you will see "Experts don't agree" referring to hardiness. This implies that maybe you *can* take your chances. You should know, however, that experts agree very well on hardiness: they know to the tenth of a degree what minimum temperature will injure a dormant bud or bloom. What they don't agree on is how to define the boundaries of a given hardiness zone because of such natural influences as elevation, big bodies of water, or exposure. Also don't assume that just because a supplier is in your hardiness zone, any plant he sells will thrive in the area. There are, for instance, many nurseries that carry the Granny Smith apple because of its popularity; but Granny Smith needs far too long a season to ripen its fruits for most northern zones.

Beware of imprecise catalog terminology. For example, some cherries are described as "sour" or "pie," and a popular plum is called the "prune plum." The taste of all cherries is a mixture of sourness and sweetness; that is, they are "tart." They are excellent for eating, and it seems a shame to imply they're only good for pies. Kids know better. "Prune" plum conjures up images of dry wrinkly fruit; it's a shame. To be called a prune plum, a plum has to have a high enough sugar content to dry properly, and that high sugar content is just what makes the European (prune) plum an incredible treat.

When you're buying from the catalogs, buy only named varieties, such as the Patriot blueberry. Some companies offer only a generic blueberry, even though blueberries come in a wide variety of shapes and sizes. To make it sound more professional, they might include the genus and species ("Buy our Blueberries—*Vaccinium corymbosum*"). It's still no good; you want an individual variety. This is particularly important when dealing with native plants that have been "improved" for better fruit—like currants, gooseberries, elderberries, bush cherries, American persimmons, and many nut trees. The unimproved ones are only fair, and subject to genetic variability. You might get a plant you're happy with, but on the other hand, you might not. What you will *not* get is the quality food you might have had. The gooseberries and currants are typical examples. They are sometimes thought of as insipid or sour, like most native types found in the woods or like somebody's grandmother had; but the improved ones are delicious. The poor gooseberries suffer doubly because the most common improved variety, Pixwell, is not much better than the native.

The catalog translation problem is compounded because most catalogs are aimed at both the home grower and the commercial grower—two markets that are often at odds, since they're usually interested in very different things. The edible landscapers live in their gardens and can concentrate on taste; commercial growers have to consider such factors as maximum productivity, mechanical picking, packing, and shipping. Commercial growers also have to consider the needs of the food processor, who has a lot of other requirements that influence the grower's variety selection. The result: food for commercial trade or processing has been hybridized for many qualities, and flavor is not one of the priority qualities. When a catalog uses terms like "good for processing or canning or cooking," be sure that's what you will use the food for.

Plant Needs that Affect Your Choices

Catalogs deal only minimally with the issue of plant health. Few really have much to say about what a good environment for a given food plant is, and how variety in sunlight, soil, and moisture affect its health and longevity. A little background in these basic issues is needed.

Plants vary a great deal in their individual needs and preferences. For example, the apples generally like the same conditions, but some varieties will put up with much more cold than others (or more heat). Some will do much better in a heavy soil than others. But to any given food plant a good home is one that:

1. Is not too cold or too hot relative to its personal requirements.
2. Has enough "out of leaf" time in winter to get an adequate rest.
3. Provides the right amount of water to meet its personal needs.
4. Has soil of good enough quality and of a compatible enough nature that the individual plant's roots can do their job of getting enough nutrients.
5. Has enough sunlight during the day and in total during the growing season to mature its fruit.

The food plants have one other need that's not strictly speaking part of a good home but which is necessary in an edible landscape—fertilization, or pollination, so you can get the fruits. Each need will be examined indi-

vidually. The detailed description of the individual plant needs will be found on the information sheets in Part 3 of this chapter.

1. Cold and Heat Tolerance

The plant's genes determine their ability to endure the cold. Specifically, the genes set the minimum temperature range that any given plant can cope with and not freeze to death or have its fruit buds killed. "Temperature range" is a more accurate term than merely "temperature" because the minimum temperature can vary somewhat, depending on the general health of the plant, cultural practices, and on weather patterns. A warm spell in late winter, for example, can trick a plant into coming out of dormancy too soon. Horticulturalists have established geographic zones of similar minimum temperatures. There are two sets of them, in fact: the U.S. Department of Agriculture zones and the traditional, or Arnold Arboretum, zones. (See pages 66–69).

The Department of Agriculture zones *should* have the letters U.S.D.A. in front of the zone number to distinguish which zoning system is being used—U.S.D.A. #6 and Arnold Arboretum #6 (traditional #6) are not the same. Look at the key on each map to see the differences. Also notice that both of these maps are based on average minimum temperatures, not cold snaps. These coldness zones, called "hardiness zones," are listed on the ornamental information sheets for all the plants described in this chapter. The Arnold Arboretum zones are used in this book. Although most nursery catalogs list hardiness zones, they often don't tell you which zoning system they're using; so you must always refer to the zoning map in any given catalog and see if they do tell you, or compare the shape of the zones to the ones here, to see which zones they're referring to. Another problem is that the zone maps in catalogs are often so small or so inaccurately drawn that it's difficult to tell exactly where you are relative to a zone. So whenever possible, make your hardiness decisions from the zone information in this book.

Bear in mind you're not looking for the hardiness of apples or peaches in general. You're looking for the hardiness of a specific variety—often called a cultivar (*culti*vated *variety*). Any one cultivar will not be as adaptable as the species taken as a whole; we can grow apples from Florida to Canada, but any given cultivar will only be good for

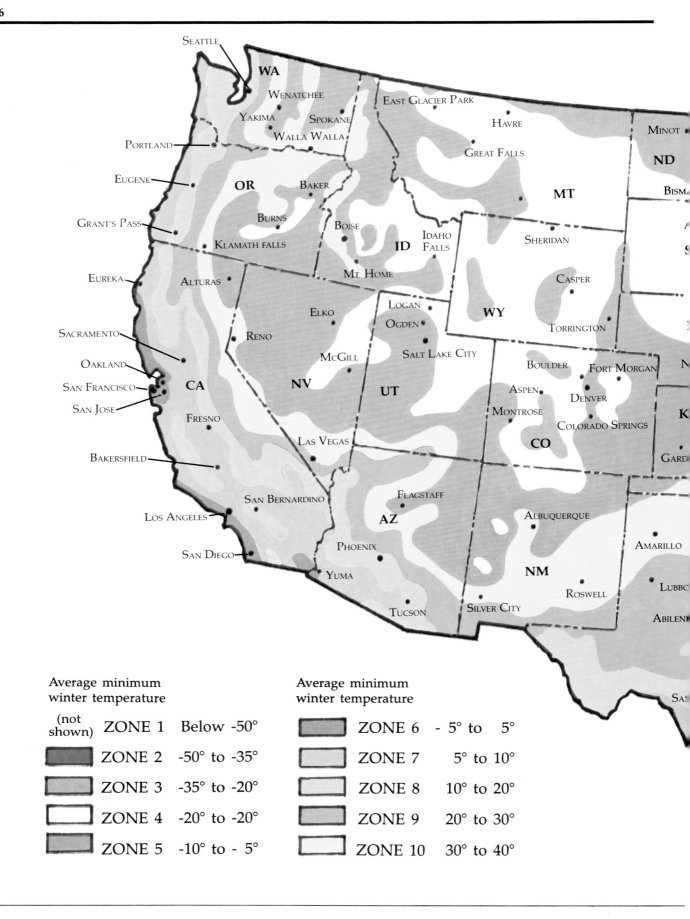

Average minimum
winter temperature

(not shown) ZONE 1 Below -50°

ZONE 2 -50° to -35°

ZONE 3 -35° to -20°

ZONE 4 -20° to -20°

ZONE 5 -10° to - 5°

Average minimum
winter temperature

ZONE 6 - 5° to 5°

ZONE 7 5° to 10°

ZONE 8 10° to 20°

ZONE 9 20° to 30°

ZONE 10 30° to 40°

ARNOLD ARBORETUM CLIMATE ZONES FOR THE USA

Reprinted with permission of the Arnold Arboretum, Jamaica Plains, Massachusetts

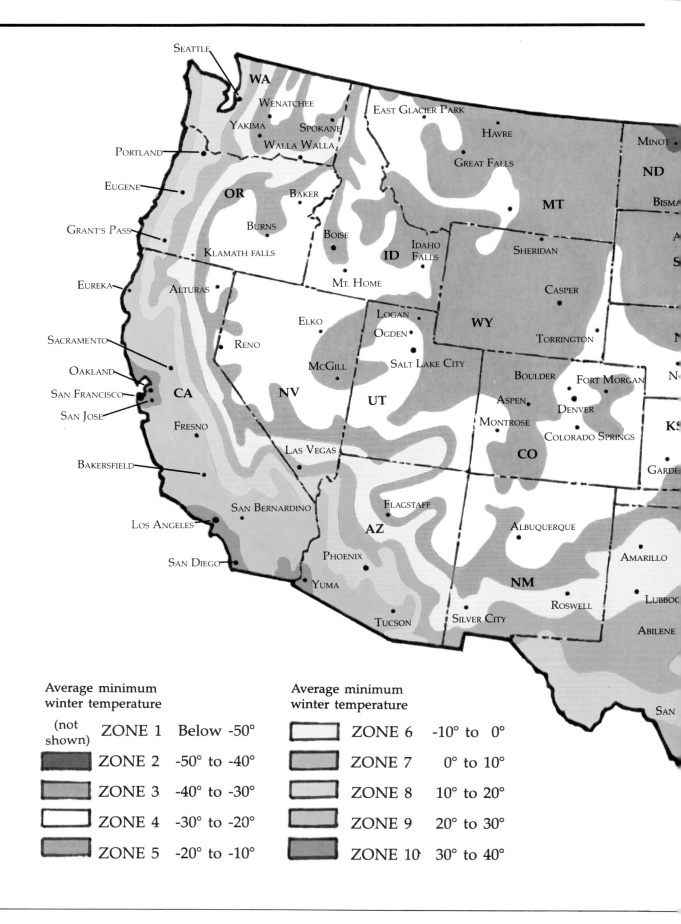

Average minimum
winter temperature

(not
shown) ZONE 1 Below -50°

ZONE 2 -50° to -40°

ZONE 3 -40° to -30°

ZONE 4 -30° to -20°

ZONE 5 -20° to -10°

Average minimum
winter temperature

ZONE 6 -10° to 0°

ZONE 7 0° to 10°

ZONE 8 10° to 20°

ZONE 9 20° to 30°

ZONE 10 30° to 40°

USDA CLIMATE ZONES FOR THE USA

part of that range. Most of us have favorite varieties and sometimes there's a strong temptation to pick a variety that's only marginally hardy. This is not a good idea. What you want is homegrown tree, bush, and vine-ripened produce. Almost *any* variety that's picked at the proper time will be better than the "best" varieties picked green for storage, shipping, or handling reasons; but a plant that's marginally hardy is less productive and takes more time to keep in good health.

The timing of spring frosts is an important cold tolerance issue. Normally it takes a lot more cold to kill the plant than it does to kill the fruit buds. Therefore, a plant can be hardy but still not be able to produce good crops. Northern gardeners are used to getting an occasional spotty crop on plants they've chosen that are near the northern extent of their range. If the choice is a spotty crop once in a while or doing without, then the choice is easy. What you *can* do if you're on the northern edge of a species range is choose a later blooming variety. Some categories will have to be given up completely; almonds and apricots, for example, bloom so early that it's not always realistic to try with these particular fruits.

As far as heat tolerance is concerned, it's a question of choosing a cultivar that's adapted to that particular southerly zone rather than trying to press a favorite variety into service. This is also important because of the plant's rest requirements.

2. Rest Needs
All plants need a rest in the winter, even the evergreen ones. Most edible landscape plants are deciduous (that is, they drop their leaves in the fall) and *really* take a rest. What they need specifically is a certain number of hours below 45 degrees F. in winter in order to get that rest. The amount of time varies, but it's at least three hundred hours for any non-tropical food plant. The cultivars that need a minimum rest are called low-chill types and it's these that edible landscapers in zones 8 and 9 should be thinking about. There's no point in picking a favorite variety if your zone doesn't meet this chill requirement.

3. The Right Amount of Water
Either too much or too little water has about the same physiological effect on plants. The nutrients in the soil are taken up in water, but in the *presence* of oxygen. The roots need to respire, or breathe, to do their job. If there is no water to take up or if the air spaces in the soil are filled up with water the roots can't function. That's why good drainage is so important. Some food plants are more tolerant of droughty conditions than others, but most thrive best with about 40″ to 50″ of rainfall per year. The homeowner in an arid region is in an enviable position. He is able to grow a wider range of varieties because he can provide supplementary water where it might not be practical for a commercial grower. Ideally, 1″ a week is what the food plants need, especially when they are maturing their fruit. That 1″ per week is not nearly enough when they're in transplant shock and adjusting to a new environment, but that will be covered in the planting section.

4. Good Enough Soil
The edible plants are fondest of the topsoil, especially one fairly rich in decayed and decaying plant material (humus). Most people will have more subsoil than topsoil and that's why a generous planting hole with the backfill mix is critical. Plants vary in their tolerance of extreme soil types—from very clayey to very sandy. A generously sized planting hole helps to a degree, but when the roots reach the edge of it they're going to have to make some kind of accommodation to the surrounding soils. If they have no natural affinity for the soil type they find there, they're going to strangle and eventually die. This is particularly true of peaches on dwarfing rootstocks. Pears and plums are generally more tolerant of heavier (clayey) soils. Almonds, blackberries, peaches, nectarines, and apricots do better in sandier soils.

5. Enough Sunlight
Plants are classified as sun-loving, shade-tolerant, and shade-loving. The vast majority of food plants are sun-loving. There's confusion about sunlight requirements because most agricultural bulletins and other literature are oriented to the commercial grower who must concentrate on maximizing production to make a living. Six hours a day of *direct* light from the sun is really enough. Not having enough total light in the season is primarily a problem with some of the vegetables, some apple varieties at the northern edge of their range, and many nuts in the same situation (particularly pecans). Some food plants (including blueberries, blackberries, raspberries, cherries,

gooseberries, wineberries, and currants) are shade-tolerant. Although shade-tolerant plants will do fine in some shade, the food yield will be a lot less (often about half) so the gardener must compensate by having twice as many plants for the same yield.

6. Fertilization (Pollination) Needs

Some food plants don't care if there's another like them nearby. Because pollen from their own flowers is enough to fertilize either their own female flowers or the female part of their flowers in cases where the sexes exist together, these plants are termed self–pollinating. (It is the base of the flower that eventually develops into the fruit.)

Some plants are self-pollinating, but only minimally. Nursery catalogs may tell you that a plant is self-pollinating, which may be technically true; but practically speaking this plant may need pollen from another plant for a decent crop. Many woody fruit plants require pollination from a different variety of the same kind of fruit or nut. To make it even more confusing, some varieties won't pollinate others, while a few are excellent pollinators for many. In addition, otherwise compatible cultivars that do not bloom at the same time can't pollinate each other. The easy way to deal with pollination needs is this: when you're choosing plants check the pollination requirements in Appendix B. The worst that can happen is that you might have to substitute one cultivar for another in your scheme. Keep in mind that food plants are most commonly pollinated by bees, not wind, so to get cross pollination you want to make sure the bee can get to the plants that need it the same day. Depending on who you read, those plants should not be more than 50' to 100' apart. Keep in mind, too, that honeybees don't fly when the daytime temperature is below 65 degrees F. or when it's too windy. That means, for example, that with the early-blooming apricots it would be prudent to choose a self-pollinating type so you don't have to depend on the bees.

The following discussion contains general recommendations on plants for specific landscaping uses—a guided tour through the wide variety of choices now available.

Plants for Specific Purposes in the Landscape

First, two very general recommendations:

1. Be aware that those tree, bush, and vine-ripened gems can be stretched out for months—not only by choosing different fruits but by choosing a succession of different varieties of each. For example, you could have fresh tree-ripened apples from mid-July to December, peaches for three months, blueberries for well over two months, and two full seasons of raspberries. It's all in choosing a succession of cultivars.

2. Among the food plants, physical appearance is not the only thing that makes a good specimen/emphasis/accent plant: cultivation needs and insect and disease problems must be considered too. There are probably better choices for those important focal points in your landscape than peaches or nectarines (for example, apples, pears, and European plums). This is true even though peaches and nectarines have exquisite blooms. These particular plants get more than their share of pest problems, which can be dealt with by pruning off the infested parts. They also require relatively severe pruning if they are to be kept bearing well. Although that's fine in a mass planting, neither requirement bodes well for a specimen plant.

Here are some specific recommendations:

Nut trees make wonderful shade trees. They're practically care free and their wood can be a valuable annuity (up to $1,000 per log for veneer wood). The small shade trees are well represented by disease-resistant type apples, some blight-free pears, the Chinese date, Northern banana, and the Japanese raisin tree.

Save the bulk of the fruits for the semidwarf and dwarf sizes that are used for privacy screening and for space forming. In these sizes their care is simple and easy. With ten minutes per application for mature semidwarfs, seven times a season for a complete residential spray program, their care can hardly be considered onerous. The two- or three-gallon pump sprayers now available are manageable for any landscaper. Organic approaches or mixed organic and chemical controls require more knowledge and attentiveness, but only marginally more time. To keep the care requirements in perspective, think how much time you spent mowing that lawn last season.

Although the northernmost foodscapers must relegate the garden or genetic dwarfs to tubs that can be moved to an unheated garage or shed in the winter, in most areas they can be planted in the ground with a care program like the dwarfs and semidwarfs. Everyone can use bush fruits. Varieties of bush cherries are excellent choices for foundation planting type use. They can be size controlled with a once-a-year pruning. Protecting the cherries from the birds is a lot easier on bushes than on trees. The smaller bramble fruits (red and black raspberries and their kin) also make nice choices. Oregon Evergreen and Black Diamond varieties are evergreen in many zones. The currants and gooseberries are attractive and trouble free. The adaptable and evergreen Oregon Holly grape and its relatives are exquisite beauties. The winter form of the beach plum is terrific. But the blueberries are the Cadillacs of the foodscape shrub world. They have beautiful foliage, take shearing if you want a clipped hedge, and have gorgeous flowers and exquisite fall coloring. November Glow has been hybridized specifically for its foliage, holding its brilliant scarlet fall color past Thanksgiving as far north as Michigan and New York. Evergreen is just that in milder climates. Other cultivars range from 16" (Tophat) to over 8' in height; and there's just about any shape you could want including vase, oval, and very broad-rounded. Ornablue (3' high with a 5" spread) and Bluetta and Northland (4' high, 5" spread) make excellent foundation type choices. Best of all, the blueberries are also trouble free (if you keep the soil pH right) and the fruits are varied and delicious.

With ground covers, the main criterion is that they be ornamentally effective for as long as possible during the year. Among the woody plants, lingonberries and creeping thyme are best for this reason. The possibilities among the herbaceous materials are endless, but plants like the perennial strawberry (not the regular one, which is short-lived and invasive), chives, and New Zealand spinach are all excellent choices as they can take some heavy frosts and are attractive much longer into the fall than most herbs. Creeping thyme even takes foot traffic.

Don't forget the vines; they are generally underused. If you want an "outdoor" natural feel, it's important to soften or hide building and other structural walls. The deciduous vines on trellises are wonderful for shade in summer too, without the waiting of fifteen years for a shade tree to mature. There are many great choices among the deciduous and the annual vines including grapes, scarlet runner beans, Northern kiwi, and climbing tomato (the last one only climbs if you tie it up as it grows). Even though the climbing roses are on this book's tertiary list because their hips are used only for jam and tea, they have to be recommended because of their great beauty. The advent of "bag-a-bugs" and milky spore disease with their ability to control Japanese beetles should place both roses and the grapes back on everyone's most wanted list.

As for those garden color, herbaceous, fresh–out-the-landscape plants, the list is truly endless, and individual taste can be the deciding factor. Vegetables, herbs, and flowers of almost every description can be used. Naturally, those listed here on the ornamental information sheets have something edible about them. Appendix F lists varieties of common vegetables that are well suited to intensive gardening (which gives an attractive, lush ornamental look) and container growing.

You can also tap the resources of your state agricultural college extension service. Every county in the United States has an agricultural agent who usually has an office in the county seat and who can give you information about good cultivars for your specific area. County agents can also identify pests and diseases if you have a problem; but don't expect them to know everything. The cultivar development work being done commercially or in other states might not be known in your area even though the climates might be similar. Most state extension services publish excellent, inexpensive pamphlets on the culture of the various fruits, nuts, and berries grown in their state. These are good sources of information as long as you keep in mind the suggestions are oriented to commercial growers rather than the home gardener.

Part 2
How to Use the Ornamental Information Sheets

All the information needed to make sound design decisions is placed in a standardized format. These blocks of information are very much like the cards or sheets a student of horticulture uses to learn landscaping plants.

In the interests of space there's one illustration and one block of information for each species or variety of plant that *looks* the same. In other words there is one listing sheet for a broad rounded shape standard size apple tree—even though over two hundred cultivars would fit that description; then all the individual cultivars are listed together later. This allows you to pick the specific plant that will fit into your garden design scheme without being overwhelmed by the choices. When you're actually ready to go out and buy the plant, or when curiosity overcomes you, you can look in the appropriate appendix and find the cultivar that has the hardiness, flavor, and timing of fruit ripening you're looking for.

These information sheets are arranged in six sections, and the plants are arranged alphabetically within each section. The first section contains everything in size from shade trees down to ground covers and vines; their common denominator is that they are all delicious nuts, fruits, berries, vegetables, and herbs. The second section covers plants that are as ornamentally attractive as those in the first section, but whose fruits are not so popular. It includes plants whose fruits are used for culinary purposes like jams, jellies, wines, and pies. The third section contains edible flowers and ornamental vegetables for color and "fleshing out." Section 4 contains additional vines with edible fruit. Sections 5 and 6 are brief and contain nonedible plants that fill in the weak areas in the edible landscape. Section 5 has the accent plants, which we use sparingly like spice in cooking. Section 6 has what are called facer plants. Heavy use of dwarf and semidwarf trees will mean a "leggy" look unless you use a low plant in front to complete the transition planting. There is not a wide variety available in the edible landscape world for this use so a few attractive ornamentals are listed.

Much of the information given in the sheets has a specific meaning. "Size at maturity" lists what are called landscape sizes rather than botanical maximums—that is to say, a size you might reasonably expect the plant to reach in the home landscape. For example, a black walnut that would normally get to 50' to 75' in height might reach 120' or more in an arboretum or perfect naturally selected spot in nature. When a wide size range is given, it's still a landscape size; the plant being described is more variable than most. Another tricky

piece of information is shape. Woody plants, and trees in particular, tend to get broader as they get older. Some also change shape as they age; the pin oak is pyramidal when young, oval when mature, and rounded in old age. The branching of trees also tends to be more horizontal and less upright in time. So under "shape," the information listed on the sheets is for the natural shape of a mature, but not an old, plant.

"Time to first crop" is an important term because plants that bear quickly are often highly prized. Many factors determine how quickly plants will bear food crops; genetics is only one. Reproduction (that is, bearing fruit or nuts) is a mature activity and some plants naturally mature more quickly than others. Some cultivars also mature more rapidly than others of the same species. As we have already mentioned, dwarfing rootstocks also play a very important role in earlier bearing. Pollination affects the timing of the first crop, as does the general health of the plant. Last, what is called the seed-type has an effect on the first and subsequent crops. The seed-type issue is the cause of much confusion for northern landscapers. Even though a species of plants may be hardy over a wide geographic area, the individual plant you buy may only be happy in a part of that range; in particular, that part of the range that has approximately the same amount of daylight as the place your individual plant was grown. Because day length is one of the big keys for plants' blooming and fruiting, dealing with a nursery or mail order house that's close to you climatically and geographically can make a difference in yield.

"Bloom date" is another item on the sheets that need clarification. The blooming dates here are for the Boston area and you must use Appendix C to adjust the blooming time for your area. Bear in mind the blooming date may vary from a few days to two weeks from year to year. The sequence of bloom will be the same. Under "seasonal interest" an attempt has been made to rate the plant on its aesthetic appeal at various times of the year. Items with a plus sign are particularly desirable, like the fall color of blueberries, the winter character of a Rhode Island Greening apple, or the bloom of any of the peaches. Even when no plus sign appears, the verbal description indicates that particular plant quality has ornamental value. A dash (generally under the entry "Winter character") indicates that the plant is not ornamentally valuable for that characteristic.

A last note of clarification: the growing zones referred to in this book are the traditional Arnold Arboretum zones. When a zone number is given in italics, it means that those zones are the limits of that particular plant's range, and that only cultivars with those zone designations listed should be chosen from the cultivar list.

THE PLANT

INFORMATION

SHEETS

Size Category	Height
shade tree	45′ +
small shade tree	20′–45′
semidwarf tree	10′–20′
dwarf tree/large shrub	6′–10′
garden dwarf tree/medium shrub	3′–6′
small shrub	18″–3′
ground cover	2″–18″
vine	by length
herbaceous material	varies

Shade Trees

45 FEET AND UP IN HEIGHT

Black Walnut Juglans Nigra

Landscaping Values

Shape oval to rounded
Time to first crop 4–8 years   **Density** average to open
Foliage medium dark green   **Texture** medium coarse
Size at maturity 50′–75′ height x 50′–75′ spread
Branching high branched, upright, and spreading

Seasonal Interest

Bloom Date —
Flowers not noticeable
Fruit 2″ diameter, nuts with thick green outer husk
Fall color weak yellow   **Winter character** —

Planting Guide

Growing zone 5 6 7 8 9
Spacing of mature plants 50′   **Root stock** seedling
Pollination weakly self-fruitful (see Appendix B)
Site considerations full sun to light shade, average or better fertility, good drainage and not shallow soil

Comments

Black Walnuts are more pyramidal when young, variable in size (sometimes to 120′) and are the fastest growing of the walnuts. The Kwik-Krop variety bears in two years.

Butternut JUGLANS CINEREA

Landscaping Values

Shape   loosely oval, somewhat flat headed
Time to first crop   3–8 years   **Density**   open to average
Foliage   medium dark   **Texture**   medium coarse
Size at maturity   40'–60' height by 30'–50' spread
Branching   stout branched, many horizontal, upright and spreading

Seasonal Interest

Bloom date   —
Flowers   not noticeable
Fruit   2" + or −, oblong with thick green outer husk
Fall color   weak yellow   **Winter character**   —

Planting Guide

Growing zone   4 5 6 7
Spacing of mature plants   30'   **Root stock**   seedling
Pollination   weakly self-fruitful
Site considerations   full sun to light shade, adaptable but needs good drainage

Comments

The hardiest of all nuts; an easy cracking variety should be bought.

Chinese Chestnut CASTANEA MOLLISIMA

Landscaping Values

Shape rounded
Time to first crop 3–5 years   **Density** dense
Foliage medium dark green   **Texture** medium coarse
Size at maturity 40'–60' height x 40'–60' spread
Branching upright spreading

Seasonal Interest

Bloom date mid-June
Flowers creamy yellow tassels
Fruit 2 or 3 in a round prickly outer husk
Fall color bronze/yellow   **Winter character** —

Planting Guide

Growing zone 4 5 6 7 8
Spacing of mature plants 40'   **Root stock** seedling
Pollination almost self-sterile; 2 different varieties are best
Site considerations full sun to light shade, adaptable but needs good drainage

Comments

The leaves are reddish when unfolding and the fall color is quite attractive. Although the tree is perfectly hardy in Zone 4, the growing season may not be always long enough to get mature nuts.

English/Persian Walnut Juglans regia

Landscaping Values

Shape   round to broad rounded
Time to first crop   4–8 years   **Density**   average to dense
Foliage   medium dark   **Texture**   medium coarse
Size at maturity   40'–60' height x 40' x 60' spread
Branching   upright spreading

Seasonal Interest

Bloom date   —
Flowers   not noticeable
Fruit   2" + diameter, nuts with thick green outer husk
Fall color   weak yellow   **Winter character**   —

Planting Guide

Growing zone   5 6 7 8 9
Spacing of mature plants   40'   **Root stock**   seedling
Pollination   weakly self-fruitful
Site considerations   full sun to light shade, average or better fertility, good drainage and not shallow

Comments

The English Walnut has a widely variable mature size depending on conditions.

Hican <small>Carya lacinosa x illinoinensis</small>

Landscaping Values

Shape loosely oval
Time to first crop 3–8 years   **Density** average to open
Foliage medium dark   **Texture** medium coarse
Size at maturity 70'–90' height x 60' spread
Branching upright, spreading, drooping

Seasonal Interest

Bloom date —
Flowers not ornamentally effective
Fruit 3" + −, oblong nut
Fall color yellow russet   **Winter character** attractive

Planting Guide

Growing zone 6 7 8
Spacing of mature plants 60'   **Root stock** seedling
Pollination weakly self-pollinating
Site considerations full sun to light shade, adaptable, moist but not wet soils, likes good drainage

Comments

The hican is a cross between the Shellbark hickory and the pecan. The Burton variety sets heavier crops than the others.

Shellbark Hickory or King Nut

Carya lacinosa

Landscaping Values

Shape loosely oval
Time to first crop 3–8 years   **Density** average to open
Foliage medium dark   **Texture** medium coarse
Size at maturity 60'–80' height x 50' spread
Branching upright, spreading, drooping

Seasonal Interest

Bloom date —
Flowers not ornamentally effective
Fruit oblong 2½" + − nut with roundish thick green outer husk
Fall color yellow russet   **Winter character** picturesque

Planting Guide

Growing zone 5 6 7 8
Spacing of mature plants 50'   **Root stock** seedling
Pollination weakly self-pollinating
Site considerations full sun to light shade, adaptable, even tolerates wet soils to a degree

Comments

The root systems of hickory trees grow much more rapidly than the tops when they're young, so don't be disappointed if they don't seem to grow much the first year or so. Buy an improved variety for better nut quality.

Pecan <small>CARYA ILLINOINENSIS</small>

Landscaping Values

Shape oval
Time to first crop 3–8 years   **Density** average
Foliage medium dark   **Texture** medium coarse
Size of maturity 75'–100' height x 50'–75' spread
Branching upright, spreading

Seasonal Interest

Bloom date —
Flowers not ornamental
Fruit oblong to 3½" in a thick husk
Fall color yellow +   **Winter character** attractive

Planting Guide

Growing zone 6 7 8 9
Spacing of mature plants 50'   **Root stock** seedling
Pollination weakly self-pollinating
Site considerations full sun to light shade, adaptable but needs good drainage

Comments

The Schley variety is a particularly beautiful tree.

Small Shade,

Large Specimen Trees

20 TO 45 FEET IN HEIGHT

Almond PRUNUS DULCIS VAR. DULCIS

Landscaping Values

Shape rounded
Time to first crop 3–4 years   **Density** average to open
Foliage medium green   **Texture** medium
Size at maturity 20'–30'
Branching upright, spreading

Seasonal Interest

Bloom date April
Flowers profuse white or pale pink
Fruit 1" nuts in hard green husks
Fall color —   **Winter character** —

Planting Guide

Growing zone 5 6 7 8 9
Spacing of mature plants 25'   **Root stock** seedling
Pollination weakly self-fertile; plant two varieties
Site considerations full sun, adaptable but well drained, drought tolerant

Comments

The self-fertile Halls Hardy almond has fragrant pink blooms. It grows in Zone 5, but most almond blooms must be protected from frost for fruits to set. A white plastic sheet clothes-pinned over the plant does the trick.

Most Apples MALUS PUMILA

Landscaping Values

Shape round to broad round
Time to first crop 4–12 years   **Density** average
Foliage medium   **Texture** medium
Size at maturity 25'–30' height x 30'–35' spread
Branching many branched—upright and spreading

Seasonal Interest

Bloom date early May
Flowers + profuse, fragrant, light pink fading to white
Fruit red and/or yellow, sometimes greenish/yellow, 2"–4" dia.
Fall color —   **Winter character** —

Planting Guide

Growing zone 3 4 5 6 7 8 9
Spacing of mature plants 25'–50'   **Root stock** seedling
Pollination some are self-pollinating; most require cross pollination
Site considerations full sun to light shade, adaptable, apples don't like wet feet

Comments

Most apples are broad-rounded in shape. Many that are not are listed on their own sheets.

(See Appendix A and Appendix B)

Northern Spy, 20-Ounce, and Macoun Apples MALUS PUMILA

Landscaping Values

Shape   loosely oval
Time to first crop   5–14 years (14 years for Northern Spy)
Density   average   **Texture**   medium
Foliage   medium
Size at maturity   30'–35' height x 20'–25' spread
Branching   upright

Seasonal Interest

Bloom date   mid to late May
Flowers   +profuse, fragrant, light pink fading to white
Fruit   red with yellow markings: 20 oz. is one of the largest apples
Fall color   —   **Winter character**   —

Planting Guide

Growing zone   4 5 6 7
Spacing of mature plants   20'   **Root stock**   seedling
Pollination   require cross pollination (see Appendix B)
Site considerations   full sun to light shade, adaptable but not shallow or clayey; don't like wet feet

Comments

Northern Spy is the most vertical apple tree. The spur types of any variety tend to be more vertical than nonspur types of the same variety.

Red and Yellow Delicious Apples

MALUS PUMILA

Landscaping Values

Shape loosely pyramidal
Time to first crop 5–8 years   **Density** average
Foliage medium   **Texture** medium
Size at maturity 35–45' height x 35' spread
Branching upright, spreading

Seasonal Interest

Bloom date early May
Flowers +profuse, fragrant, pink fading to white
Fruit 3–4" diam., all red or all yellow, or nearly so
Fall color —   **Winter character** —

Planting Guide

Growing zone 5 6 7 8
Spacing of mature plants 30'   **Root stock** seedling
Pollination weakly self-pollinating
Site considerations full sun to light shade, adaptable but not clayey; don't like wet feet.

Comments

There are many varieties for both fruit color and spur growth. Red Bouquet Delicious has medium pink blooms which stay quite pink. Kandil Sinap is also quite pyramidal and smaller.

Rhode Island Greening Apple MALUS PUMILA

Landscaping Values

Shape mounded
Time to first crop 6–8 years   **Density** average
Foliage medium   **Texture** medium
Size at maturity 30' height x 40' spread
Branching upright spreading

Seasonal Interest

Bloom date early May
Flowers +profuse, fragrant, light pink fading to white
Fruit light yellowish green, 3"–4" diameter
Fall color —   **Winter character** +picturesque

Planting Guide

Growing zone 4 5 6 7
Spacing of mature plants 50'   **Root stock** seedling
Pollination requires cross pollination
Site considerations full sun to light shade, adaptable but not too clayey; doesn't like wet feet

Comments

This is probably the most beautiful apple with its broad, spreading, majestic form. May be the best of the cooking apples. Roxbury Russet is also mounded in form.

Tydeman Type Apples MALUS PUMILA

Landscaping Values

Shape   loosely broad vase
Time to first crop   5 years   **Density**   open to average
Foliage   medium   **Texture**   medium
Size at maturity   30'–40' height x 35'–45' spread
Branching   lanky, somewhat sparsely branched

Seasonal Interest

Bloom date   early May
Flowers   +profuse, fragrant, light pink fading to white
Fruit   3–4" diameter, red with yellow markings
Fall color —   **Winter character**   picturesque

Planting Guide

Growing zone   5 6 7 8
Spacing of mature plants   45'   **Root stock**   seedling
Pollination   requires cross pollination
Site considerations   full sun to light shade, adaptable but not too clayey;
don't like wet feet

Comments

Tydeman types are similar to the tea crab apple in character. A beautiful
apple to act as a foil in front of a structure you don't want to hide
completely.

Apricot Prunus armeniaca

Landscaping Values

Shape broad vase
Time to first crop 4–5 years
Foliage medium dark green
Size at maturity 20′–25′
Branching upright spreading

Density average
Texture medium

Seasonal Interest

Bloom date late April
Flowers 1″ profuse pink or white
Fruit 1½–2″ round, orange
Fall color variable red or yellow

Winter character gnarled branches

Planting Guide

Growing zone 4 5 6 7 8
Spacing of mature plants 30′   **Root stock** seedling
Pollination some self-fertile; some require cross fertilization (see Appendix A)
Site considerations full sun to light shade, adaptable but they like lots
of organic material

Comments

The apricot is not as early a bloomer as the almond, but it's close and just
about as susceptible to spring frost damage. Protect with white plastic.
Self-pollinating ones are probably better in colder climates because the bees
(pollinators) don't fly if it's too cold.

Montmorency Tart Cherry PRUNUS CERASUS

Landscaping Values

Shape vase
Time to first crop 3–5 years   **Density** average
Foliage medium   **Texture** medium
Size at maturity 15'–30' height x 15'–30' spread
Branching upright

Seasonal Interest

Bloom date early May
Flowers +profuse, white, to 1" diameter
Fruit round, 1" + or − diameter, glossy medium red
Fall color yellow   **Winter character** —

Planting Guide

Growing zone 5 6 7
Spacing of mature plants 20'   **Root stock** Mahaleb
Pollination self-fertile
Site considerations full sun to medium shade, adaptable but intolerant of wet soil

Comments

These so-called "sour" or "pie" cherries are really more tangy than sour.

Morello Tart Cherries Prunus cerasus

Landscaping Values

Shape rounded
Time to first crop 3–5 years
Foliage medium
Size at maturity 15′–30′ height x 15′–30′ spread
Branching upright, spreading

Density average
Texture medium

Seasonal Interest

Bloom date early May
Flowers +profuse, white, to 1″ diameter
Fruit round, 1″ + or −, medium red
Fall color yellow

Winter character —

Planting Guide

Growing zone 4 5 6 7
Spacing of mature plants 20′
Pollination self-fertile
Site considerations full sun to medium shade, adaptable but wet soil intolerant

Root stock Mahaleb

Comments

The Morellos are the tartest of the cherries. Better for baking than eating out of hand.

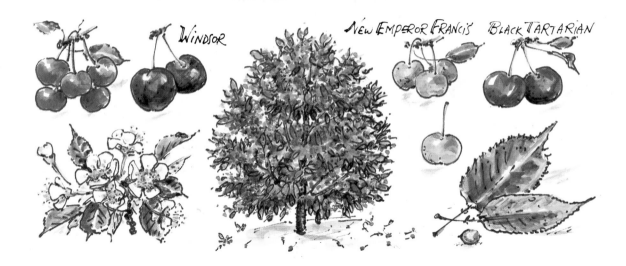

Sweet Cherries PRUNUS AVIUM

Landscaping Values

Shape loosely pyramidal
Time to first crop 5–6 years   **Density** average
Foliage medium dark, glossy   **Texture** medium coarse
Size at maturity 30'–40' height x 30' spread
Branching upright, spreading, strong central stem

Seasonal Interest

Bloom date early May
Flowers profuse, white
Fruit 1" + or − diameter, pale yellow, blush red to deep red (See Appendix A)
Fall color bronze/yellow   **Winter character** —

Planting Guide

Growing zone 5 6 7 8
Spacing of mature plants 30'   **Root stock** seedling
Pollination weakly self-pollinating (see Appendix B)
Site considerations full sun to medium shade, adaptable but intolerant of wet soil

Comments

The sweet cherries are the most shade-tolerant of the shade trees.

Chinese Date (Jujube) Ziziphus jujuba

Landscaping Values

Shape oval
Time to first crop 4–5 years   **Density** average
Foliage glossy, medium green   **Texture** medium-fine
Size at maturity 25'–30'
Branching drooping

Seasonal Interest

Bloom date May
Flowers not ornamentally effective
Fruit 1½"–2" shiny reddish-brown datelike in September & October
Fall color —   **Winter character** attractive
branching

Planting Guide

Growing zone 7 8 9
Spacing of mature plants 20'   **Root stock** seedling
Pollination weakly self-fertile; two or more varieties best
Site considerations full sun to light shade, adaptable and tolerant of heavy soils, better in wet soils than most

Comments

Lang and Li are the only two varieties easily available and their shapes are not typical of the species, both being a beautiful weeping form. Fruits should be picked when wrinkled for storage, earlier for candying.

Japanese Raisin Tree Hovenia dulcis

Landscaping Values

Shape oval to rounded
Time to first crop 6–8 years   **Density** average
Foliage handsome glossy green   **Texture** medium coarse
Size at maturity 30'
Branching upright, spreading

Seasonal Interest

Bloom date June and July
Flowers white clusters
Fruit brownish red pea-sized swollen flower stalks
Fall color yellowish green   **Winter character** —

Planting Guide

Growing zone 5 6 7
Spacing of mature plants 20'   **Root stock** seedling
Pollination self-fertile
Site considerations full sun to light shade, very adaptable, drought tolerant

Comments

Fruit tastes like the Bergamot pear; clean, very attractive tree with nice foliage.

Mulberry MORUS NIGRA

Landscaping Values

Shape rounded
Time to first crop 3–4 years   **Density** dense
Foliage medium dark green   **Texture** coarse
Size at maturity 30'–50'
Branching irregular, slender branches

Seasonal Interest

Bloom date —
Flowers not ornamentally effective
Fruit ½"–1" white, pinkish or purplish, similar to blackberry
Fall color —   **Winter character** —

Planting Guide

Growing zone 4 5 6 7 8
Spacing of mature plants 45'   **Root stock** seedling
Pollination self-fertile
Site considerations full sun to light shade, extremely adaptable, very poor soil and drought tolerant

Comments

Plant only improved cultivars. Black Beauty has a somewhat weeping form. Wellington is a good choice. Mulberries are the favorite of birds; their presence helps keep birds away from cherries. Mulberries are fast growing, but messy fruited.

Northern Banana (Pawpaw) ASIMINA TRILOBA

Landscaping Values

Shape pyramidal
Time to first crop 7–8 years
Foliage light green
Size at maturity 25'–30'
Branching upright, spreading

Density average–dense
Texture coarse

Seasonal Interest

Bloom date May
Flowers 2" diameter maroon/purple
Fruit 3"–7" oblong
Fall color —

Winter character —

Planting Guide

Growing zone 5 6 7 8 9
Spacing of mature plants 20'   **Root stock** seedling
Pollination weakly self-fertile, plant two or more for best crops
Site considerations full sun to medium shade, good soil

Comments

The fruits should be harvested like pears—picked when slightly soft and ripened indoors to almost custardlike consistency. Excellent fresh. Darker fleshed ones are tastier. Pollination is iffy.

Asian or Salad Pear PYRUS PYRIFOLIA

Landscaping Values

Shape loosely oval
Time to first crop 3–4 years   **Density** dense
Foliage glossy medium dark green   **Texture** medium
Size at maturity 25'–40'
Branching upright spreading

Seasonal Interest

Bloom date early to late April
Flowers extremely profuse, 1¼" diameter white
Fruit apple like shape
Fall color purplish red   **Winter character** interesting
branching

Planting Guide

Growing zone 6 7 8 9
Spacing of mature plants 25'   **Root stock** P. calleryana betulaefolia
Pollination requires cross-pollination from another Asian or early- to
mid-European pear
Site considerations full sun to light shade

Comments

The oriental pears are even more profuse bloomers than the European
pears and have nicer fall color. The flesh of the Oriental pears is "fresh"
tasting but blander and grittier than their European counterparts. Should
be tree ripened.

Bosc Pears PYRUS COMMUNIS

Landscaping Values

Shape Oval
Time to first crop 6–8 years   **Density** average
Foliage glossy medium dark green   **Texture** medium
Size at maturity 20'–25'
Branching upright, spreading

Seasonal Interest

Bloom date late April, early May
Flowers profuse, ½" diameter white
Fruit elongated neck, med. sized brown and golden russet
Fall color yellow   **Winter character** upright branching

Planting Guide

Growing zone 5 6 7 8
Spacing of mature plants 18'   **Root stock** seedling
Pollination requires cross pollination from another variety
Site considerations full sun to light shade, adaptable, more clayey soil and poor drainage tolerant than most common fruits

Comments

These are crisp, excellent eating and cooking pears. They're very susceptible to fire blight, however.

Most Pears PYRUS COMMUNIS

Landscaping Values

Shape loosely oval
Time to first crop 4–18 years   **Density** average
Foliage glossy, medium dark green   **Texture** medium
Size at maturity 25'–40'
Branching quite upright, some spreading

Seasonal Interest

Bloom date late April, early May
Flowers profuse ½" diameter, white
Fruit 2"–8" pear-shaped in fall
Fall color yellow

Winter character very upright branching

Planting Guide

Growing zone 4 5 6 7 8 9
Spacing of mature plants 25'   **Root stock** seedling
Pollination require cross pollination from another variety
Site considerations full sun to light shade, adaptable, more clayey soil and poor drainage tolerant than most common fruits

Comments

Fire blight–resistant varieties are best for the homeowner. Like apples, they are more easily trained for espalier than most common fruits. Collete has a very long bloom period. Pears take shearing for hedge use better than most.

Seckel Pear PYRUS COMMUNIS

Landscaping Values

Shape pyramidal
Time to first crop 6–8 years   **Density** average
Foliage glossy medium dark green   **Texture** medium
Size at maturity 20'–25'
Branching upright

Seasonal Interest

Bloom date late April, early May
Flowers profuse ½" diameter, white
Fruit yellowish, brown, small for pears
Fall color yellow   **Winter character** interesting
                                          branching

Planting Guide

Growing zone 4 5 6 7 8
Spacing of mature plants 18'   **Root stock** seedling
Pollination requires cross pollination from another variety (not Bartlett)
Site considerations full sun to light shade, adaptable, more clayey soil and
poor drainage tolerant than most common fruits

Comments

Like all pears they should be harvested when they are full size but still a
bit green, then ripened in storage. Its close relative Chapin is quite
pyramidal in form.

American Persimmon Diospyrus virginiana

Landscaping Values

Shape oval
Time to first crop 4–5 years
Foliage dark green
Size at maturity 40'–50'
Branching horizontal

Density average to open
Texture medium coarse

Seasonal Interest

Bloom date May
Flowers 3/5", whitish
Fruit 1"–2" diameter Pome, yellowish to pale orange & reddish purple
Fall color variable yellow

Winter character attractive branching

Planting Guide

Growing zone 4 5 6 7 8
Spacing of mature plants 25'   **Root stock** seedling
Pollination sexes separate, females fruitful, need pollination from a male
Site considerations Full sun to light shade, very adaptable, low fertility and pollution tolerant.

Comments

Planting holes should be deep. Meader variety does not need pollination to bear and when not pollinized will bear seedless fruit. Cultivated persimmons are absolutely not astringent when allowed to ripen until soft.

Oriental Persimmon Diospyros kaki

Landscaping Values

Shape rounded
Time to first crop 3 years
Foliage glossy dark green
Size at maturity 25'–30'
Branching upright and spreading

Density average
Texture medium coarse

Seasonal Interest

Bloom date May
Flowers 1"–2" yellowish white
Fruit 4"–5" tomato-shaped, red-orange
Fall color orange-red

Winter character "blocky" bark

Planting Guide

Growing zone 6 7 8 9 10
Spacing of mature plants 25'   **Root stock** seedling
Pollination sexes separate—females self-fruitful
Site considerations full sun—light shade, adaptable, drought tolerant.

Comments

The fruit must be fully mature to be good and it's larger in size than the American persimmon. It is a very attractive tree although the flowers are not particularly showy.

Semidwarf

Trees

10 TO 20 FEET IN HEIGHT

Semidwarf Almond PRUNUS DULCIS VAR. DULCIS

Landscaping Values

Shape rounded
Time to first crop 3 years
Foliage medium green
Size at maturity 14'–20'
Branching upright spreading

Density average to open
Texture medium

Seasonal Interest

Bloom date April
Flowers profuse white or pale pink
Fruit 1½″ nuts in hard green husks
Fall color —

Winter character —

Planting Guide

Growing zone 6 7 8 9
Spacing of mature plants 15'   **Root stock** seedling
Pollination weakly self-fertile; plant two varieties
Site considerations full sun, adaptable, likes good drainage,
drought tolerant

Comments

All the almonds do much better in more arid than more humid climates;
semidwarf size varieties include All-in-one (self-fertile) and Price.

Semidwarf Apple Malus pumila

Landscaping Values

Shape   see standard size sheets
Time to first crop   3–4 years   **Density**   average
Foliage   medium green   **Texture**   medium
Size at maturity   12–18′ depending on variety
Branching   many branched, upright and spreading

Seasonal Interest

Bloom date   early May
Flowers   + profuse, fragrant, light pink fading to white
Fruit   red and/or yellow, sometimes greenish yellow, 2–4″ diam.
Fall color   —   **Winter character**   —

Planting Guide

Growing zone   3 4 5 6 7 8 9
Spacing of mature plants   12′–15′   **Root stock**   —
Pollination   some are self-pollinating, most require cross-pollination
from another variety (see Appendix B)
Site considerations   full sun to light shade, adaptable, don't like wet soils

Comments

The spur-type varieties are small in the size range while 'Black Gilliflower'
and the Pearmains are among the largest. The semi-dwarfs bear a lot more
quickly than the standard size trees, usually in 2 to 3 years.

Semidwarf Cherry PRUNUS AVIUM

Landscaping Values

Shape loosely pyramidal
Time to first crop 3–4 years   **Density** average
Foliage medium dark glossy green   **Texture** medium coarse
Size at maturity 10'–20' depending on variety
Branching upright spreading

Seasonal Interest

Bloom date early May
Flowers profuse white
Fruit 1" + or − diameter yellow, blush red to deep red
Fall color bronze/yellow   **Winter character** —

Planting Guide

Growing zone 5 6 7 8
Spacing of mature plants 30'   **Root stock** seedling
Pollination ones listed below are self-fertile
Site considerations full sun to light shade, adaptable, more tolerant of wet soils in spring than most fruits

Comments

Cherries in the semidwarf size range include sweet kinds like Starkcrimson, Compact Stella (10'–14') and Stella (15'–25'). The tarts (sours) attain 15'–30' in height except Meteor, which is 10'–15', and North Star, which gets to about 10'.

Fig FICUS CARICA

Landscaping Values

Shape broad rounded
Time to first crop 3–4 years   **Density** dense
Foliage medium green   **Texture** coarse
Size at maturity 15'–25'
Branching upright spreading, clubby

Seasonal Interest

Bloom date summer
Flowers inconspicuous
Fruit 1"–3" fleshy, oblong, black, brown, purplish, white
Fall color yellow   **Winter character** —

Planting Guide

Growing zone 7 8 9
Spacing of mature plants 25'   **Root stock** seedling
Pollination self-fertile
Site considerations full sun to light shade, average to poor and neutral soil, drought tolerant when established

Comments

It is a much smaller tree if it's in cooler areas of its range because of winter die back, or if it's maintained as a multistemmed specimen instead of a single trunk. Some varieties bear twice a year. Heavy mulching helps if you have nematodes in your area.

American Filbert CORYLUS AMERICANA

Landscaping Values

Shape loosely vase
Time to first crop 4 years   **Density** average
Foliage dark green   **Texture** medium
Size at maturity 10'
Branching upright, multistemmed shrubby tree

Seasonal Interest

Bloom date April
flowers inconspicuous
Fruit 1–6 nuts in a group with frilly green covering
Fall color —   **Winter character** —

Planting Guide

Growing zone 4 5 6 7 8 9
Spacing of mature plants 8'   **Root stock** seedling
Pollination weakly self-fertile; plant two or more different varieties
Site considerations full sun to light shade, adaptable but well drained

Comments

The American Filbert nuts are smaller and not as tasty as the European types, but the flowers and buds are hardier. Both these and the European types sucker easily.

European Filbert <small>Corylus avellana</small>

Landscaping Values

Shape loosely vase
Time to first crop 4 years   **Density** average
Foliage dark green   **Texture** medium
Size at maturity 15'–20'
Branching upright, spreading, often multistemmed

Seasonal Interest

Bloom date April
Flowers inconspicuous, easily frost damaged
Fruit 1–4 nuts in a group with frilly green coverings
Fall color —   **Winter character** —

Planting Guide

Growing zone 5 6 7 8 9
Spacing of mature plants 15'   **Root stock** seedling
Pollination weakly self-fertile; plant two or more varieties
Site considerations full sun to light shade, adaptable but well drained

Comments

In the East a European/American cross is best because of blight. Beautiful ornamentals like the purple or dark bronzy leafed and corkscrew hazels have fewer, less tasty, and very variable nuts.

Medlar Mesipilus germanica

Landscaping Values

Shape slightly broad rounded
Time to first crop 4–6 years   **Density** average
Foliage medium green   **Texture** medium coarse
Size at maturity 15'–20'
Branching irregular

Seasonal Interest

Bloom date mid-May
Flowers 1½" white fading to pink on branch tips
Fruit roundish greenish brown
Fall color red   **Winter character** zig-zag branching

Planting Guide

Growing zone 5 6 7 8
Spacing of mature plants 18'   **Root stock** hawthorn, common pear
Pollination self-fruitful
Site considerations full sun to light shade, very adaptable

Comments

Fruit should be picked when greenish-brown after frost and ripened in storage like pears. Unusual in that the graft should be planted below the ground. Use improved varieties only. Nottingham is available.

Nectarine PRUNUS PERSICA

Landscaping Values

Shape broad rounded
Time to first crop 4–6 years   **Density** average
Foliage medium green   **Texture** medium
Size at maturity 12′–18′ and 15′–20′ spread
Branching upright spreading

Seasonal Interest

Bloom date late April
Flowers +profuse pink, 1–1½″ diameter
Fruit 2″–4″ round, yellow and/or reddish fuzzless
Fall color yellow   **Winter character** —

Planting Guide

Growing zone 5 6 7 8 9
Spacing of mature plants 15′   **Root stock** many (see Appendix D)
Pollination self-fertile
Site considerations full sun to light shade, adaptable but very fussy about getting wet feet, prefers sandier soils

Comments

Like the peaches, the bloom tempts homeowners to use them as specimen plants, but they should be relegated to the mass planting because of the care and cultural practices; they'll almost always get brown rot in a wet year.

Dwarf Peach PRUNUS PERSICA

Landscaping Values

Shape broad rounded
Time to first crop 3–5 years   **Density** average
Foliage medium green   **Texture** medium
Size at maturity 10'–12' x 12'–15' spread.
Branching upright spreading

Seasonal Interest

Bloom date late April
Flowers + profuse pink
Fruit 2"–4" round yellow and/or reddish
Fall color yellow   **Winter character** —

Planting Guide

Growing zone 5 6 7 8 9
Spacing of mature plants 12'   **Root stock** Prunus tomentosa
Pollination almost all self-fertile (see Appendix B)
Site considerations full sun to light shade, adaptable but much prefers lighter (sandier) soils

Comments

The standard peaches are kept fairly small because of the pruning needs. It is probably not worth it to buy the dwarfs for the modest size reduction because they are even shorter lived than the standards. The dwarfs do somewhat better in heavier soils, however.

Peach <small>Prunus persica</small>

Landscaping Values

Shape broad rounded
Time to first crop 4–6 years   **Density** average
Foliage medium   **Texture** medium
Size at maturity 12'–18' height x 15'–20' spread
Branching upright spreading

Seasonal Interest

Bloom date late April
Flowers +profuse, pink, 1"–1½" diameter
Fruit 2"–4" round, yellow and/or reddish
Fall color yellow   **Winter character** —

Planting Guide

Growing zone 5 6 7 8 9
Spacing of mature plants 15'   **Root stock** many (see Appendix D)
Pollination almost all self-fertile (see Appendix B)
Site considerations full sun to light shade, adaptable but doesn't like wet feet, prefers sandier soils

Comments

The bloom tempts homeowners to use the peaches as specimen plants, but it's better to use them in mass plantings because they're the fussiest of the fruit trees for care requirements. Cultural practices limit the specimen value.

Semidwarf and Dwarf Pear PYRUS COMMUNIS

Landscaping Values

Shape see standard size sheets
Time to first crop 3–8 years   **Density** average
Foliage glossy medium dark green   **Texture** medium
Size at maturity 10′–20′
Branching quite upright, some spreading

Seasonal Interest

Bloom date late April, early May
Flowers profuse, ½″ diameter, white
Fruit 2″–8″ pear shaped in fall
Fall color yellow   **Winter character** very upright
branching

Planting Guide

Growing zone 4 5 6 7 8 9
Spacing of mature plants 10′ or 15′   **Root stock** quince/old home
Pollination require cross-pollination from another variety
Site considerations full sun to light shade; pears grafted on quince stock
are not as tolerant of clayey or poorly drained soils as standard pears

Comments

Seckel and Chapin succeed very well on dwarfing root stock. Both the
semidwarf pear (15′–20′) and the dwarf pear (10′–15′) are in the semidwarf
size range.

All Red Plum (Japanese) PRUNUS SALICINA

Landscaping Values

Shape   narrow vase
Time to first crop   4–6 years   **Density**   average
Foliage   + bronze/red   **Texture**   medium
Size at maturity   15'–20' height x 10'–15' spread
Branching   upright

Seasonal Interest

Bloom date   early May
Flowers   + profuse, white
Fruit   2"–3" diameter, round, bright red with red flesh
Fall color   bronze/red   **Winter character**   —

Planting Guide

Growing zone   6 7 8 9
Spacing of mature plants   15'   **Root stock**   Halford
Pollination   requires pollination by another Japanese plum
Site considerations   full sun to light shade, adaptable but needs adequate drainage, prefers light soils

Comments

Although it is often bought for its novel leaf color, its fruits are excellent Japanese plums; holds leaves well into fall.

Burbank Plum (Japanese) Prunus salicina

Landscaping Values

Shape broad rounded
Time to first crop 4–6 years   **Density** average to open
Foliage medium green, glossy   **Texture** medium
Size at maturity 12'–15' height x 15'–20' spread
Branching upright, spreading, drooping

Seasonal Interest

Bloom date early May
Flowers +profuse, white, ½–¾" diameter
Fruit 2"–3" round, bright to medium red
Fall color +bronze/red   **Winter character** —

Planting Guide

Growing zone 5 6 7 8 9
Spacing of mature plants 20'   **Root stock** Halford
Pollination requires pollination by another Japanese plum
Site considerations full sun to light shade, very adaptable but prefers adequate drainage and lighter soils

Comments

The Burbank plum tree can get somewhat flat topped at maturity.

California Blue Plum (European)

PRUNUS DOMESTICA

Landscaping Values

Shape narrow vase
Time to first crop 4–6 years   **Density** average
Foliage medium green, glossy   **Texture** medium
Size at maturity 15'–20' height x 10'–15' spread
Branching very upright

Seasonal Interest

Bloom date early May
Flowers +profuse, white ½"–¾" diameter, clustered along spurs
Fruit 3' +or −, blue/black, oval
Fall color —   **Winter character** —

Planting Guide

Growing zone 5 6 7 8
Spacing of mature plants 12'   **Root stock** Halford
Pollination weakly self-pollinating
Site considerations full sun to light shade, very adaptable but needs adequate drainage, prefers heavier (more clayey) soils

Comments

The California Blue has a rare shape among the food-bearing plants. It lends itself to forming small scaled allées or against buildings where limited space is available between windows or doors.

Cocheco Plum <small>PRUNUS DOMESTICA</small>

Landscaping Values

Shape broad round
Time to first crop 4–6 years   **Density** average
Foliage bronze purple   **Texture** medium
Size at maturity 15′–20′ x 20′ spread
Branching upright spreading

Seasonal Interest

Bloom date early May
Flowers + profuse white
Fruit 2″–3″ diameter, round reddish purple
Fall color bronzy purple   **Winter character** —

Planting Guide

Growing zone 5 6 7 8
Spacing of mature plants 20′   **Root stock** Halford
Pollination needs pollination by another Japanese plum
Site considerations full sun to light shade, adaptable but needs adequate drainage.

Comments

A very beautiful ornamental plum, the fruits are similar to Methley.

European Plums Prunus domestica
(Stanley, Damson, Seneca, Iroquois)

Landscaping Values

Shape vase
Time to first crop 4–6 years   **Density** average
Foliage medium green, glossy   **Texture** medium
Size at maturity 15'–20' height x 12'–18' spread
Branching upright spreading

Seasonal Interest

Bloom date early May
Flowers + profuse, white ½"–¾" diameter on spurs
Fruit 2"–3" diameter, blue/black, oval (Damson types 1" + or − round)
Fall color —   **Winter character** —

Planting Guide

Growing zone 5 6 7 8
Spacing of mature plants 15'   **Root stock** Halford
Pollination self-fruitful
Site considerations full sun to light shade, very adaptable but needs adequate drainage, prefers heavy soils

Comments

The Iroquois is the broadest spreading of the vase shaped European plums. The Damson types are prized for their tart flavor (which turns sweet when dead ripe). Stanley is the hardiest of this group.

Frontier Plum (Japanese) PRUNUS SALICINA

Landscaping Values

Shape oval
Time to first crop 4–6 years   **Density** average
Foliage medium green, glossy   **Texture** medium
Size at maturity 15'–20' height x 12'–18' spread
Branching upright spreading

Seasonal Interest

Bloom date early May
Flowers +profuse, white, ½"–¾" diameter, clustered on spurs
Fruit 2–3" blue/black, round
Fall color bronze/red   **Winter character** —

Planting Guide

Growing zone 5 6 7 8 9
Spacing of mature plants 15'   **Root stock** Halford
Pollination requires pollination by another Japanese plum
Site considerations full sun to light shade, very adaptable but needs
adequate drainage, prefers light soils

Comments

The Frontier plum is often mistaken for a European type plum because of its fruit color. If a pollinator is not provided, it won't bear fruit.

The Gages and Grand Prize Plum

PRUNUS DOMESTICA

Landscaping Values

Shape oval
Time to first crop 4–6 years   **Density** average
Foliage medium green, glossy   **Texture** medium
Size at maturity 15′–20′ height x 12′–18′ spread
Branching upright spreading

Seasonal Interest

Bloom date early May
Flowers +profuse, white, ½″–¾″ diameter, clustered along spurs
Fruit red or pale yellow–green
Fall color —   **Winter character** —

Planting Guide

Growing zone 5 6 7 8
Spacing of mature plants 15′   **Root stock** Halford
Pollination weakly self-fruitful
Site considerations full sun to light shade, very adaptable but need adequate drainage, prefer heavy soils

Comments

Grand Prize is the most narrowly oval in shape and the one that will grow in Zone 8. The Gages include Green Gage (or Reine Claude), Yellow Transparent Gage, and Red Reine Claude (or Conducta).

Japanese Plum PRUNUS SALICINA

(Elephant Heart, Red Heart, Shiro, Formosa, Duarte)

Landscaping Values

Shape vase
Time to first crop 4–6 years   **Density** average
Foliage medium green, glossy   **Texture** medium
Size at maturity 15′–20′ height, x 15′–20′ spread
Branching upright spreading

Seasonal Interest

Bloom date early May
Flowers +profuse white, ½″–¾″ diameter, clustered in spurs
Fruit 2″–3″ round, bright red (Shiro is golden yellow)
Fall color +bronze/red   **Winter character** —

Planting Guide

Growing zone 5 6 7 8 9
Spacing of mature plants 20′   **Root stock** Halford
Pollination requires pollination by another Japanese plum
Site considerations full sun to light shade, very adaptable but prefers adequate drainage, lighter soils

Comments

Shiro and Formosa tend to be more broad than the Elephant Heart and Red Heart. Shiro grows in cooler areas of Zone 9. Formosa holds its leaves late into the fall.

Mirabelle and Damson Plum PRUNUS INSTITIA

Landscaping Values

Shape rounded
Time to first crop 4–5 years   **Density** average
Foliage glossy medium green   **Texture** medium
Size at maturity 12'–15'
Branching upright spreading

Seasonal Interest

Bloom date early May
Flowers profuse white
Fruit Damson—small purple; Mirabelle—small golden
Fall color —   **Winter character** —

Planting Guide

Growing zone 5 6 7
Spacing of mature plants 15'   **Root stock** seedling
Pollination Damsons self-fertile; Mirabelle requires cross-pollination
Site considerations full sun to light shade, very adaptable but needs good drainage

Comments

The Damsons are quite tart, making excellent tarts and preserves. The Mirabelles are small but very sugary and excellent eating.

Mohawk Plum (European) PRUNUS DOMESTICA

Landscaping Values

Shape broad rounded
Time to first crop 4–6 years   **Density** average
Foliage medium green, glossy   **Texture** medium
Size at maturity 12′–15′ height x 15′–20′ spread
Branching upright spreading

Seasonal Interest

Bloom date early May
Flowers +profuse, white, ½″–¾″ diameter, clustered on spurs
Fruit 3″ + or − , blue/black
Fall color —   **Winter character** —

Planting Guide

Growing zone 5 6 7 8
Spacing of mature plants 20′   **Root stock** Halford
Pollination weakly self-fruitful
Site considerations full sun to light shade, very adaptable but needs adequate drainage, prefers heavy soils

Comments

Mohawk has very pronounced spur growth.

Ozark Premier Plum (Japanese)

PRUNUS SALICINA

Landscaping Values

Shape mounded
Time to first crop 4–6 years   **Density** average
Foliage medium green, glossy   **Texture** medium
Size at maturity 12′–15′ height x 15′–20′ spread
Branching upright spreading

Seasonal Interest

Bloom date early May
Flowers +profuse white, ½″–¾″ diameter, clustered on spurs
Fruit 3″ + or −, round, bright red
Fall color bronze/red   **Winter character** attractive form

Planting Guide

Growing zone 5 6 7 8 9
Spacing of mature plants 20′   **Root stock** Halford
Pollination self-fertile (unusual for Japanese plums)
Site considerations full sun to light shade, very adaptable but needs adequate drainage, prefers light soils

Comments

Ozark Premier has the largest fruits and is one of the most beautiful plums.

Semidwarf Plum PRUNUS DOMESTICA

Landscaping Values

Shape   see standard size sheets
Time to first crop   3–4 years
Foliage   medium green, glossy
Size at maturity   10'–14'—varies
Branching   upright spreading

Density   average
Texture   medium

Seasonal Interest

Bloom date   early May
Flowers   +profuse white, ½"–¾" on spurs
Fruit   2"–3" oblong or round, red to blue-black
Fall color —   **Winter character** —

Planting Guide

Growing zone   5 6 7 8
Spacing of mature plants   10'   **Root stock**   Julien A. common plum
Pollination   see standard sheets
Site considerations   full sun to light shade, very adaptable to soil type
but needs adequate drainage, prefers heavier soils

Comments

Both the standard and semidwarf plums are in the semidwarf size range.
One supplier, Southmeadow Fruit Gardens, offers the plums on dwarf size
range root stock (6'-to-10' at maturity).

Weeping Santa Rosa Plum <small>PRUNUS SALICINA</small>

Landscaping Values

Shape mounded
Time to first crop 4–5 years   **Density** average
Foliage medium dark green   **Texture** medium
Size at maturity 12′–15′
Branching slender, gracefully weeping

Seasonal Interest

Bloom date mid-May
Flowers profuse white
Fruit 3″ diameter deep red
Fall color bronzy red   **Winter character** attractive
branching

Planting Guide

Growing zone 5 6 7 8
Spacing of mature plants 20′   **Root stock** seedling
Pollination self-fruitful
Site considerations full sun to light shade, very adaptable but needs
adequate drainage, prefers light soils

Comments

The Santa Rosas are reputed to be shy bearers in the East, but the spicy
flavor is excellent. The weeping ones bloom a little later than the
others so that can be an advantage for northern landscapers.

Pomegranate Punica granatum

Landscaping Values

Shape   broad vase
Time to first crop   4–5 years   **Density**   average
Foliage   light green, mostly   **Texture**   medium
deciduous
Size at maturity   12′–20′
Branching   upright spreading

Seasonal Interest

Bloom date   see comments
Flowers   brilliant orange red, alone or in clusters
Fruit   bright red
Fall color   yellow   **Winter character**   interesting form

Planting Guide

Growing zone   8 9 10
Spacing of mature plants   18′   **Root stock**   seedling
Pollination   self-fertile
Site considerations   full sun to light shade, very adaptable, tolerant of
alkaline and slow drainage conditions, but fruit quality suffers

Comments

The Pomegranate blooms in two or three main periods from March to
September in Zone 9, sometimes as much as six weeks at a time. It suckers
easily and can be maintained as a large shrub.

Quince CYDONIA OBLONGA

Landscaping Values

Shape rounded
Time to first crop 7–8 years
Foliage medium green
Size at maturity 12'–20'
Branching upright spreading

Density average
Texture medium

Seasonal Interest

Bloom date early May
Flowers profuse 2" white and pale pink
Fruit yellow pear shaped (Pineapple is round)
Fall color yellow

Winter character —

Planting Guide

Growing zone 5 6 7 8 9
Spacing of mature plants 15'
Pollination self-fertile

Root stock seedling

Site considerations full sun to light shade, very adaptable, will tolerate slow drainage, fruiting adversely affected in very clayey or very sandy soil

Comments

The fruit is great cooked, candied, or in jelly. The quince suckers easily. It is susceptible to fire blight in humid areas of warm zones.

Dwarf Trees

and Large Shrubs

6 TO 10 FEET IN HEIGHT

Garden Dwarf Almond PRUNUS DULCIS VAR. DULCIS

Landscaping Values

Shape vase
Time to first crop 3–4 years   **Density** average to dense
Foliage medium green   **Texture** medium
Size at maturity 6′–8′ height x 8′ spread
Branching upright spreading

Seasonal Interest

Bloom date April
Flowers profuse clustered pink
Fruit 1½″ nuts in hard green husks
Fall color —   **Winter character** —

Planting Guide

Growing zone 7 8 9
Spacing of mature plants 8′   **Root stock** seedling
Pollination self-pollinating
Site considerations full sun, adaptable but needs well-drained soil, drought tolerant, likes low humidity

Comments

The Garden Dwarf almond is well suited to container growing but requires about two hundred days to mature nuts. Garden Prince is the first on the market.

Dwarf Apple MALUS PUMILA

Landscaping Values

Shape   see standard size sheets
Time to first crop 3–4 years   **Density**   average
Foliage medium green   **Texture**   medium
Size at maturity 6'–10'
Branching   many branched, upright and spreading

Seasonal Interest

Bloom date   early May (see Appendix A)
Flowers   +profuse, fragrant, light pink fading to white
Fruit   red and/or yellow, sometimes greenish yellow, 2"–4" diameter
Fall color —   **Winter character** —

Planting Guide

Growing zone   3 4 5 6 7 8 9
Spacing of mature plants 8'   **Root stock**   m9, m26
Pollination   some are self-pollinating, most require cross-pollination from another variety (see Appendix B)
Site considerations   full sun to light shade, adaptable, don't like wet feet

Comments

Dwarf apples should be inconspicuously staked all their life to avoid breakage. Most varieties are available on dwarf root stocks. The m26 will produce a dwarf size-range tree with some spur-type or less vigorous cultivars.

Garden Dwarf Apple MALUS PUMILA

Landscaping Values

Shape loosely pyramidal
Time to first crop 4–5 years
Foliage medium green
Size at maturity 6'–8' height x 6' spread
Branching upright spreading

Density average
Texture medium

Seasonal Interest

Bloom date early May
Flowers +profuse, fragrant, light pink fading to white
Fruit 2" +, red
Fall color dull yellow

Winter character —

Planting Guide

Growing zone 5 6 7 8
Spacing of mature plants 6'
Pollination weakly self-fruitful
Site considerations full sun to light shade, adaptable

Root stock seedling

Comments

The Garden Dwarf apples are only marginally smaller than grafted dwarf apples, which offer infinitely greater variety. They are also slow growing.

Dwarf Apricot PRUNUS ARMENIACA

Landscaping Values

Shape broad vase
Time to first crop 3–4 years
Foliage medium dark green
Size at maturity 8'–10'
Branching upright spreading

Density average
Texture medium

Seasonal Interest

Bloom date late April
Flowers 1″ profuse pink or white
Fruit 1½″–2″ round orange
Fall color variable red or yellow

Winter character gnarled branches

Planting Guide

Growing zone 4 5 6 7 8
Spacing of mature plants 10'   **Root stock** Manchurian
Pollination some self-fertile, some require cross pollination
Site considerations full sun to light shade, adaptable but likes good organic soil

Comments

Early blooms must be protected from frost by wrapping with white plastic. The Manchurian root stock imparts hardiness.

Garden Dwarf Apricot <small>PRUNUS ARMENIACA</small>

Landscaping Values

Shape broad vase
Time to first crop 3–4 years   **Density** average
Foliage medium dark green   **Texture** medium
Size at maturity 6'–8' height x 6'–8' spread
Branching upright spreading

Seasonal Interest

Bloom date late April
Flowers 1" profuse white
Fruit 1½"–2" round orange
Fall color yellow   **Winter character** —

Planting Guide

Growing zone 5 6 7 8 9
Spacing of mature plants 8'   **Root stock** seedling
Pollination self-pollinating
Site considerations full sun to light shade, adaptable but fussy about good drainage; prefers lighter, organic soils

Comments

Garden Annie is on the market now, others will follow. It is larger than the other garden dwarfs. Some die back of branch tips should be expected.

Manchurian Apricot <small>PRUNUS AMENIACA VAR. MANCHURIACA</small>

Landscaping Values

Shape rounded
Time to first crop 4–5 years   **Density** average
Foliage medium dark glossy green   **Texture** medium
Size at maturity 8'–10' height x 8'–10' spread
Branching upright spreading

Seasonal Interest

Bloom date late April
Flowers +profuse 1" pink, fragrant
Fruit 1½"–2" diameter round—orange
Fall color yellow   **Winter character** —

Planting Guide

Growing zone 4 5 6 7 8
Spacing of mature plants 10'   **Root stock** seedling
Pollination self-pollinating; two or more is better
Site considerations full sun to light shade, adaptable but needs well-drained soil

Comments

These are very hardy plants but the blooms can be killed if not protected from late frosts. Often called Manchurian bush apricot; even though it gets quite large, it can be size controlled with pruning for shrub use.

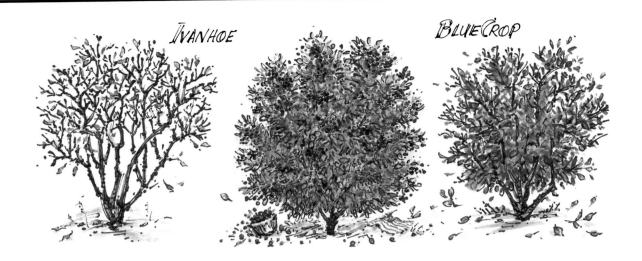

IVANHOE   BLUECROP

Oval Blueberry VACCINIUM CORYMBOSUM

Landscaping Values

Shape oval
Time to first crop 2–3 years   **Density** average
Foliage deciduous, medium dark   **Texture** medium
      green
Size at maturity 6'–8'
Branching upright spreading

Seasonal Interest

Bloom date mid-May
Flowers profuse clusters, white or white tinged pink
Fruit clustered blue-black berries
Fall color +scarlet red   **Winter character** —

Planting Guide

Growing zone 4 5 6 7 8 9
Spacing of mature plants 4'–6'   **Root stock** seedling
Pollination mostly weakly self-fertile; two or more varieties best
Site considerations full sun to medium shade; moist acidic well-drained
soil with lots of peat moss and mulch

Comments

Do not plant blueberries after they leaf out but do before the last frost. 1½
lb. of garden sulfur should be added per 100 sq. ft. for each point of soil
pH above 5.5. Patriot is broad oval (6' height x 5' spread). Bluehaven is
a small one (4' x 3' spread).

Vase Blueberry Vᴀᴄᴄɪɴɪᴜᴍ ᴄᴏʀʏᴍʙᴏsᴜᴍ

Landscaping Values

Shape vase
Time to first crop 2–3 years
Foliage deciduous, medium dark
      green
Size at maturity 8' + or −
Branching upright spreading

Density average/open
Texture medium

Seasonal Interest

Bloom date mid-May
Flowers profuse clusters, white or white tinged with pink
Fruit clustered blue-black berries
Fall color +scarlet red

Winter character —

Planting Guide

Growing zone 4 5 6 7 8 9
Spacing of mature plants 6'   **Root stock** seedling
Pollination weakly self-fertile; two or more varieties best
Site considerations full sun to medium shade, moist, acidic well-drained soil with lots of peat moss and mulch

Comments

Rubel and Spartan both have the vase form; but of the two, Spartan has by far the largest berries and is the tastiest. Rubel is fussier than most other blueberries about acidity.

Cherry Plum PRUNUS NATIVE CROSSES

Landscaping Values

Shape broad rounded
Time to first crop 3–4 years   **Density** average
Foliage deciduous, medium green   **Texture** medium texture
Size at maturity 4'–8' height x 6'–10' spread
Branching upright spreading

Seasonal Interest

Bloom date early May
Flowers white
Fruit 1" diameter red to purple
Fall color yellow   **Winter character** —

Planting Guide

Growing zone 3 4 5 6 7
Spacing of mature plants 6'–10'   **Root stock** seedling
Pollination mostly self-fertile
Site considerations full sun to light shade, adaptable

Comments

The cherry plums are shaped the same but the cultivars vary in size with Compass the largest at 8' and Delight the smallest at about 4' to 5'. They can be size-controlled with pruning.

Nanking or Manchu Cherry Prunus tomentosa

Landscaping Values

Shape rounded
Time to first crop 2–3 years   **Density** average to dense
Foliage deciduous, medium green   **Texture** medium
Size at maturity 6'–8' height x 6'–8' spread
Branching upright spreading

Seasonal Interest

Bloom date late April
Flowers profuse white with a red base
Fruit profuse ½" diameter round red
Fall color —   **Winter character** —

Planting Guide

Growing zone 3 4 5 6 7
Spacing of mature plants 8'   **Root stock** seedling
Pollination self-fertile
Site considerations full sun to medium shade, adaptable

Comments

Nanking cherries are attractive ornamentals in fruit and flower; they make excellent informal hedges. Fruits are only for pies, sauces, and canning.

Elderberry SAMBUCUS CANADENSIS

Landscaping Values

Shape mounded
Time to first crop 2–3 years   **Density** dense
Foliage medium green   **Texture** medium
Size at maturity 6′–10′
Branching spreading, arching

Seasonal Interest

Bloom date late June
flowers 6″–10″ white clusters, fragrant
Fruit purple/black ½″ drupe in large clusters
Fall color —   **Winter character** —

Planting Guide

Growing zone 3 4 5 6 7 8 9
Spacing of mature plants 10′–12′   **Root stock** seedling
Pollination self unfruitful; plant two varieties
Site considerations full sun to medium shade, adaptable but needs moist soil, tolerates wet feet

Comments

The elderberries are beautiful ornamentals. It's important to buy only named varieties. Red-berried natives have toxic fruit. A little pruning helps keep the attractive mounded shape.

Dwarf Fig FICUS CARICA

Landscaping Values

Shape broad rounded
Time to first crop 3–4 years   **Density** dense
Foliage medium green   **Texture** coarse
Size at maturity 6'–10'
Branching upright, spreading, clubby

Seasonal Interest

Bloom date summer
Flowers inconspicuous
Fruit 1" to 3" fleshy, oblong, black, brown, purplish, white
Fall color yellow   **Winter character** —

Planting Guide

Growing zone 7 8 9
Spacing of mature plants 8'   **Root stock** seedling
Pollination self-fertile
Site considerations full sun to light shade, average to poor but neutral soil, drought tolerant when established

Comments

Hardiness is not the only consideration with figs. If you live in a cooler climate, choose a variety that will sweeten as it ripens without hot summers.

Juneberry AMELANCHIER FLORIDA

Landscaping Values

Shape oval
Time to first crop 2–3 years
Foliage medium green
Size at maturity 6'–8'
Branching upright spreading can be shrubby or small tree

Density average
Texture medium

Seasonal Interest

Bloom date late April—4–5 days
Flowers profuse white, 1" diameter
Fruit ½" to ¾" bluish black, berrylike
Fall color orange/red

Winter character —

Planting Guide

Growing zone 2 3 4 5 6
Spacing of mature plants 6'
Pollination self-fertile
Site considerations full sun to medium shade, adaptable but likes acidic soil

Root stock seedling

Comments

Many Amalanchier species are sold as the Saskatoon or the Juneberry, so stick to one of the named varieties or at least be sure it's A. Alinifolia. The fruit is very sweet. They have beautiful blooms, but a short bloom period.

Dwarf Nectarine <small>Prunus persica</small>

Landscaping Values

Shape broad rounded
Time to first crop 3–5 years
Foliage medium green
Size at maturity 6'–8'
Branching upright spreading

Density average
Texture medium

Seasonal Interest

Bloom date late April
Flowers profuse pink, 1"–1½" diameter (see Appendix D)
Fruit 2"–3" round fuzzless peach
Fall color yellow

Winter character —

Planting Guide

Growing zone 5 6 7 8 9
Spacing of mature plants 8'
Pollination self-fertile

Root stock Prunus Tomentosa

Site considerations full sun to light shade, adaptable but very fussy about getting wet feet, prefers sandier soils

Comments

Like the peaches they could really use at least eight hours of full unobstructed sun rather than the usual minimum of six. Also like the peaches they are short lived (8–20 years) on dwarfing stock—more reason to use them in a border than as an accent.

Wineberries Rubus phoenicolasius

Landscaping Values

Shape mounded
Time to first crop 2 years
Foliage medium green
Size at maturity 6'–8'
Branching arching canes

Density average to dense
Texture medium

Seasonal Interest

Bloom date mid-late May
Flowers small pink to white
Fruit red raspberry-like, but seedless
Fall color —

Winter character —

Planting Guide

Growing zone 4 5 6 7
Spacing of mature plants 2'–4'
Pollination self-fertile
Site considerations light to deep shade, very adaptable

Root stock seedling

Comments

Wineberries should be allowed to ripen to a deep burgundy wine red before picking. They have excellent flavor and are a much underused plant.

Garden Dwarf Trees

and Medium Shrubs

3 TO 6 FEET IN HEIGHT

Beach Plum PRUNUS MARITIMA

Landscaping Values

Shape broad rounded
Time to first crop 3–4 years   **Density** dense
Foliage medium green   **Texture** medium
Size at maturity 4'–6'
Branching upright spreading

Seasonal Interest

Bloom date early May
Flowers white, single or double
Fruit round purple, sometimes deep red
Fall color —   **Winter character** +attractive
branching

Planting Guide

Growing zone 3 4 5 6 7
Spacing of mature plants 7'   **Root stock** seedling
Pollination self-pollinating
Site considerations full sun to light shade, adaptable, salt tolerant

Comments

Sometimes Eastham, Hancock, and Premier can be found locally in New England. They all have larger, better quality fruits.

Broad Rounded Blueberry VACCINIUM CORYMBOSUM

Landscaping Values

Shape broad rounded
Time to first crop 2–3 years   **Density** average/dense
Foliage deciduous, medium dark   **Texture** medium
          green
Size at maturity 3'–4' height x 4'–6' spread
Branching upright spreading

Seasonal Interest

Bloom date mid-May
Flowers profuse clusters, white or white tinged with pink
Fruit clustered blue-black berries
Fall color +scarlet red   **Winter character** —

Planting Guide

Growing zone 4 5 6 7
Spacing of mature plants 4'–6'   **Root stock** seedling
Pollination weakly self-fertile
Site considerations full sun to medium shade, moist acidic, well-drained
soil, lots of peat moss and mulch

Comments

Bluetta is dense and Ornablue (3' height x 5' spread) has tarter wild
flavor. All the blueberries are good ornamentals for medium
shade but the yields are much reduced.

Round Blueberry VACCINIUM CORYMBOSUM

Landscaping Values

Shape round
Time to first crop 2–3 years   **Density** average
Foliage deciduous, medium dark   **Texture** medium
          green
Size at maturity 4'–6' height x 4'–6' spread
Branching upright spreading

Seasonal Interest

Bloom date mid-May
Flowers profuse clusters, white or white tinged pink
Fruit clustered blue-black berries
Fall color + scarlet red   **Winter character** —

Planting Guide

Growing zone 4 5 6 7 8 9
Spacing of mature plants 4'–6'   **Root stock** seedling
Pollination weakly self-fertile; two or more varieties best
Site considerations full sun to medium shade, moist acidic well-drained soil

Comments

Evergreen (4' x 4'), Collins, Darrow, and Northland (4' x 4') are rounded.
Evergreen is an extremely attractive ornamental.

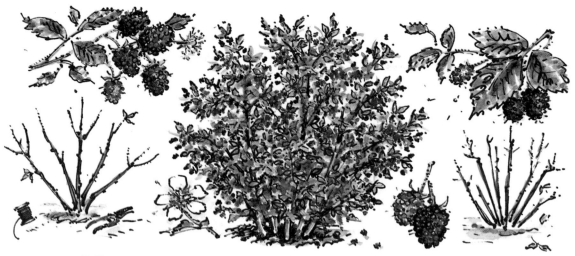

Upright Blackberries and Black Raspberries RUBUS OCCIDENTALIS

Landscaping Values

Shape mounded
Time to first crop 2 years
Foliage medium green
Size at maturity 4'–6'
Branching arching canes

Density average to dense
Texture medium

Seasonal Interest

Bloom date early June
Flowers profuse 1" white to pink
Fruit black, purple 1" + or − berry
Fall color —

Winter character —

Planting Guide

Growing zone 3 4 5 6 7 8
Spacing of mature plants 2'–4'

Root stock seedling, virus free only

Pollination self-fertile
Site considerations full sun to medium shade, adaptable but like high organic content and good drainage pH of 5.5 to 7

Comments

Purple raspberries are particularly tall and more upright. The yield is greatly reduced in half-shade. The brambles will suffer if they stand in water for more than two or three days during spring rains. Keep taller varieties to 6' with pruning.

Garden Dwarf Cherry

Landscaping Values

Shape vase
Time to first crop 4–6 years   **Density** average
Foliage medium dark green   **Texture** medium coarse
Size at maturity 4'–6' height x 3'–4' spread
Branching upright

Seasonal Interest

Bloom date early May
Flowers profuse white
Fruit 1" + or − diameter dark red
Fall color yellow   **Winter character** —

Planting Guide

Growing zone 6 7 8 9
Spacing of mature plants 4'   **Root stock** seedling
Pollination self-pollinating
Site considerations full sun to medium shade, adaptable but does not like wet feet, prefers fertile soil

Comments

Particularly vigorous limbs should be pruned back. These plants are a little sparse at the bottom for hedge use. Garden Bing is a good one.

Improved Western Sand Cherries

PRUNUS BESSEYI

Landscaping Values

Shape broad rounded
Time to first crop 2–4 years   **Density** average
Foliage medium green   **Texture** medium
Size at maturity 4'–6' height × 6'–8' spread
Branching upright spreading

Seasonal Interest

Bloom date early May
Flowers + profuse ½" white
Fruit ½" diameter round
Fall color yellow, variable
                                Winter character —

Planting Guide

Growing zone 3 4 5 6 7
Spacing of mature plants 6'   **Root stock** seedling
Pollination requires cross-pollination from another sand cherry
Site considerations full sun to medium shade, very adaptable

Comments

It is very important to only buy the named improved varieties; even then
they're not as good as the cultivated kind. They are attractive ornamentals
in their size range and excellent in the colder zones. Good varieties include
South Dakota Ruby, Black Beauty, and Golden Boy.

Currants RIBES SATIVUM

Landscaping Values

Shape oval
Time to first crop 2–3 years
Foliage medium green
Size at maturity 3'–5'
Branching upright

Density average
Texture medium

Seasonal Interest

Bloom date early May
Flowers small greenish white
Fruit clusters of red, white or black berries
Fall color —   **Winter character** —

Planting Guide

Growing zone 3 4 5 6 7
Spacing of mature plants 4'   **Root stock** seedling
Pollination self-pollinating
Site considerations full sun to fairly heavy shade, likes mulch and high organic content in soil, prefers some shade in hotter zones.

Comments

Except for Consort, black currants are alternate hosts for white pine blister rust. Call your county agent to make sure they're okay to plant in your area. White or red types are conservative choices.

Gooseberries RIBES SPECIES

Landscaping Values

Shape   mounded
Time to first crop   2–3 years   **Density**   average
Foliage   medium green   **Texture**   medium
Size at maturity   3'–5'
Branching   spreading, sometimes arching

Seasonal Interest

Bloom date   early May
Flowers   small greenish white to violet
Fruit   1" round green red or white depending on variety
Fall color —   **Winter character** —

Planting Guide

Growing zone   3 4 5 6 7
Spacing of mature plants   6'   **Root stock**   seedling
Pollination   self-pollinating
Site considerations   full sun to fairly heavy shade; likes organic material but otherwise adaptable, needs good drainage, prefers some shade in hot summer areas, responds well to mulch

Comments

These plants have very attractive foliage. Good varieties include Welcome, Whitesmith (European), and Champion. The American varieties are hardier than the European types. Spinefree is thornless and good tasting.

Garden Dwarf Nectarine PRUNUS PERSICA

Landscaping Values

Shape loosely mounded
Time to first crop 2–3 years   **Density** dense
Foliage medium dark green   **Texture** coarse
Size at maturity 4'–6' height x 4'–6' spread
Branching upright spreading

Seasonal Interest

Bloom date late April
Flowers +profuse 1" + or −, pink
Fruit 2–4" round yellow and/or red
Fall color yellow   **Winter character** —

Planting Guide

Growing zone 6 7 8 9
Spacing of mature plants 6'   **Root stock** seedling
Pollination self-pollinating
Site considerations full sun to light shade, adaptable but doesn't like wet feet, prefers sandier soils

Comments

Garden Beauty is double flowered. The fruit is not as showy on the garden dwarfs; it tends to hide under the branches. Even though they're well suited to container growing they still need about 150 days to ripen their fruit.

Garden Dwarf Peach PRUNUS PERSICA

Landscaping Values

Shape loosely mounded
Time to first crop 2–3 years   **Density** dense
Foliage medium dark green   **Texture** coarse
Size at maturity 4′–6′ height x 4′–6′ spread
Branching upright spreading

Seasonal Interest

Bloom date late April
Flowers + profuse 1″ + or −, pink
Fruit 2″–4″ round yellow and/or red
Fall color yellow   **Winter character** —

Planting Guide

Growing zone 6 7 8 9
Spacing of mature plants 6′   **Root stock** seedling
Pollination self-pollinating
Site considerations full sun to light shade, adaptable but doesn't like wet feet, prefers sandier soils

Comments

These should be spaced about 3′ apart for use as a dense hedge. Well suited to container growing—whiskey half-barrels work well—but they still need about 150 days to ripen fruit.

Red Raspberries Rubus idaeus

Landscaping Values

Shape mounded
Time to first crop 2 years
Foliage medium green
Size at maturity 4'–6'
Branching arching canes

Density average to dense
Texture medium

Seasonal Interest

Bloom date —
Flowers + profuse 1" white to pink
Fruit 1" + or − berry red or yellow
Fall color —

Winter character —

Planting Guide

Growing zone 3 4 5 6 7 8
Spacing of mature plants 2'–4'

Root stock seedling-virus-free only

Pollination self-fertile
Site considerations full sun to medium shade, some afternoon shade is best in hot summer areas, prefers pH of 5.5 to 7, good drainage and high organic content in soils

Comments

Chief is extremely hardy; Milton and Latham are virus resistant. Latham is quite low growing (about 4').

Small Shrubs

1½ TO 3 FEET IN HEIGHT

Northsky and Northblue Blueberries

VACCINUM CORYMBOSUM X ANGUSTIFOLIUM

Landscaping Values

Shape broad rounded
Time to first crop 2–3 years   **Density** average–dense
Foliage deciduous, medium dark   **Texture** medium
          green
Size at maturity 2'–3' height x 4' spread
Branching upright spreading

Seasonal Interest

Bloom date mid-May
Flowers + profuse clusters, white or white tinged pink
Fruit clustered blue-black berries
Fall color + scarlet red   **Winter character** —

Planting Guide

Growing zone 4 5 6 7
Spacing of mature plants 4'   **Root stock** seedling
Pollination weakly self-fertile
Site considerations full sun to medium shade, moist, acidic, well drained
soil, lots of peat moss and mulch

Comments

Northsky is slightly smaller (2–2½' x 3–4'), Northblue is 2½–3' x 4' spread.
Both are highbush/lowbush crosses with fruit flavor that has some character
to it.

Top Hat Blueberry Vaccinum corymbosum x angustifolium

Landscaping Values

Shape round
Time to first crop 2–3 years
Foliage deciduous, medium dark green
Size at maturity 18″ x 18″ spread
Branching upright spreading

Density dense
Texture medium

Seasonal Interest

Bloom date mid-May
Flowers profuse white clusters
Fruit clustered blue-black berries
Fall color + red

Winter character nearly evergreen

Planting Guide

Growing zone 3 4 5 6 7
Spacing of mature plants 1′
Pollination self-fertile
Site considerations full sun to medium shade, moist, fertile, acidic, well-drained soil

Root stock seedling

Comments

Spacing them a foot apart will create a solid cover; 1½′ spacing will give it a mounded look. They have a 3–4 week blooming period.

Ground Covers

6 INCHES TO 1½ FEET IN HEIGHT

Bush Beans PHASEOLUS VULGARIS

Landscaping Values

Shape broad rounded
Time to first crop 40–60 days   **Density** average
Foliage medium green   **Texture** medium
Size at maturity 12″–18″ x 18″ spread
Branching upright spreading

Seasonal Interest

Bloom date —
Flowers not ornamentally effective
Fruit mostly green, horticultural or purple podded types are ornamentally effective
Fall color —   **Winter character** herbaceous annual

Planting Guide

Growing zone 2 3 4 5 6 7 8 9
Spacing of mature plants 12″   **Root stock** —
Pollination self-fertile
Site considerations full sun to light shade, average or better garden soil

Comments

The herbaceous annuals should be used in conjunction with an attractive mulch such as bark chips and spring bulbs for more year-round interest. Bush type string, wax or horticultural (shell) beans can be used. Bush lima beans are somewhat larger, up to 2′ in height.

Chives Allium Schoenoprasum

Landscaping Values

Shape mounded
Time to first crop 60 days
Foliage dark green
Size at maturity 10″–12″
Branching ornamental grass–like

Density dense
Texture medium fine

Seasonal Interest

Bloom date June
Flowers 1″ round light purple
Fruit —
Fall color green

Winter character herbaceous perennial

Planting Guide

Growing zone 2 3 4 5 6 7 8 9
Spacing of mature plants 12′
Pollination self-fertile
Site considerations full sun to medium shade, adaptable

Root stock —

Comments

Similar in character to garlic chives and garlic, both of which get too large for ground covers, although they are fine for edging (garlic chives to 3′ with white late summer flowers and garlic with small pink flowers to 2′). All hold their foliage until very late into fall.

Creeping Blueberry VACCINIUM CRASSIFOLIUM

Landscaping Values

Shape spreading
Time to first crop 2–3 years
Foliage deciduous, medium dark
   green
Size at maturity 6″–8″
Branching horizontal

Density dense
Texture fine

Seasonal Interest

Bloom date Mid-May
Flowers white or tinged pink
Fruit clustered blue-black berries
Fall color scarlet red

Winter character —

Planting Guide

Growing zone 5 6 7
Spacing of mature plants 12″
Pollination weakly self-fertile
Site considerations full sun to medium shade; moist, acidic, well-drained soil; lots of peat moss and mulch

Root stock seedling

Comments

Very beautiful ornamentals with limited berry production. 'Wells Delight' and 'Bloodstone' with its bright red twigs are currently available. The similar Lingonberry (*Vaccinium vitis-idaea var. minimum*) is highly prized in Northern Europe for its distinctive jam, and is available from seed.

New Zealand Spinach TETRAGONIA EXPANSA

Landscaping Values

Shape spreading
Time to first crop 55 days
Foliage light green
Size at maturity 9″–12″
Branching prostrate and trailing

Density dense
Texture medium

Seasonal Interest

Bloom date —
Flowers inconspicuous
Fruit —
Fall color green

Winter character herbaceous perennial

Planting Guide

Growing zone 2 3 4 5 6 7 8
Spacing of mature plants 8″
Pollination self-fertile
Site considerations full sun to medium shade, adaptable

Root stock —

Comments

This plants tastes like spinach but it is a perennial and tolerates heat well without going to seed. Old leaves are tough. It is attractive in hanging baskets or on container edges because of the trailing habit.

Parsley OETROSELINUM CRISPUM

Landscaping Values

Shape mounded
Time to first crop 70–80 days
Foliage medium dark green

Density dense
Texture fine (moss curled); medium fine (Italian)

Size at maturity 8″–10″ (moss curled) 1½′ (Italian)
Branching upright spreading

Seasonal Interest

Bloom date —
Flowers not ornamentally effective
Fruit —
Fall color green

Winter character biennial

Planting Guide

Growing zone all
Spacing of mature plants 6″

Root stock —

Pollination —
Site considerations full sun to medium shade, average garden soil, but moist

Comments

The small flowers should be picked off to ensure full attractive foliage. Soak seeds overnight before planting or start indoors early. Only Italian dries well.

Runnerless Strawberries Fragaria vesca

Landscaping Values

Shape mounded
Time to first crop 120 days
Foliage medium green
Size at maturity 8″–12″
Branching upright spreading

Density dense
Texture medium

Seasonal Interest

Bloom date summer
Flowers small white with yellow center
Fruit red 1″ oblong berry
Fall color green

Winter character herbaceous perennial

Planting Guide

Growing zone 3 4 5 6 7 8 9
Spacing of mature plants 8″
Pollination self-fertile

Root stock —

Site considerations full sun to medium shade, average or better garden soil, likes being fertilized three or four times a year

Comments

Much better for landscape use than regular strawberries, which are often marketed for edging or ground cover use but which are invasive and troublesome because of the runners. The larger-berried regular types are also biennial where these are perennial. Frais-de-bois and Baron Solemacher are good choices.

Thyme THYMUS VULGARIS

Landscaping Values

Shape mounded
Time to first crop 3 months
Foliage evergreen, varies
Size at maturity 6″–15″ height, depending on cultivar
Branching spreading

Density dense
Texture fine

Seasonal Interest

Bloom date Common: late May; Caraway: mid-summer; Creeping: all summer
Flowers white, pink or lavender spikes
Fruit —
Fall color green

Winter character perennial— sometimes woody

Planting Guide

Growing zone 5 6 7 8 9
Spacing of mature plants varies
Pollination self-fertile
Site considerations full sun to light shade, adaptable

Root stock —

Comments

The thymes are attractive almost year round. Many forms have silvery or variegated foliage. Creeping thyme (2″-3″ height fine textured) takes foot traffic and is excellent for joints in dry-laid garden walks. All have fragrant leaves. Creeping thyme is quite hardy to Zone 3.

Hanging Baskets

Cascading Strawberry FRAGARIA CHIOLENSIS

Landscaping Values

Shape mounded
Time to first crop 60 days   **Density** dense
Foliage medium dark green   **Texture** medium
Size at maturity 2′ (top of plant to longest runner)
Branching pendulous (in hanging basket)

Seasonal Interest

Bloom date late May–early June
Flowers small white
Fruit bright red or white, somewhat conical berries
Fall color green   **Winter character** herbaceous
                                                          biennial

Planting Guide

Growing zone 3 4 5 6 7 8 9
Spacing of mature plants 3 plants   **Root stock** seedling
in 10″ basket
Pollination self-fertile
Site considerations full sun to medium shade, needs commercially prepared
potting soil with stones in the bottom for drainage

Comments

These are biennial type regular strawberries with profuse long runners that
fruit without rooting; they'll normally last three years. Good varieties include
Harvest Hangup, Snow King (white fruit), and Paris Spectacular (everbearing).
The white-fruited variety is much less interesting to birds.

Cascading Tomato Lycopersicon esculentum

Landscaping Values

Shape low mounded
Time to first crop 60–80 days   **Density** average
Foliage light green   **Texture** medium
Size at maturity 3'–4'
Branching spreading—pendulous in a basket

Seasonal Interest

Bloom date summer
Flowers yellow, not profuse
Fruit red, 1"–2" diameter
Fall color dull yellow   **Winter character** annual

Planting Guide

Growing zone all
Spacing of mature plants —   **Root stock** —
Pollination self-fertile
Site considerations full sun to light shade; for a basket grow in potting soil with lots of 5-10-5 fertilizer

Comments

Sweet 100 is by far the best of the cascading type tomatoes. It has beautiful clusters of fruit on the vine and a flavor that will spoil you. Use it in larger sized baskets or containers. Keep well watered; unattractive if allowed to dry out.

Patio Tomato <small>LYCOPERSICON ESCULENTUM</small>

Landscaping Values

Shape loosely mounded
Time to first crop 52–80 days
Foliage light green
Size at maturity 1½'–2' height x 2' spread
Branching spreading

Density average to open
Texture medium

Seasonal Interest

Bloom date summer
Flowers yellow, not profuse
Fruit pink to red round, 1"–2" diameter
Fall color dull yellow

Winter character annual

Planting Guide

Growing zone all
Spacing of mature plants 2'
Pollination self-fertile
Site considerations full sun to light shade, fairly rich garden soil

Root stock —

Comments

Many of the patio varieties mature extremely quickly. Fruit can be had much sooner by spraying with Blossom Set. The shape of the plant can be helped with a stake on even the smaller varieties.

Vines

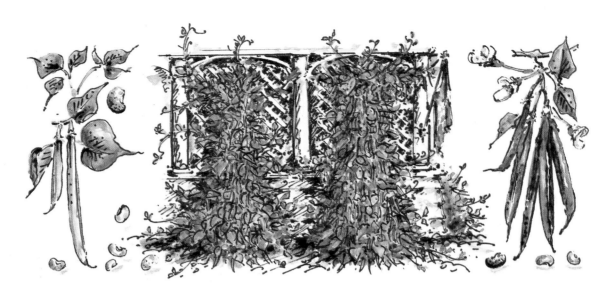

Pole Bean Phaseolus vulgaris

Landscaping Values

Shape vine
Time to first crop 55–60 days
Foliage medium green
Size at maturity 6′
Branching twining vine

Density average
Texture coarse

Seasonal Interest

Bloom date 5 weeks after planting
Flowers ½″–¾″ white, not profuse
Fruit green or yellow 6″ pod
Fall color —

Winter character —

Planting Guide

Growing zone 3 4 5 6 7 8 9
Spacing of mature plants 10″–12″
Pollination self-fertile
Site considerations full sun to light shade, good garden soil, pick often, likes fertilizing

Root stock —

Comments

Pole beans are more productive than their more attractively flowered relatives, the scarlet runner bean. They can be planted with annual flowering vines or tall cosmos if you want a better flower show.

Scarlet Runner Bean Phaseolus coccineus

Landscaping Values

Shape vine
Time to first crop 65 days
Foliage medium green
Size at maturity 8'–10'
Branching twining vine

Density average
Texture medium coarse

Seasonal Interest

Bloom date 6 weeks after planting
Flowers scarlet red
Fruit 6" long green pod
Fall color —

Winter character tender perennial

Planting Guide

Growing zone 3 4 5 6 7 8 9
Spacing of mature plants 8"
Pollination self-fertile

Root stock —

Site considerations full sun to light shade, good garden soil, pick frequently, likes being fertilized

Comments

These have very beautiful flowers and must be treated as an annual. One close relative, Thomas, a white Dutch runner bean, has large beautiful white flowers; another pole bean, Royalty, has purple flowers and pods.

Trailing Blackberries RUBUS URSINUS AND OTHERS

Landscaping Values

Shape mounded
Time to first crop 2–3 years   **Density** average
Foliage medium dark green   **Texture** medium
Size at maturity 6'–20' depending on cultivar
Branching spreading, trailing

Seasonal Interest

Bloom date early June
Flowers white, 1" diameter
Fruit 1" oblong cluster, black
Fall color dull yellow   **Winter character** —

Planting Guide

Growing zone 6 7 8 9
Spacing of mature plants 4'–6'   **Root stock** seedling
Pollination self-fertile
Site considerations full sun to medium shade, fertile well-drained soil, likes high organic content, responds well to mulch

Comments

All trailing brambles should be treated as vines and trained on walls, posts, or fences. Some can be trained in espalier patterns. Thornless Evergreen and Himalaya are very long; plant 10'–12' apart.

Bower Actinidia (Northern Kiwi)
ACTINIDIA ARGUTA

Landscaping Values

Shape vine
Time to first crop 2–3 years **Density** dense
Foliage glossy dark green, red **Texture** medium coarse
petioles
Size at maturity 30'
Branching twining vine

Seasonal Interest

Bloom date —
Flowers not ornamentally effective
Fruit 1" oblong green
Fall color yellow green **Winter character** —

Planting Guide

Growing zone 4 5 6 7 8
Spacing of mature plants 8' **Root stock** seedling
Pollination few fruits without pollination from a male plant
Site considerations full sun to medium shade, very adaptable, responds
well to mulching

Comments

The Northern kiwi is not nearly as fussy about watering, drainage and fertility
as its larger, fruited relative, the kiwi; the fruits are used the same way.

Grapes <small>VITIS SPECIES</small>

Landscaping Values

Shape vine
Time to first crop 2–3 years
Foliage medium green
Size at maturity 80'
Branching vine

Density average/dense
Texture coarse

Seasonal Interest

Bloom date —
Flowers not ornamentally effective
Fruit 1" + or − round
Fall color dull yellow

Winter character peeling bark

Planting Guide

Growing zone 4 5 6 7 8 9
Spacing of mature plants 8'   **Root stock** seedling
Pollination self-fertile except some muscadine types, which require pollination from a male
Site considerations full sun to light shade, adaptable but should be fertilized in early and late spring for best fruit production

Comments

The mature length would never be reached because of pruning practices but it means there would be enough length for any overhead arbor or trellis situation. Leaves for salads or wrapping specialities should be picked in early summer. Seedless types in particular should be grown in protected southern exposure spots in the colder zones; Scupperlong types only in zones 8 and 9.

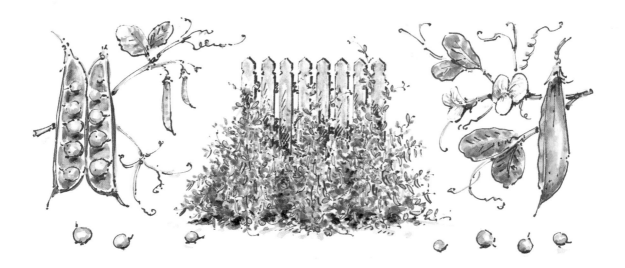

Trellis Pea Pisum sativum

Landscaping Values

Shape vine
Time to first crop 75 days
Foliage medium dark
Size at maturity 6′
Branching vine

Density average
Texture medium

Seasonal Interest

Bloom date 8 weeks after planting
Flowers ¾″ white, similar to sweet pea
Fruit 4″ straight green pod
Fall color —

Winter character annual

Planting Guide

Growing zone 3 4 5 6 7 8 9
Spacing of mature plants 10″
Pollination self-fertile
Site considerations full sun to light shade, rich garden soil

Root stock —

Comments

The best trellis variety is Alderman, also known as Tall Telephone. Spacing of 10″ will give a solid screen and good production, and 1½′ to 2′ spacing will "foil" structures rather than block them entirely.

Climbing Tomato LYCOPERSICON ESCULLENTUM

Landscaping Values

Shape vine
Time to first crop 70 days   **Density** average
Foliage medium green   **Texture** medium
Size at maturity 12'–15'
Branching vine

Seasonal Interest

Bloom date 4 weeks
Flowers 1½" yellow
Fruit 4"–5" round red
Fall color —   **Winter character** annual

Planting Guide

Growing zone 4 5 6 7 8 9
Spacing of mature plants 6'   **Root stock** —
Pollination self-fertile
Site considerations full sun, rich garden soil

Comments

Trip-L-Crop is probably the best of the climbers. It can get to 20' or more. It must be tied up or grown in a frame for vine use.

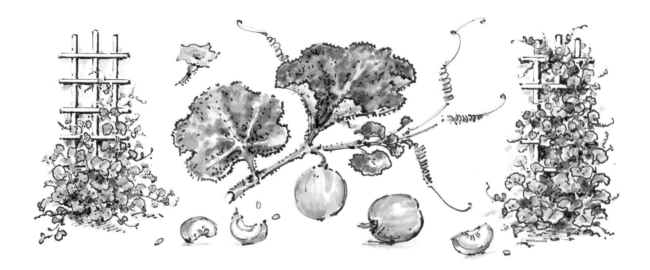

Vine Peach (Cucumber Melon)

CUCUMIS MELO VAR. CHITO

Landscaping Values

Shape vine
Time to first crop 80 days
Foliage medium green
Size at maturity 6'–10'
Branching only slightly twining

Density average
Texture medium coarse

Seasonal Interest

Bloom date 4 weeks from starting
Flowers 1" yellow
Fruit 2"–3" round greenish yellow
Fall color —

Winter character annual

Planting Guide

Growing zone 4 5 6 7 8 9
Spacing of mature plants 3'
Pollination self-fertile
Site considerations full sun to average garden soil, prefers sandier soils

Root stock —

Comments

This plant is also called Mango-melon or Lemon-cucumber. It's a cucumber/melon relative having nothing to do with peaches. It is used as a sweet vegetable, in salads, or pickled. It must be tied to supports for use as a vine.

Attractive

Ornamentals For

Culinary Use

Black Gum
(Nyssa Sylvatica)

A 90′ deciduous pyramidal tree with dense dark-green lustrous foliage. Beautiful tree with brilliant orange/scarlet fall color, one of the best trees anywhere for fall color. Small blue berries on females (pollination required from male) good for jams, jellies. Zones 4 to 8, transplant when small with root ball, wet soil tolerant.

Hackberry
(Celtis australis & occidentalis)

European hackberry or honeyberry and common hackberry or sugarberry respectively. 70′ deciduous vase-shaped tree. Although occidentalis has the larger fruits of the two, it is troubled by witches' broom, which is unsightly, common, and incurable. Zones 4 to 8. Fruits on female plants are very sweet and highly prized in the Middle East. (Male needed for effective pollination.) Very drought tolerant.

Chinquapin
(Castanea pumilia)

45′ shrubby broad rounded small tree. Coarse, dense foliage. Zones 5 to 9. A close relative of the American chestnut but with much inferior nuts. Good bronzy yellow fall color. Resistant to chestnut blight.

Heartnut

(*Juglans cordiformis*)

A 60' rounded deciduous tree. Coarse texture; close relative of the walnut. Flowers not showy, and has no fall color, but nuts are tasty and easily cracked. Zones 4 to 8. Self-fertile.

Shagbark Hickory

(*Carya ovata*)

An 80' loosely oval tree. Medium coarse texture. Small but highly flavorful nuts. Wood used in smoking meats. Transplant when young because of its taproot; grows slowly at first while root establishes itself. Interesting bark in winter landscape. Always dropping branchlets. Zones 4 to 8.

Japanese Walnut

(*Juglans sieboldiana*)

Similar to the heartnut. A 60' rounded deciduous tree with coarse texture. The Japanese walnut and heartnut are attractive ornamentals. Both are heavy feeders and like fertilizing for good nut production. Comes into bearing early for a nut tree (4 years). Zones 4 to 8. Self-fertile.

Sugar Maple
(Acer saccharum)

70'–120' height, oval. Zones 3 to 7. Has vivid yellow/orange/red fall color. Beautiful shade tree and cultivars are available for even better fall color. Not for polluted environments and very sensitive to road salt. The boiled-down sap makes the best maple syrup.

Crabapples
(*Malus pumila* and others)

15'–25' height, various shapes from low mounded to narrow upright and pendulous. Zones 4 to 8, except Siberian Crab, which is Zone 2. Flowers are available in white, pink, rose, and red. The flowers are very showy and some double forms are available. The fruits are good pickled or in jelly. Dolgo, Whitney, and Chestnut are good fruiters.

European Mountain Ash
(*Sorbus aucuparia*)

45' height, oval to rounded. Zones 2 to 7. Very attractive ornamental tree. The fruits are bright orange and clustered. A form with yellow fruits is available. The fruits are excellent in preserves.

Cornelian Cherry
(Cornus mas)

Actually a member of the Dogwood genus. 25' height, rounded. Zones 4 to 8. Often multistemmed shrubby tree and one of the first flowerers in spring with profuse yellow blooms in March. Nice red fall color. Will take a fair amount of shade. Fruits used for tarts and are good candied as well as for flavoring sherbet.

Buffaloberry
(Shepherdia argentea)

6'–10', rounded deciduous shrub. Medium texture. Silvery green leaf color like that of the Russian olive, its relative. Flowers are not showy but small orangey berries on females effective in early to mid-summer. Need male for fertilization. Very hardy. Zones 2 to 8. Tolerant of poor soil, drought, and salt. Berries used to make jams and jellies.

Nannyberry
(Viburnum lentago)

15'–20' height. Oval shrub. Medium texture and color; variable purple/red fall color. Nice creamy white flowers in early to mid-May. Blue-black fruits the best of the viburnums for jams and jellies along with the blackhaw viburnum. Very adaptable to varying soil types. Suckers freely. Needs full sun to nearly full shade. Also very hardy. Zones 2 to 8.

American Highbush Cranberry

(Viburnum, trilobum)

Not a cranberry but a viburnum, it's an 8'–10' broad rounded deciduous shrub with medium texture and leaf color. Beautiful white flat flower clusters in late May followed by profuse clusters of bright red berries throughout the fall. Very attractive ornamental; a little pruning for appearance helps in winter. Zones 2 to 8. Hardier with much tastier berries than more commonly used European Cranberrybush.

Oregon Hollygrape

(Mahonia aquifolium)

3'–5' broad-leafed evergreen shrub. Broad rounded in form, one of the few evergreen edibles. Small bluish-black berries make good jams and jellies. Beautiful yellow flowers in early May. Zones 5 to 8. Likes moist, acidic well-drained soil. Light to full shade.

Dwarf Oregon Hollygrape

(Mahonia aquifolium compacta and Mayhan strain)

Beautiful large-scaled ground cover. These two types are very broad rounded relatives of the standard Oregon Hollygrape. Neither gets over a foot to 1½ feet in height. Has the same flower and fruit as its relative and likes the same conditions. Beautiful glossy leaves that turn purplish bronze during cold winters.

Southern Magnolia

(Magnolia grandifolia)

80′ dense pyramidal broadleaf evergreen tree. Very beautiful ornamental with 8″ fragrant white flowers in late May. Takes 10–15 years to come into flower. Flower petals used in salad or steamed. Zones 7 to 9. Full sun to medium shade.

Some Oaks

(Quercus species)

Tannin causes the bitterness in acorns and can be leached out but some species have naturally sweeter nuts. These include the chestnut, willow, and live oak in the East and California, live (field) and Rocky Mountain scrub oak in the West.

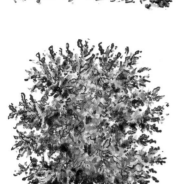

Carolina Silverbell

(Halesia carolina)

30′ rounded deciduous tree. White clusters of flowers in mid-May. Fruit eaten raw when ripe (light brown) or pickled while still green. Zones 5 to 8. Moist, acidic well-drained soil. Beautiful native tree.

Eastern Redbud

(Cercis canadensis)

20′–30′ rounded shrubby tree. Coarse glossy medium-dark foliage with very showy rosy pink flowers in late April. Flowers are used in salads. Zones 4 to 8. Full sun to medium shade. Very adaptable to soil type.

English Hawthorne
(*Crataegus oxacantha*)

15'–20' rounded deciduous tree. Beautiful in leaf and bloom. Profuse white flowers in mid-May, bright red ½"–¾" fruits in September. Fruits good for jelly, sometimes used for making wine. Zones 4 to 8. Gets serious pest problems. Full sun to light shade, adaptable.

Shrub Rose
(*Rosa* species)

The shrub roses are far less troublesome than the hybrids. The Alpine Rose (3', Zone 5) and Apple Rose (6', Zone 5) have particularly large fruits. Rugosa Rose (6', Zone 2) has fragrant rosy purple flowers all summer; its 1" red fruits make excellent jelly.

Spice Bush
(*Lindera benzoin*)

10'–12' rounded deciduous shrub. Yellow flowers in mid-April and bright red berries in September. The leaves make a nice tea and the dried fruits make an allspice substitute. Zones 5 to 9. Full sun to heavy shade. Adaptable to differing soil conditions.

Rose of Sharon
(*Hibiscus syriacus*)

10'–12' vase-shaped small tree. Hibiscus-like flowers all summer in white, red, purple, or violet, depending on the cultivar. Leaves made into tea or eaten young. Zones 5 to 9. Full sun to medium shade, adaptable, but needs moist soil.

Nandina
(*Nandina domestica*)

8' rounded evergreen shrub with large clusters of white flowers in late July. Profuse red or purplish berries in fall and winter. Bright red fall color. Fruit used for jams and jellies. Zones 7 to 9. Full sun to light shade. Adaptable.

Myrtle
(*Myrtus communis*)

5'–10' rounded evergreen shrub. Small white flowers all summer, blue-black berries in fall. Dried fruit and flower buds used as a spice, particularly in Northern Italian cooking. Zones 8 and 9. Full sun, light shade, adaptable. Drought tolerant.

Cotoneaster
(*Cotoneaster* species)

A large group of attractive spreading shrubs ranging in height from under 3' to over 18', depending on the species chosen. All fine textured, sometimes semi-evergreen with bright red berries and white or pink flowers. Fruits used for jelly. Zone varies with cultivar. Full sun to light shade.

Pyracantha
(*Pyracantha coccinea*)

10'–18' irregularly shaped semi-evergreen shrub. Often used as an informal espalier. Profuse white flowers in early June, orange-red berries in fall. Fruit can be eaten fresh when ripe. Zones 6 to 8. Full sun, light shade, adaptable. Choose a variety resistant to fire blight.

Evergreen Barberry

(Berberis buxifolia)

Magellan Barberry (1½' height, Zone 5) and *Berberis darwinii* (Darwin barberry; 10' height, Zone 7) have the best fruits, which are used for making pies and tarts. The popular Japanese barberry is the worst for fruit. Full sun to medium shade, very adaptable.

Snowberry

(Symphoricarpos albus)

3'–6' rounded deciduous shrub with cool green foliage. Pink flowers not showy but white berries in fall are quite attractive. Berries used for jam and jellies. Zone 3. Full sun to full shade. Beautiful plant for full shade. Very adaptable to varying soil types and fertility.

Evergreen Hollys

(Ilex cassine)

Dahoon, Zone 7; (*I. vomitoria*) Yaupan Holly, Zone 7; (*I. glabra*); Inkberry, Zone 3; and deciduous (*I. verticillata*) Winterberry, Zone 3, all have leaves that make a good tea. Flowers not showy but profuse red fruits in fall persisting into winter are attractive on female plants. Full sun to medium shade. Moist soil.

Dwarf Cotoneaster

(Cotoneaster horizontalis and *damneri)*

Many varieties of these two species make excellent ground covers, seldom getting above a foot in height. Fine-textured glossy leaves. *Damneri* is nearly evergreen. Attractive red fruits used for jelly. Zone 5. Full sun to light shade. Very adaptable.

Edible Flowers

and Ornamental

Vegetables

Tea Rose
(*Rosa* hybrids)

The most popular of the hybrid roses, they still exhibit a shrub form and are less fussy than other hybrids. The hips are good for tea and jelly and the flowers provide color over a long season as they continue to bloom.

Creeping Bellflower (*Rampion*) (*Campanula rapunculoides*)

Practically a grocery store, its roots are used raw in salad or cooked as a vegetable, young shoots steamed like asparagus, leaves used in salads or cooked as a vegetable. 3' tall perennial with 1" blue flowers all summer. Will be invasive under right conditions.

Balloon Flower
(*Platycodon grandiflorum*)

Young shoots can be steamed like asparagus; flowers make a nice addition to salads. 2½' tall perennial with blue-white or pink 2"–3" bell-shaped flowers from June until frost. Very dependable, not fussy; full sun to medium shade.

Pot Marigold
(*Calendula officinalis*)

The flower petals are used for seasoning soups and stews as well as giving color. 1'–2' tall plants with yellow-orange pale yellow or creamy white 4" flowers all summer long, exceptionally good for container growing. Full sun to light shade. Annual.

Ornamental Kale

Beautiful 15″ height bedding plant for fall into winter to replace frost-killed annuals. Available in red on green or white on green. Colors up well after first frost. Looks attractive in all weather conditions. Use as you would use regular kale. Treat as annual.

Ornamental Eggplant

Also called Japanese eggplant. 3′ tall plant with purple blooms and many egg-sized fruits over a two-month period. Often sold as a novelty but many prefer its flavor to regular eggplant. Use as you would use regular eggplant.

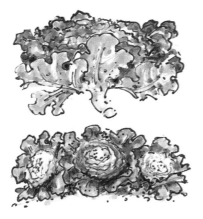

Ornamental Cabbage

Many varieties of red-headed cabbage are available. They mature in 80 to 95 days and vary in their keeping ability. Some forms retain their green outer leaves and a few yellow-headed forms exist.

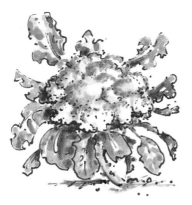

Ornamental Cauliflower

The same size and shape as standard cauliflower but with a striking purplish tinge. Early Purple Head does not need blanching and the purple color disappears when it's cooked.

Nasturtium

(*Tropaeolum majus*)

Flowers and leaves good in salad, taste like watercress. Seeds eaten while green and young, good for pickling, an excellent substitute for capers. 1'–4' single- and double-flowered types available. There are climbing types (to 10'), bush types or dwarf annuals.

Primrose

(*Primula veris* and *Primula vulgaris*, [English primrose])

Leaves eaten in salads or used for potherbs. Flowers of *vulgaris* used when just opened to make liquor (fermented with water and sugar). Early flowering, 6"–9" plants in spring, many colors available, fragrant, like woodland soils, take half shade. Perennial.

Oriental Poppy

(*Papaver orientale*)

Flower heads eaten when green, raw or fried; very spicy. Over one hundred varieties, 2'–4' height, white, pink, and red colors available. Blooms May and June, foliage disappears during late summer. Some annuals, most perennial.

Ice Plant

(*Mesembryanthemum crystallinum*)

Leaves boiled like spinach, too acidic to eat raw. Small white, pink, red, and yellow daisylike flowers on 6" tall plants with silver-flecked foliage. Full sun, prefers sandier soils, not fussy about fertility.

Caladium

(*Caladium bicolor*)

The tubers are steamed or boiled as a vegetable. It's possible to eat the leaves boiled, but raw they have enough prussic acid to be poisonous. 6"–24" leaves in a variety of red, green, and white combinations. Take full shade. Treat as annual.

Hollyhock

(*Althea rosea*)

Young leaves eaten in salads or cooked as a vegetable. Young flowers and fruits also edible. Sometimes 8' or more tall, available in red, pink, yellow, and white with some doubles. A few modern varieties will flower the first year on this traditional biennial.

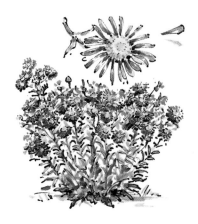

Garden Huckleberry

(*Physalis* species)

2'–4' plants with small patio tomato-like fruits in husks are used in pies, sometimes eaten fresh. The papery fruit cases (Chinese Lanterns) are used in dried flower arrangements. Not a particularly attractive ornamental. Sometimes weedy-looking. Treat like an annual.

Aster

(*Aster* species and hybrids)

Young leaves must be cooked to be eaten. Young flowers okay raw in salads. A large group of perennials, mostly treated as annuals. From 8" to 5' in height, depending on species; available in white, pinks, reds, and blues.

Bee Balm

(*Monarda didyma*)

Leaves used for seasoning soups and stews or for making tea. This 4' tall native perennial has exotic pink flowers and blooms from June to August. A brilliant red cultivar, Cambridge Scarlet, is available. Hummingbirds love it. Full sun to light shade.

Asiatic Lilies

(*Lilium* species)

The bulbs are commonly cooked and eaten as a vegetable in the East. The tiger lily in particular is cultivated for this purpose in northern Japan. 1'–6' in height with a wide variety of flower colors available. Each blooms a few weeks but the species choices can be made to ensure bloom all summer.

Siberian and Japanese Iris

(*Iris sibirica* and *kaempferi*)

The roots are used for their starch in the East. Both species are 2' in height. Both available in blue, purple, lavender, and white. *Sibirica* blooms in June and *kaempferi* in July. Both withstand fairly wet soils and medium shade.

Day Lilies

(*Hemerocallis* species)

Everything edible, raw or cooked. Flowers eaten in salads, pickled, breaded, and fried. Dried they're used to flavor soups. Bulbs cooked as a vegetable. Leaves in salads. 1½'–6'; all colors except blue and white. Species can be chosen for a succession of bloom from May to October.

Impatiens

(*Impatiens sultanii* and *balsamina*)

Leaves must be cooked, flowers can be eaten in salads. 1'–2½' plants treated as annuals; available in white, pinks, reds, oranges, and purples. Beautiful plant for bedding because they "drift." Good for shade. Pinching helps keep full. Attractive all summer.

Bachelor Buttons

(*Centaurea cyanus*)

Flowers a beautiful addition to salad. 2½' tall annual also called cornflower. Available in blue, pink, or white. Doubles particularly attractive. Prefer sandier soil and full sun. Cut off spent flower heads for second bloom.

Peony

(*Paeonia* species)

Roots can be cooked or generally treated like parsnips. Extremely dependable and trouble-free group of perennials. Available in rose, pink, white, red; singles and doubles in late May and June. Attractive foliage best propped up with peony hoops. Full sun to medium shade, well-drained soil. Long-lasting cut flowers.

Tulip

(*Tulip* species and hybrids)

Bulbs can be steamed or boiled. Flowers and leaves good for salads. Tremendous variety available; most tulips do not naturalize well so are good prospects for the cooking pot after two or three years. Unsurpassed for spring color. Deer love them.

Edible Chrysanthemum
(*Chrysanthemum coronarium*)

Delicious young shoots can be eaten in salads or cooked as vegetable. Also called Shungiku or Crown Daisy chrysanthemum. 1½'–3' height. Dense, profuse bloomer Tom Thumb grows to 1' height. Beautiful annual for container culture.

Oxeye Daisy
(*Chrysanthemum leucanthemum*)

Leaves and flowers eaten in salads. This 2' perennial with white petals and a yellow eye is a common wild flower blooming in June and July. Not at all fussy. Full sun to light shade.

Butterfly Weed
(*Asclepias tuberosa*)

Must be cooked. Young shoots steamed like asparagus are very tasty. 3' tall plant with orange flowers in late summer. Grows well in sandy soils. Drought tolerant. Full sun to light shade. Perennial.

Ornamental Pepper

Peppers both attractive and tasty but hot. Come in long, narrow, and round types. Excellent plant for container culture or borders. 6"–9" tall compact plants with attractive foliage. Bring inside as houseplants before first frost. Full sun to light shade. Annual.

Jerusalem Artichoke
(*Helianthus tuberosus*)

The tubers can be sliced raw for salads and are commonly boiled or creamed. At their best when steamed until the skins peel easily then dipped in melted butter. 6'–8' height. Perennial with bright yellow flowers. Full sun to light shade. Attractive, quick-growing screen.

Sunflower
(*Helianthus annus*)

Seeds tasty in trail mix or by themselves. Exceptionally nutritious. 6'–10' annual. Yellow flowers with brown, reddish-brown, or purple center. Some varieties have flower heads over 1' in diameter. Full sun to light shade. Adaptable to soil type.

Dahlia
(*Dahlia* species)

Flowers eaten fresh in salads, tuberous roots cooked. 2'–8' height. Tender perennial with 1"–18" flowerheads. Available in white, red, purple, yellow, and combinations. Full sun to light shade. Adaptable but need moist soil. Bloom in late summer.

Fall-Blooming Crocus
(*Crocus sativus*)

Saffron comes from the stigma of this plant. 3"–6" tall perennial with lilac or white flowers in autumn. Full sun to light shade. Plant in spring. Hardy to Zone 6.

Vines

with Edible Fruits

Five-Leaved Akebia

(*Akebia quinata*)

Semi-evergreen twining vine, 30'–40'. Nice cool green foliage; Zones 4 to 7; can be invasive; fragrant rosy purple flowers in May with 2"–3" edible pods in fall which are somewhat sweet. Pick young. Female plants require pollination from a male for fruits.

Climbing Roses

(*Rosa* species)

8'–16' long; need proper support to climb well. The rose hips of the climbing type roses are often not as large as some others but still make nice tea and jelly. The beauty of the climbers is unsurpassed among the vines. The species types are much less troublesome than the fussy hybrids.

Variegated Actinidia

(*Actinidia kolomikta*)

15'–20' climbing vine. Male plants needed for pollination have variegated foliage with white to pink blotches. Fruits on females are smaller and less tasty than those of Bower Actinidia but white fragrant flowers much nicer. Blooms mid-May. Zones 4 to 8.

Asparagus Bean

(*Vigna sinensis sesquipedalis*)

Annual pole bean often sold as a novelty because its pods are 3' long. Actually very tasty with a hint of asparagus flavor. Attains 6' height. Must be supported for trellis use. Flowers white, not showy. 70 days to table.

Nonedible

Accent Plants

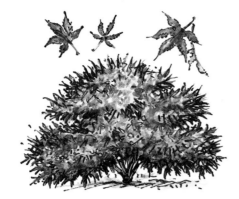

Japanese Maple
(*Acer palmatum*)

15′–25′ tall mounded-form small tree. Flowers not effective but one of the most beautiful plants for foliage and form. Both green- and red-leaved forms available as are cut-leaved types. Full sun to medium shade. Zone 5 or 6 depending on variety.

Double-Flowering Cherry
(*Prunus serrulata*)

20′–25′ tall vase-shaped small tree. Flowers available in white, light pink, or deep pink depending on cultivar. Very beautiful in bloom. Tend to be short lived, about 25–30 years. Zone 5 or 6 depending on the cultivar; full sun to light shade.

Bradford Pear
(*Pyrus calleryana*)

3′–50′ oval tree although some seed types tend to be more loosely pyramidal. Beautiful profuse white flowers in early May. Nice glossy green foliage, scarlet/purple fall color. Not susceptible to fire blight like many other pears. Full sun to light shade, Zone 4.

Weeping Cherry
(*Prunus subhirtella var. pendula*)

20′–40′ mounded tree, gracefully weeping, with single pink flowers (double on Yae-Shidare Higan) in late April. Full sun to light shade. Zone 5.

Double-Flowering Crabapple

(*Malus* species)

Forms vary with variety chosen. Range from 8' to more than 30'. Available in white, pinks, and reds. The double-flowered types seldom have valuable fruits but the blooming periods tend to be longer. Full sun to light shade. Zone varies with variety.

Yucca

(*Yucca filamentosa*)

3' mounded shrub with stiff evergreen swordlike leaves from the base. Creamy white spike of flowers in mid-July. Extremely attention-gathering plant. Full sun. Drought tolerant. Zone 4.

Weeping Hemlock

(*Tsuga canadensis var. sargentii*)

8'–10' tall broad mounded evergreen shrub. Beautiful form and fairly fast growing for an evergreen. Full sun to heavy shade. Zone 3.

White Birch

(*Betula pendula* and *papyrifera*)

The 50' European white (*pendula*) is the common clump-type birch. Both a weeping and a cut-leaf weeping form are available. The 70' paper birch is broader spreading with white branchlets and peeling bark. Zone 2. Full sun to light shade.

Nonedible

Facer Plants

Dwarf Holly

(*Ilex* species)

Green Island and Hetzi are 3'–4' cultivars of *I. crenata* and Compact Inkberry holly. They are all beautiful evergreen facer plants. Compact Inkberry is Zone 3. The others are Zone 5. Blackberries on the females in the fall. All withstand medium shade and will take shearing. Prefer moist soil.

Lavender

(*Lavendula officinalis*)

Beautiful 3' mounded plant with fragrant lavender spikes of flowers in late June. Semi-evergreen. Zone 5. Full sun to light shade. Prefers fairly sandy soil. Dried flowers are fragrant for many months.

Dwarf Spirea

(*Spirea* species)

The Japanese White (1½", Zone 4) blooms late June. Anthony Waterer (2', Zone 5), with deep pink flowers, blooms all summer. Both have profuse flowers and mounded form. Full sun to medium shade, but flowers best in full sun. Adaptable to varying soil types.

Dwarf Weigela

(*Weigela florida, variegata nana*)

A 3' tall, rounded, deciduous with attractive and attention-getting variegated foliage which has yellow edges. Pink flowers all June with sporadic blooming throughout summer. Zone 5. Full sun to light shade. Adaptable.

Rockspray Cotoneaster

(*Cotoneaster horizontalis*)

Very spreading, 2'–3' tall, semi-evergreen shrub with small light pink flowers in mid-June and profuse red berries in the fall. Attractive horizontal branching pattern. Zone 4. Full sun to light shade. Adaptable to varying soil types.

Heaths and Heathers

(*Erica* species and *Calluna vulgaris*)

Both upright-growing 1'–2' tall plants which form extensive thick masses. Heather (Zone 4) is evergreen (or nearly so depending on climate) with purplish-pink flowers all summer. The heathers' hardiness, flower color, blooming date, and height all vary with the species. Both require full sun to medium shade and soil that is moist, acidic, well-drained but low in fertility.

Gum-Rock Rose

(*Cistus ladaniferus*)

Mounded evergreen, 3'–4' tall shrub in Zone 7 and farther south. 3½" white flowers with red splotches throughout summer. Difficult to transplant. Full sun to light shade. Adaptable, but prefers well drained soil.

St. Johnswort

(*Hypericum* species)

Many of the St. Johnsworts are facer plant size, 2'–3', and some are quite hardy. *H. Prolificum*, shrubby St. Johnswort, is mounded, 3', Zone 4, with bright yellow flowers in late summer. Full sun to light shade. Very adaptable, especially to drought.

6

Taking Care of the Plants

*T*he three parts of this chapter will provide you with the information you need to get a beautiful and practical plan into the ground and to take care of it once it's installed. Covered are planting techniques, information on the care of the plants during those early days, and an explanation of the general maintenance needs over the years. Pest and disease problems will be covered in Part 3. The planting part is partly focused on handling and installing plants you would get through mail order.

Part 1
Planting and Establishing

Planting

There are so many flower and vegetable varieties available from seed that it's beyond the scope of this book to cover them all effectively. Fortunately the best information source is usually the seed packet itself. As every home gardener knows, the packages normally contain information on planting dates, planting depths,

and spacing. It is only the last that should be adjusted. Spacings given on most vegetable packages are for standard American row-type gardens. If you cut any spacing recommended by a third, you will get a much more attractive look as well as higher yields in less space. These closer spacings are usually referred to as Chinese or French-intensive spacings.

Many people like to start their seeds indoors as early as possible in the spring. It is a particularly good idea for areas covered only by wood mulch in the spring; getting the summer vegetable ground cover in the ground as early as possible can only help the looks of your garden. Again, there is much helpful literature in print on seed starting.

Flats of flower and vegetable seedlings are becoming more and more popular. The costs of these trays of young plants are usually modest, and the earlier food production and attractive look make them particularly appropriate for an edible landscape. Make your wishes known to your local greenhouse grower in the fall so that you stand a better chance of getting exactly what you want. Too often the selection in the spring is limited to only the most popular flowers and vegetables. If you wait until the spring to make your choice, make sure you shop early.

Planting the herbaceous seedlings is easy. Your supplier can tell you the spacing you should plant. Explain that you are using intensive spacing for the vegetables and that you want a full look where the flowers are concerned. If you observed the spacing of many common bedding annuals in public show gardens, you would find it was more like four inches than the commonly recommended six to eight inches. There are few keys to success with the plant seedlings but each is important. First, plant each seedling with the ground line the same place it was in the flat. The only exception should be tomatoes; they should be planted so the very hairy part of the lower stem is below ground. Handle the plants by their small root balls as much as possible. Squeezing is not good for the young stems. Once the seedling is in the ground it should be pressed firmly into place by hand to eliminate air pockets and then thoroughly watered in. Invest in a nozzle for the hose that sprinkles rather than bombs the young plant.

Handling the woody plants requires more explanation because of the different ways they can be bought. If you get your plants from a mail order nursery, they'll be shipped with a soilless packing material around the roots to keep them moist. If you get the plants locally, they'll probably have a dirt ball around the roots wrapped in burlap or plastic. They also may come in plastic or metal containers. All three methods are acceptable, but containers are generally best because they protect the bond between the roots and the soil. Larger,

landscape-size material should definitely be purchased with soil around the roots because as plants become more mature they become less able to accommodate a change in the environment. A one- or two-year-old plant can be yanked out of the ground, chopped up, and shipped around the country; but older plants need that soil ball or a protective container.

Giving a plant a good start is extremely important; it will affect the plant's health and productivity for years. Good general health, in turn, means less susceptibility to disease and insect problems. They will also recover better from such environmental injury as extreme weather temperatures. With a good start in mind, the first issue you have to confront when you get your plants is not the planting, but making sure they do not dry out until you *do* plant them. Most of what you see when you look at the roots is just a transporting device. It is the fine root hairs and other small parts that actually collect the water and nutrients for the plant. If these fine hairs dry out, they die and the plant has to make new ones to get established.

With bare root stock, open the package and make sure the packing material is moist. Then water the packing material and roots, and keep the plant in as cool and dark a place as you can find until you're ready to plant. If the material has a soil ball, water it and store it the same way. Handle the ball carefully so you don't break it. Continue keeping the packing material or soil ball moist until you plant. If more than three days lapse, "heel in" the plants; that is, cover the bare roots thoroughly in a cool, shady place, like this:

HEELING-IN TECHNIQUE

Pick a shady area for your heeling-in spot.

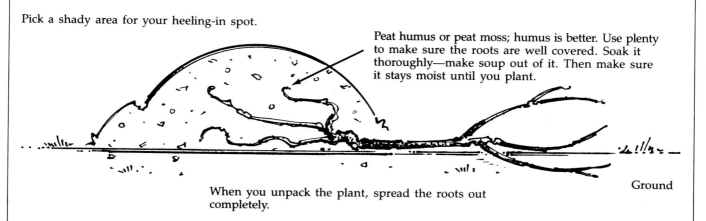

Peat humus or peat moss; humus is better. Use plenty to make sure the roots are well covered. Soak it thoroughly—make soup out of it. Then make sure it stays moist until you plant.

When you unpack the plant, spread the roots out completely.

Ground

PLANTING DETAIL: BARE-ROOT TREE

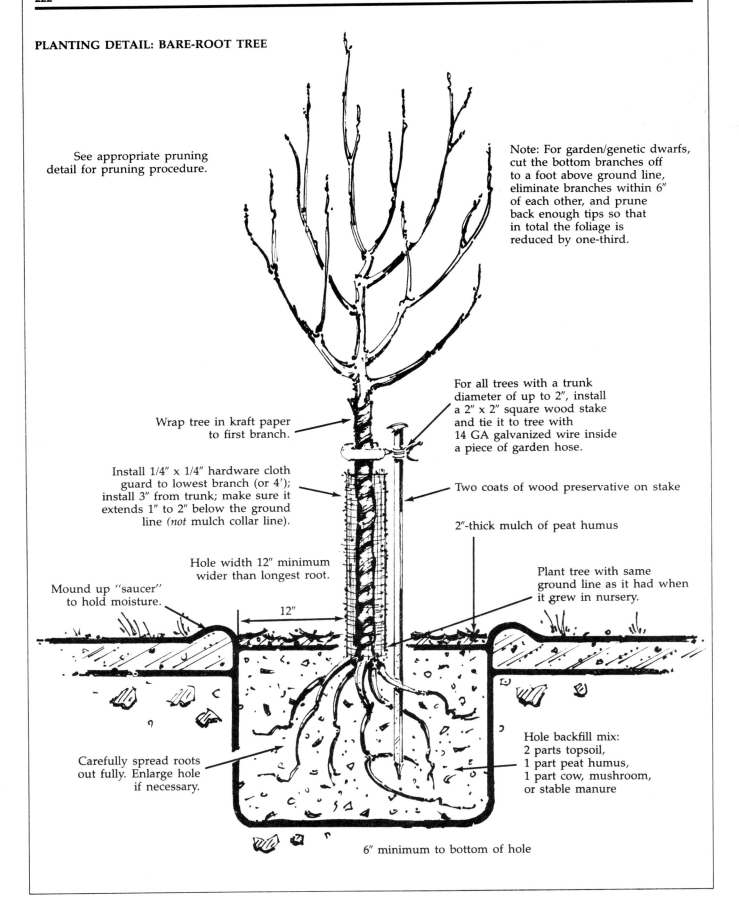

See appropriate pruning detail for pruning procedure.

Note: For garden/genetic dwarfs, cut the bottom branches off to a foot above ground line, eliminate branches within 6" of each other, and prune back enough tips so that in total the foliage is reduced by one-third.

For all trees with a trunk diameter of up to 2", install a 2" x 2" square wood stake and tie it to tree with 14 GA galvanized wire inside a piece of garden hose.

Wrap tree in kraft paper to first branch.

Two coats of wood preservative on stake

Install 1/4" x 1/4" hardware cloth guard to lowest branch (or 4'); install 3" from trunk; make sure it extends 1" to 2" below the ground line (*not* mulch collar line).

2"-thick mulch of peat humus

Hole width 12" minimum wider than longest root.

Plant tree with same ground line as it had when it grew in nursery.

Mound up "saucer" to hold moisture.

12"

Carefully spread roots out fully. Enlarge hole if necessary.

Hole backfill mix: 2 parts topsoil, 1 part peat humus, 1 part cow, mushroom, or stable manure

6" minimum to bottom of hole

Before you plant bare root material, soak the roots in water for a minimum of two hours—overnight is ideal, but do not soak them longer than twenty-four hours. You can enrich the water by throwing a handful of dried cow manure into the bucket of water.

Do your planting according to the appropriate sketch from the following group. Treat a

container plant the same as a balled and burlapped plant. Occasionally a container-grown plant will be allowed to grow too long in its container and roots will grow in a circular pattern. Eventually the roots will girdle and strangle the plant. If you see this be sure to spread the roots out thoroughly when you plant.

PLANTING DETAIL: BARE-ROOT SHRUB

Remove any fruits if present.
Cut red (but not black) raspberries back to crown.

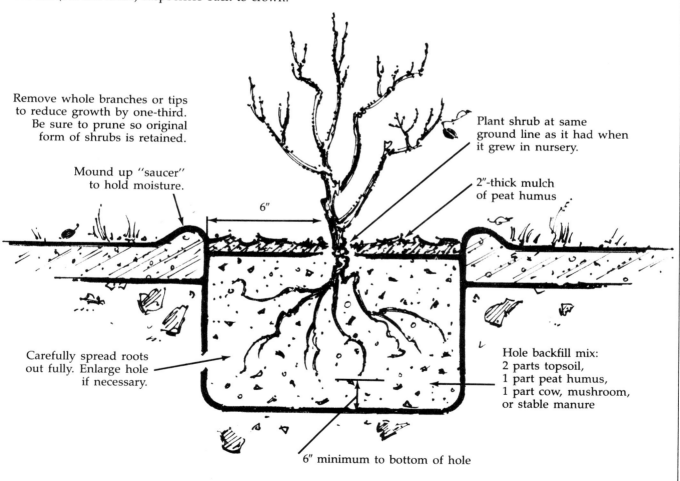

Remove whole branches or tips
to reduce growth by one-third.
Be sure to prune so original
form of shrubs is retained.

Mound up "saucer"
to hold moisture.

6"

Carefully spread roots
out fully. Enlarge hole
if necessary.

Plant shrub at same
ground line as it had when
it grew in nursery.

2"-thick mulch
of peat humus

Hole backfill mix:
2 parts topsoil,
1 part peat humus,
1 part cow, mushroom,
or stable manure

6" minimum to bottom of hole

PLANTING DETAIL: BALLED-AND-BURLAPPED TREE

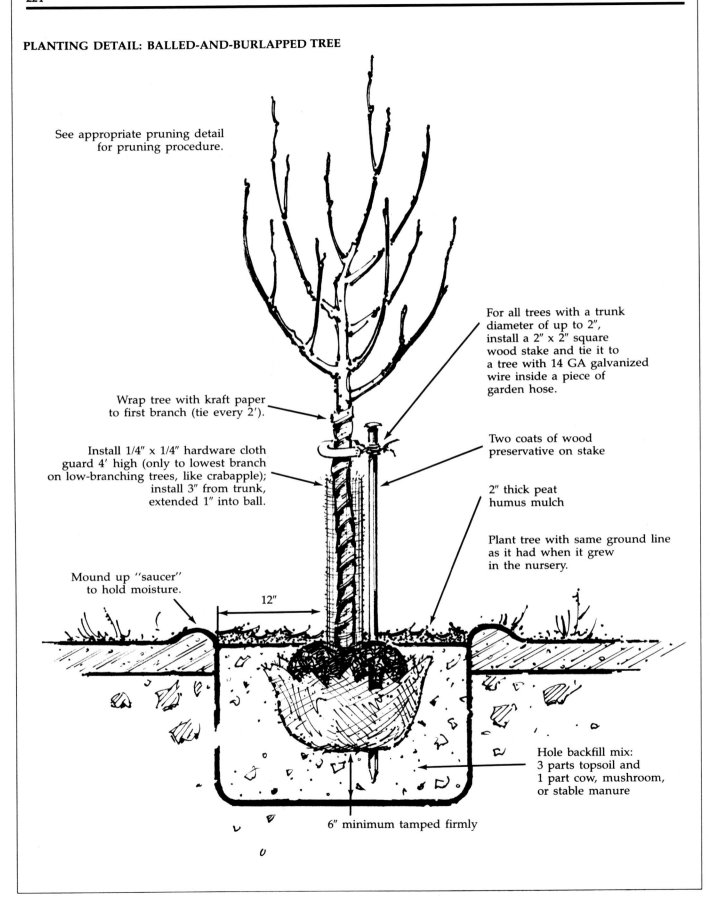

See appropriate pruning detail
for pruning procedure.

For all trees with a trunk
diameter of up to 2″,
install a 2″ x 2″ square
wood stake and tie it to
a tree with 14 GA galvanized
wire inside a piece of
garden hose.

Wrap tree with kraft paper
to first branch (tie every 2′).

Two coats of wood
preservative on stake

Install 1/4″ x 1/4″ hardware cloth
guard 4′ high (only to lowest branch
on low-branching trees, like crabapple);
install 3″ from trunk,
extended 1″ into ball.

2″ thick peat
humus mulch

Plant tree with same ground line
as it had when it grew
in the nursery.

Mound up "saucer"
to hold moisture.

12″

Hole backfill mix:
3 parts topsoil and
1 part cow, mushroom,
or stable manure

6″ minimum tamped firmly

PLANTING DETAIL: CONTAINER-GROWN OR BALLED-AND-BURLAPPED SHRUB

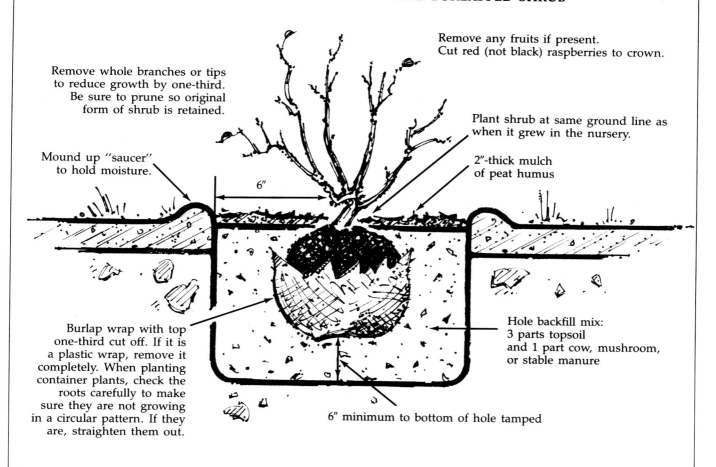

Remove any fruits if present.
Cut red (not black) raspberries to crown.

Remove whole branches or tips
to reduce growth by one-third.
Be sure to prune so original
form of shrub is retained.

Plant shrub at same ground line as
when it grew in the nursery.

Mound up "saucer"
to hold moisture.

2"-thick mulch
of peat humus

6"

Burlap wrap with top
one-third cut off. If it is
a plastic wrap, remove it
completely. When planting
container plants, check the
roots carefully to make
sure they are not growing
in a circular pattern. If they
are, straighten them out.

Hole backfill mix:
3 parts topsoil
and 1 part cow, mushroom,
or stable manure

6" minimum to bottom of hole tamped

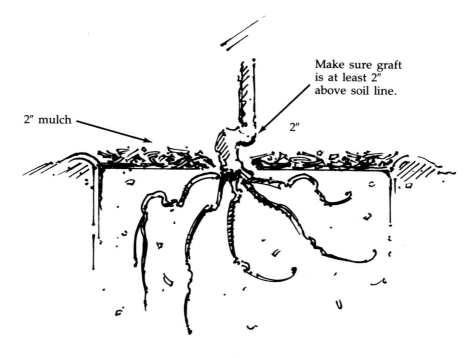

Make sure graft
is at least 2"
above soil line.

2" mulch

2"

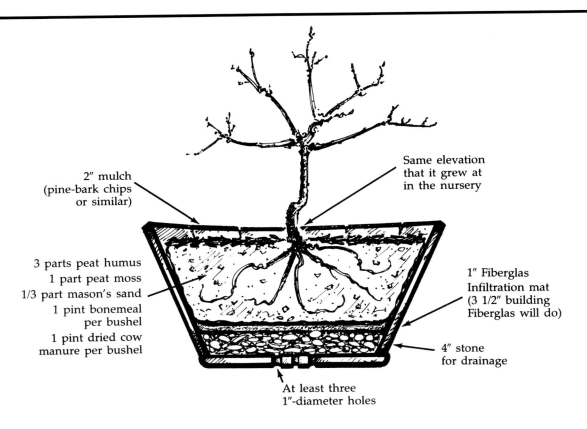

2″ mulch
(pine-bark chips
or similar)

3 parts peat humus
1 part peat moss
1/3 part mason's sand
1 pint bonemeal
per bushel
1 pint dried cow
manure per bushel

Same elevation
that it grew at
in the nursery

1″ Fiberglas
Infiltration mat
(3 1/2″ building
Fiberglas will do)

4″ stone
for drainage

At least three
1″-diameter holes

Do not cheat on these planting details. The big hole is important because the young plant will be in transplant shock for a long time—probably a year. During that time it will be losing tremendous amounts of moisture through the leaves and stems—a process called transpiration. That big hole with the backfill mix will make a good moisture holder and supplier as well as an easy growth medium for the roots during this difficult period. The kraft paper and hardware cloth wrap for the trunk is recommended for many reasons: the brown paper is very good for preventing sun scald and controlling transpiration. Its black inside-moisture barrier also absorbs heat, so when the winter sun is blocked quickly (as when it disappears over the horizon or behind a building) the temperature drop won't be so fast as to crack the bark. Painting tree trunks with white latex paint is often recommended for this, but it is a rather obtrusive way to solve the problem.

The plastic tree guards are being viewed with increasing suspicion; insects like to spend the winter under them, and rabbits and mice have been known to lunch on the bark below their base. Bear in mind that the plants' moisture and nutrients travel up to the leaves all around the outside of the stem, just under

the bark. If a small animal chews around it (girdles it) it is dead. All that money and time will be wasted. Therefore, think of the hardware cloth wrap as an insurance policy.

When you plant be sure to put the backfill mix in the hole about 6″ at a time and soak it thoroughly: make a soup out of it.

The stakes for the dwarf and semidwarf trees are serious business. The semidwarfs need them while they are getting established unless they are tied up in espalier; dwarfs *always* need them. Locate the stakes on the least obtrusive side of the trunk.

The best time for planting is early spring. It's not so critical in zones 6 through 9 where early fall plantings are all right too; but it is important in zones 3 to 5 (U.S.D.A. zones: 3′–6). Spring planting gives the plants the maximum chance to get established before they have to endure winter. Very low early temperatures or January thaws and then very cold spells could mean the difference between success and setback or failure with fall planted material. Late spring planting means the leaves will get too much of a jump on the roots, delaying bearing and slowing overall growth. Late planting is particularly hard on raspberries. So, as soon as possible after the frost is out of the ground, you should be out there planting. This means doing your planning and placing your plant orders in the fall and winter.

Don't be so enthusiastic about early planting that you try it in wet soils. Good soils have a lot of air space; an ideal soil is 25 percent air, 25 percent water, 45 percent mineral material, and 5 percent organic material. If the soil is too wet when you work it or walk on it, you compress it and eliminate the air spaces the roots need. Unfortunately, clay soils dry out the slowest and are precisely the ones that have air space problems *before* they become compacted. In fact, if you are one of those unfortunate few with heavy clay soils, no attempt should be made at edible landscaping without providing underground drainage as shown in Appendix E.

Establishing the Plants

Initial Work

Once the plants are in the ground too many people are inclined to figure their work is finished. Remember, it's a difficult adjustment period for the plants. The herbaceous plants, for instance, should be watered enough to keep them from wilting. Fertilizing them every two weeks is recommended if you use a granular form; less if you use a slow-release form. Do it according to the direction given on the package. So-called complete fertilizers are the best; these are fertilizers containing nitrogen, phosphorous, and potassium. Numbers on the packages tell you what percentage of each is present. So the most useful fertilizer, 5-10-5, is 5 percent nitrogen, 10 percent phosphorus, and 5 percent potassium. The other 80 percent is filler. Sometimes local suppliers carry different ratios that are designed to complement local soil conditions. Many gardeners prefer slow-release fertilizers for slowly maturing crops like melons, corn, and squash. The same could be said for perennial flowers and vegetables like asparagus. Slow-release types are also best for the woody plants, which, unlike the herbaceous plants, don't get fed initially at all.

Once the woody plants are planted you'll have to spend another five or ten minutes on pruning. The following pruning instructions will apply whether you're working on bare root plants or plants with a soil ball around them.

Both initial and regular maintenance pruning techniques vary. What is recommended

here are methods that will give a balance between productivity and attractive appearance. Even commercial orchardists do less vigorous pruning nowadays, and are more respectful of the natural plant forms.

Exact pruning techniques vary among species, so no single technique covers everything. Plants can be grouped, though, and three generalizations made: first, no matter what kind of pruning you do, you should always cut back to the bud:

PRUNING TO BUD

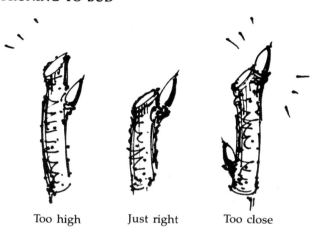

| Too high | Just right | Too close |

Second, where *some* pruning is recommended, it is best that you do it. In their zeal to have an instant landscape, many people are afraid to cut back their already small plants. However, in a few months, to say nothing of a few years, it's *not* pruning that will have a bad effect. Although plants with soil balls are less affected than those shipped with bare roots, in neither case can the reduced roots support all the top growth. Not pruning early, as shown in the following series of sketches, will in every case mean a less attractive and less productive plant.

Third, whenever you prune, whether it's for training or pest control, *always* soak your pruning shears in full-strength, undiluted chlorine laundry bleach. Until scientists understand more about the spread of viruses and other smaller organisms, you must be cautious.

With all this in mind, the following sketches will cover the tree crops; the initial pruning on the bush and the cane plants is as indicated on the planting details. The grapes are cut back to the one strongest cane with just two buds left on it.

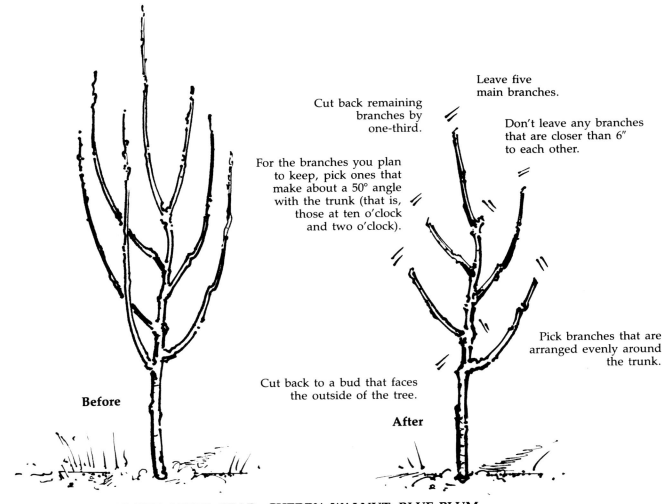

Cut back remaining branches by one-third.

Leave five main branches.

Don't leave any branches that are closer than 6″ to each other.

For the branches you plan to keep, pick ones that make about a 50° angle with the trunk (that is, those at ten o'clock and two o'clock).

Cut back to a bud that faces the outside of the tree.

Pick branches that are arranged evenly around the trunk.

Before

After

INITIAL PRUNING FOR APPLE, PEAR, CHERRY, WALNUT, BLUE PLUM

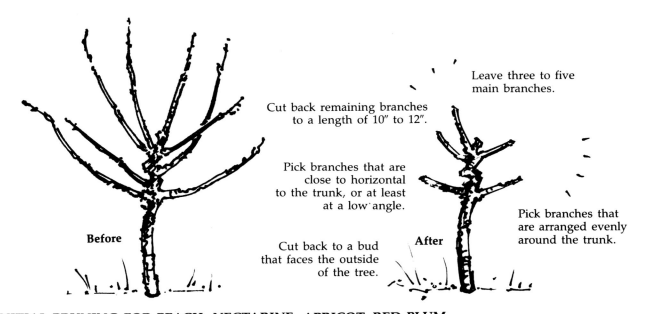

Cut back remaining branches to a length of 10″ to 12″.

Leave three to five main branches.

Pick branches that are close to horizontal to the trunk, or at least at a low angle.

Cut back to a bud that faces the outside of the tree.

Pick branches that are arranged evenly around the trunk.

Before

After

INITIAL PRUNING FOR PEACH, NECTARINE, APRICOT, RED PLUM

Once the planting, pruning, and initial fertilizing is done, your work is mostly through for the first year. If you're using planting masses, it's a good idea to expand the mulch saucer shown in the planting details to create a continuous mulch cover in the planting bed. Beyond that, you need only water the plants when they're dry and prune off any new stems coming up from the roots. They need a minimum of an inch of water a week after their first year; two inches is better. (See Appendix J for the procedure to calculate precise water amounts.) Most people don't water enough: if you're not sure, thoroughly soak the ground. Better still, if you have a lot of plants, use a soaker hose or sprinkler so you don't have to stand around. If you really want to make it easy, buy an automatic timer. In any case, from time to time, dig a hole after you have watered to see if you really are moistening the soil to the proper depth.

Part 2
Maintaining the Plants

Since annual plants, by definition, only last one year, this section addresses the needs of the woody plants. After the first full year in the ground, the plants need further fertilizing and another important pruning. In succeeding years some modest further pruning, feeding, and thinning of the fruit will be needed. This is what the first year pruning looks like for different plants:

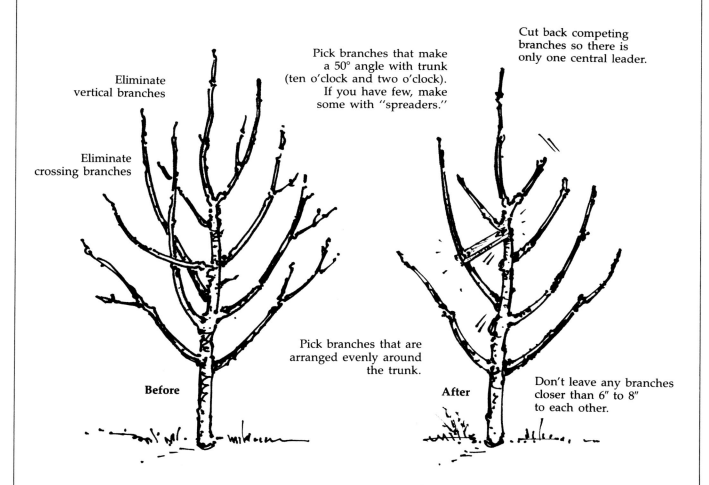

Eliminate vertical branches

Eliminate crossing branches

Pick branches that make a 50° angle with trunk (ten o'clock and two o'clock). If you have few, make some with "spreaders."

Cut back competing branches so there is only one central leader.

Pick branches that are arranged evenly around the trunk.

Don't leave any branches closer than 6″ to 8″ to each other.

Before

After

FIRST-YEAR PRUNING FOR APPLE, PEAR, CHERRY, WALNUT, BLUE PLUM

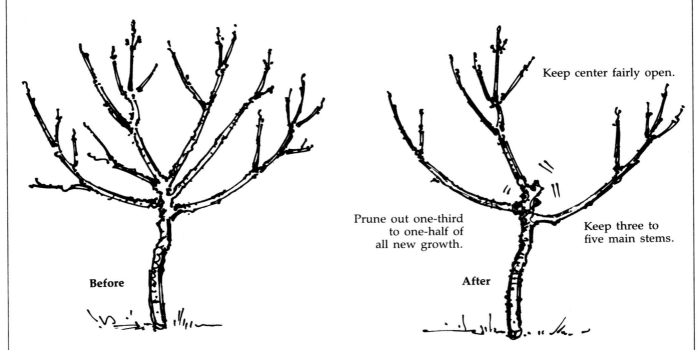

Keep center fairly open.

Prune out one-third
to one-half of
all new growth.

Keep three to
five main stems.

Before

After

FIRST-YEAR PRUNING FOR PEACH, NECTARINE, APRICOT, PLUM

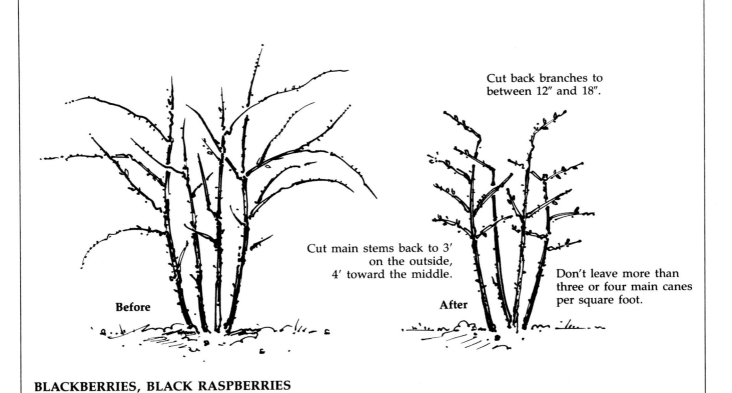

Cut back branches to
between 12″ and 18″.

Cut main stems back to 3′
on the outside,
4′ toward the middle.

Don't leave more than
three or four main canes
per square foot.

Before

After

BLACKBERRIES, BLACK RASPBERRIES

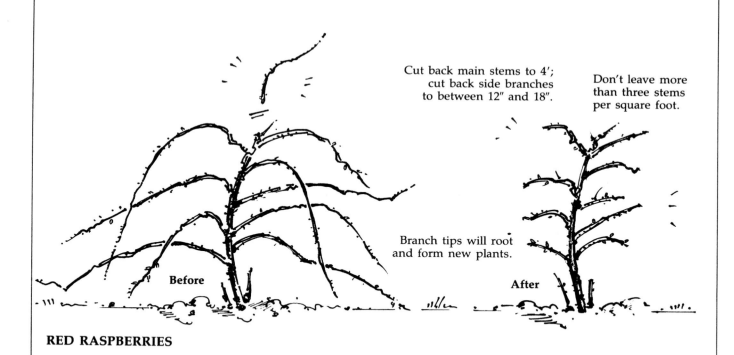

Cut back main stems to 4'; cut back side branches to between 12" and 18".

Don't leave more than three stems per square foot.

Branch tips will root and form new plants.

Before

After

RED RASPBERRIES

Cut canes back to 3' to 4'.

Cut out any canes with diameters as small as a pencil or smaller.

Before

After

THORNLESS BLACK RASPBERRIES, DEWBERRIES, LOGANBERRIES

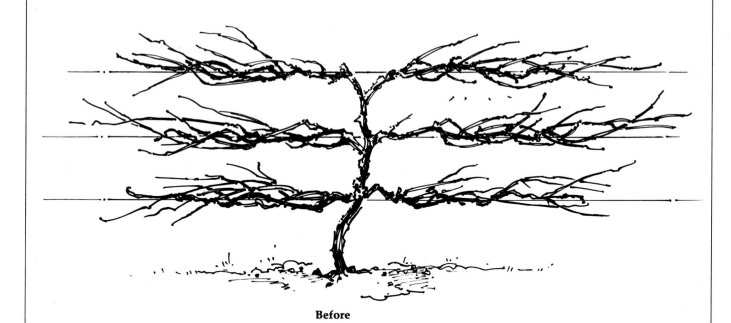

Before

Leave one cane (which will eventually become
old-wood, nonfruiting arms) and one stub
per wire. Leave two buds on the stub.

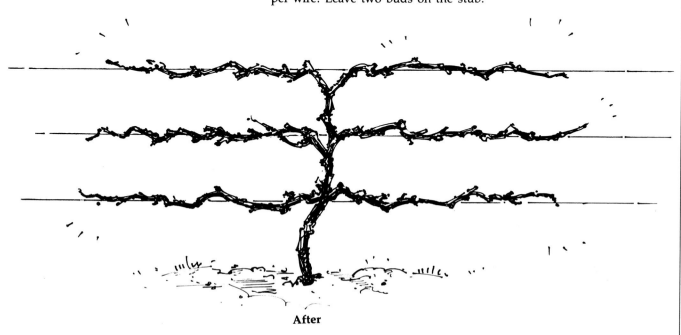

After

MOST NORTHERN GRAPES

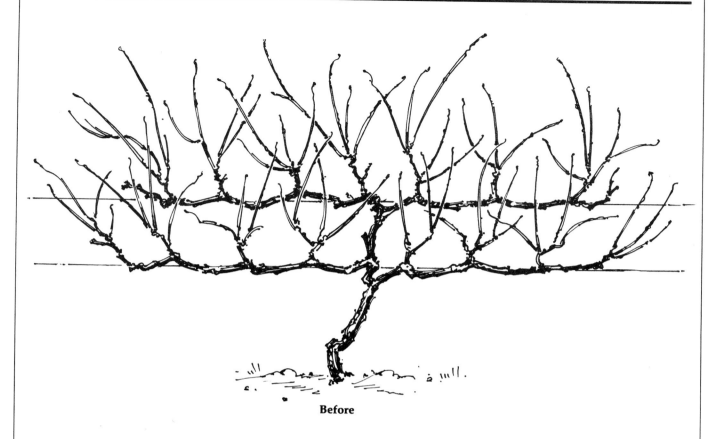

Before

Allow about 6 to 8
buds per cane.

Allow about 8 side
arms per wire.

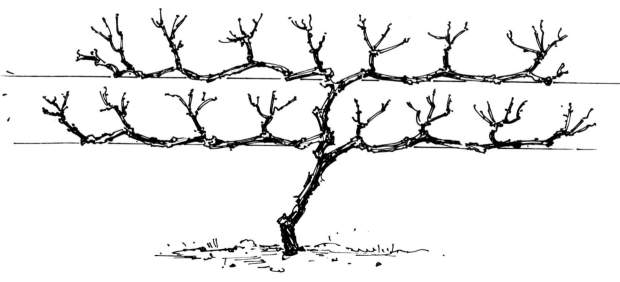

After

MUSCADINE GRAPES

Be sure to cut off all the new stems (sucker growth) that come up from the soil. The spreaders shown are just notched pieces of wood, wedged in place. They are used to increase bearing.

Fertilize them with a slow-release 5-10-5 fertilizer after six months and again after one year. After the first year, the only watering you'll have to do is during drought periods, especially within six to eight weeks of harvest. As for thinning the fruit, you won't have to worry about the nuts, berries, and cherries at all. The rest of the fruits vary in their favorite spacing, but you can make a general rule of keeping the space between fruits a little wider than the back of your hand. Plants that have spur growth (short stubs that the fruit grows on) can be thinned to one fruit per spur. Let the work go until mid- to late June; by then some of the plants will have done most of this work for you. It may seem like a peculiar thing to do, but this thinning is important work. Plants have been hybridized over the years for maximum fruit production, and the hybridization has been so successful that the fruits tax both the food-making ability of the plant and the physical strength of its branches.

Feeding

After the first year, feed the plants once a year. Do this as soon as possible each spring. A 5-10-5 fertilizer is good for ensuring general health and productivity. Fruit plants in particular will be very sparse bearers if nutrients are in short supply in the soil or are out of balance. To some, the best reason to fertilize is that it speeds up the growth process and gives a mature look to the landscape more quickly. Fertilizer spikes—little stakes of timed-release fertilizer you pound into the ground with a hammer—are especially beneficial. They are foolproof; you can't overfertilize and burn anything. Nor do they affect the plant's ability to go dormant at the proper time. Package directions will tell you how many to use for any given size plant. Organic gardeners will want to spread about a 4" depth of well-rotted manure around the base of the plant—to just beyond its outermost branches. Then cultivate it in. If dried manure is used, one inch in depth will do.

Regular Maintenance Pruning

Generally speaking, if you prune when you plant, and again after the first year, little additional pruning will be required. The grapes and cane fruits (red raspberries, blackberries) will benefit from annual pruning, although many people do not do this. It is certainly worth the limited time and effort for the extra quantity and quality food you get and for the lusher ornamental look that will result. Unlike other fruit crops, the peaches and nectarines bear their fruit on new growth, so they need to have any new growth cut back by about one-third each year to continue producing well. The ongoing pruning requirements for the rest of the food plants are quite modest: take out one-third of the most vertical new growth over all. As the years roll by they won't need as many major branches, so periodically remove one or two. The blueberries and other bush fruits don't really need any pruning until they're older, when some of the oldest and more central canes can be taken out to rejuvenate growth. Assuming you picked the right size plant for the right size space in the first place, you won't have to worry about size control pruning—there won't be any. You *will* have injury from time to time: broken branches and perhaps some winter kill in colder areas. Just prune these off as soon as you notice the damage. You will also need to prune out and burn wood that's infected with disease. Whenever you prune, keep a mental image of the overall shape of the plant in your mind's eye. If you take out big limbs or some damaged or diseased wood in one spot, you might want to take some healthy wood out in another spot to balance the plant out and preserve its attractive appearance. This won't hurt the plant in any way; horticulturalists tend to keep plants growing vigorously by doing more pruning than the average homeowner anyway. Should you discover that you're becoming an edible landscaping enthusiast, there are interesting pruning practices you can adopt. For one thing, there is a difference between keeping a healthy, productive landscape and maximizing your yield. Maximizing your yield involves a greater depth of knowledge about pruning and pruning philosophies; included are such tricks as notching, pinching back, and disbudding. Then there's the kind of espalier training shown earlier in the Idea Sketchbook. If espalier pruning techniques are new to you, you'll probably have the best luck working with apples or pears. Check the examples of what can be done in Appendix H. You can also graft branches of different cultivars onto one plant for economy, variety, and better pollination. Though they're beyond the scope of this book, none of the techniques are hard and there are good sources of information available. The Rodale Press offers many of these.

Part 3
Pest and Disease Control

Very few of us step back far enough to put pest and disease problems into proper perspective. We need to take a more basic view. There are only three categories of organisms in the world: 1. The food makers: those that take basic compounds from the soil, water, and air to make food (the plants); 2. The food eaters: those organisms that in turn eat the food makers or other food eaters; and 3. The decomposers: the very tiny organisms that eat the parts of plants and animals that are left when they die. Unfortunately, out of the hundreds of thousands of decomposer organisms, there are some renegades who have got into the bad habit of not waiting until their host dies. In fact, the weaker the host is in the first place, the more desirable these organisms find it to be. These pathogens, or disease organisms, can be so small we can't see them even with electron microscopes. Insects fall into the category of food eaters and use the fruits and nuts for food as we do. However, like pathogens, they tend to go after the weaker plants. So the old adage that an ounce of prevention is worth a pound of cure is at least as true with plants as it is with humans. Maintaining the general health of the plants must be the first concern of pest control.

Pest and disease control techniques vary. There are three basic schools of thought: the chemical users, the organic growers, and a combination of the two, known as the integrated pest management group. You will have to spend *some* time and energy protecting your food from the depredations of the various creatures. How much time and for what result is a matter of choosing your place in the philosophical camps.

Pest Control Philosophies

Chemical Use

For most of us, chemical sprays are the most time-efficient and successful technique for the tree and bush fruits that need protection. But it's important that you develop reasonable expectations about what the crop should look like. A typical home spray program is seven sprayings a season (five minutes for each dwarf and ten minutes for each semidwarf) as opposed to more than a dozen applications in some cases for commercial growers. The growers' expensive spray program is foisted on them by our buying habits. We Americans are visually oriented; the fruits and vegetables that look the nicest, sell the best. But seeing all that perfect-looking produce in the stores gives a false impression of the real farm world. We don't see the produce that was cut for processing, used for juices, jams, and jellies, or the produce that was discarded completely. In order for commercial growers to make money they have to keep crop losses down to a few percentage points of the total crop, and they do. They do it with complete focus and attention to what is going on in the fields and orchards and with a vast armada of chemicals. Chemicals are sprayed for almost every pest, then an "insurance" spraying is conducted later to make sure no pest has been missed. There are also a few miscellaneous sprays for thinning, weed control, growth regulation, increasing color and firmness, and preventing premature fruit drop. Every pest and every problem is a direct threat to the commercial orchardist's economic survival; and thus commercial growers belong to the chemical use group for economic as well as philosophical reasons.

Homeowners, on the other hand, are not required to meet the demand that 95 to 98 percent of the crop look perfect. Let the other creatures of the world have a few nibbles of your food. You're doing fine if you get half or more perfect fruit, and another third or so has a few spots or worms that can be cut out and then be used for slices, pies, canning, or freezing. Burn or ship out the remainder with the garbage man. *Do not throw them into the compost pile.* Actually, most homegrowers end up with better than five-sixths usable fruit with a seven-sprayings home program. The main reason is that a home foodscape differs in one important respect from an orchard: its diversity. It is harder for the pest population

Hose attachment type   2 quart size   1 gallon size   2 gallon size (good foodscape size)

PUMP TYPES

to increase if their lunch is not concentrated in one spot.

The popular and effective home orchard sprays are a combination of fungicides with insecticides and are readily available through mail order and garden centers. They also contain poison, so keep them locked up when they're not in use. Read the label every time you use them as a question of both safety and effectiveness. You will need one other material: a dormant oil to be used once a year in the early spring. These petroleum-based oils smother insect eggs before they hatch. One brand, Scalecide, is readily available. There are specific sprays for individual pests, but most people prefer not spending the time mixing their own pesticides for the modest savings that result.

There are many reasonably priced pieces of equipment available to apply the spray with. Here's what some of the smaller easy-to-use rigs for home use look like. These are designed to provide spray coverage without the use of a ladder for semidwarf, dwarf, garden dwarf, and bush fruit. The two-gallon or three-gallon size is probably best for small gardens; invest in a pump type if you are considering more than a dozen or two plants.

Here's what a spraying schedule looks like. It may seem complicated, but remember, all that is required for a whole season is a total of one-half hour for each dwarf and an hour for each semidwarf.

Those plants listed in tables are the only ones that need such regular care. The rest of the plants, including the nut trees, gooseberries, raspberries, currants, and blueberries, can be treated as ornamentals; that is, they can be left alone unless they develop a problem. When you have dormant oil in the spray rig and you are spraying other things anyway, the bush fruits, grapes, and roses would certainly benefit from a treatment at the same time. The dormant oil is used even by most organic fruit growers. If you are presented with a problem not covered in this book, make use of your local county agricultural extension agent; other homegrowers have probably encountered the same problem before you.

Apple, Pear, Quince

	Timing	Spray*
First spray	Early spring before buds open and after average daytime temperatures are 40-50° F. Best time is when buds are starting to swell, but before they show pink. You don't want temperature to drop below freezing before the spray dries.	miscible oil, superior oil, Scalecide: different names for the same product.
Second spray	When the buds color up pink and just before they start to open.	Fruit Tree** or Orchard spray**: two names for the same product.
Third spray	From when two-thirds of the flower petals on the bloom have fallen to no later than a week after they've all fallen	Fruit Tree spray
Fourth spray	Ten days after your petal fall spray.	Fruit Tree spray
Fifth spray	Two weeks after your fourth spray.	Fruit Tree spray
Sixth spray	Two weeks after fifth spray.	Fruit Tree spray
Seventh spray	Two weeks after sixth spray.	Fruit Tree spray

Nectarine, Peach, Plum, Cherry, Apricot

	Timing	Spray *
First spray	Early spring, before buds open and after average daytime temperatures are 40-50° F. Best time is when buds are starting to swell, but before they show pink. You don't want temperature to drop below freezing before the spray dries.	miscible oil, superior oil, Scalecide: different names for the same product.
Second spray	When the buds color up pink and just before they open.	Fruit Tree or Orchard spray: two names for the same product.
Third spray	From when about two-thirds of the flower petals have fallen until they've all fallen-not later.	Fruit Tree spray
Fourth spray	Two weeks after third spray.	Fruit Tree spray

For Peaches and Nectarines Only

Fifth spray	Two weeks after fourth spray.	Fruit Tree spray
Sixth spray	Check when your particular variety of fruit is mature and spray four weeks before that date.	Fruit Tree spray

* Always read the label completely, noting any precautions. The recommended strength will always be given on the label of any given product; be sure to use it. Don't spray when it's windy or rainy.

** These are combination sprays to take care of most or all of the various insects and diseases without the mess or bother of a lot of individual compounds. Use Starks, or ask your local county agricultural agent which brands he thinks is best for your area.

Organic Pest Control

Much has been written about organic growing of herbaceous material. *Organic Gardening* magazine is a fountainhead of information and there are many excellent books on the subject. Raising trees and bushes organically is more difficult because the plants remain year after year, giving the diseases or pests a chance to build up. There are those who claim that it is impossible to raise fruit organically, but it seems there are plenty of people doing it. Clearly they are content with fewer perfect fruits. When I was growing up nobody I knew sprayed; I thought bumps, holes, and worms were a normal part of fruit growing. Nobody seemed to mind them.

Organic growers look at it this way. First of all, a home landscape is a polyculture, not a monoculture. That is, it is a diverse landscape rather than the one-plant landscape of the orchard. Second, there are many beneficial practices they are philosophically comfortable with. Spraying a dormant oil in early spring helps

some. There are biological insecticides that work to a degree. Insects that feed on fruits and nuts have their own predators and parasites. Taken on balance, most bird species do more good than harm because of the insects they eat. Bad weather kills some insects. Although a long warm rainy spell might mean losing most of a susceptible fruit on a given tree one year, the next it might not be affected. When you're all through there is plenty of food for yourself, your friends, and your helpers in the ecosystem. So the organic growers' view is, why use poison? Let the ecosystem work for you instead of against you.

The important thing about organic growing is that to do it well requires knowledge of the insects and diseases' appearance, their life cycles and feeding habits, and their place in the food chain. Once you're informed, the care is no more time consuming than a standard chemical spray program. Here are some common pest controls used by organic growers.

ORGANIC PEST CONTROLS

Compound or Organism	Pest
Ryania	Coddling moth, aphids, Japanese beetles
Dormant oil	Aphids, scale, pear psylla, mites
Tobacco dust, nicotine sulfate	Aphids, pear psylla
Dormant oil and water under pressure	Pear psylla
Rotenone	Aphids, general insecticide
Sapodilla	Aphids, general insecticide
Pyrethrum	Aphids, general insecticide
Wood creosote (not coal-derived as that found in wood preservative)	Borers, especially peach tree
Mothballs or crystals (napthalene type only)	Borers, deer
Tanglefoot strips around trunks	Borers, moths
Red tanglefoot-coated fishing bobbins or other spheres hanging in tree. Use six or more	Apple maggot
Yellow tanglefoot-coated squares hanging in tree	Fruit fly, aphid
White tanglefoot-coated squares hanging in tree	Sawflies
Wettable sulfur	Scab, fruit rot

Lime-sulfur	Scale, blistermites, scab leaf spot, brown rot (depends on timing)
Bordeaux mixture	General fungus problems
Vedalia beetle	Scale
Ladybug	Aphids, scale (useful only if native population has been killed or limited by spraying; California types not very effective in the East)
Praying mantis	General insect eater (of questionable value)
Aphis lion (green lacewing larvae)	Aphids, mealybugs, scale, some mites
Aphis wolf (brown lacewing larvae)	Mealybugs, aphids, scale, some mites
Fireflies	Slugs, snails
Ichneumon wasps	Miscellaneous caterpillars, sawfly
Tricogramma wasps	Mealybugs, soft scale, oriental fruit moth
Braconid wasps	Aphids, moths
Chickadees	General headstart on early insect populations
Redheaded, downy, and hairy woodpeckers	Coddling moth, miscellaneous insects
Dried egg solids	Deer
Dried blood	Rabbits
Milky spore disease	Japanese beetles
Granulosis virus	Coddling moth
Vinegar (2 parts) and molasses (1 part)	Coddling moth
Sex lures (Pheromone traps)	Coddling moth, Japanese beetles

In addition to organic pest controls, organic gardeners rely heavily on specific gardening practices to control pests. These include using a deep layer (at least 4") of mulch to hold in soil moisture and applying natural fertilizer (manure) rather than chemical types that they believe have the effect of throwing the soil nutrients and ecosystem out of balance. Organic growers make a practice of keeping the planting area clean, which includes removing loose bark and checking for egg masses underneath. They also rake up and burn all dead leaves in the fall. They pick off any fruit that looks infested during the season, and they remove any fruit drops from the area. Banding woody plants with tanglefoot is also considered to be a good idea. This sticky substance catches many damaging pests on their way up the trunk. Burning any dead or diseased branches or caterpillar tents is also considered to be necessary. Besides adding organic matter, soil improving techniques include adding earthworms (for aeration and their castings), and a spray of soil micro-organisms for general health. (Bio-dynamic soil starter is available from Pfeiffer Institute, Spring Valley, N.Y.)

Integrated Pest Management
Proponents of the compromise group, or I.P.M. (for integrated pest management), talk about a three-tiered approach to pest control. The first line of defense is heredity, the second is general health (including preventive measures) and the third, treatment. Even in treatment, ear-

ly discovery is stressed. When the I.P.M. group treats a problem, they use physical or biological measures before resorting to poisoning and other chemicals.

For edible landscapers, heredity means choosing the cultivars that are intrinsically the most disease resistant. The excellent quality of homegrown produce chosen for flavor and picked ripe cannot be overstated; whichever variety you choose will be far superior to what you can usually buy. With that being the case, why not choose varieties that are disease resistant to begin with? There are plenty of choices; see the cultivar description in the Variety List in Appendix A. Also, go through the ornamental information sheets and find pest-free plants.

The I.P.M. group claim stress is as much of an issue with plants as it is with people. Therefore, in making your choice, pay special attention to cold hardiness. Do not allow poor drainage or planting in wet areas; and conversely, be sure to water during droughts.

Preventive measures include the same ones the organic group uses, including burning leaves and using dormant oil. The I.P.M. group will resort (eventually) to whatever measure solves their problem, including any of the various poisons used by the chemical group. You should be aware, however, that once the problem becomes obvious, spraying could be too late to help much on the current year's crop. The I.P.M. group takes the attitude that they will be satisfied with the year's losses and be ready for the pest next year. In the author's view, it is the integrated pest management group that has the most to offer the edible landscaper.

The Individual Woody Plant Pests

If you go to seminars on food-producing plants, you would think the plant world was different from the human world in that while humans get mostly colds and headaches, the plants get mostly cancer and heart disease. It is not that way, of course. Some pests and diseases are serious but some are not.

In the plant world, the problems that affect the plant itself in a major way are the only really serious ones. Some problems affect the fruit only, so each year is a new game. Here are some common, often serious pests; they are arranged from the smallest to the largest creature. Where orchard spray is given as a control,

you can assume the timing of one of those sprayings mentioned in the home spray program was to control that particular pest.

Bramble Fruit Viruses The various types are a common and serious problem with red and black raspberries. Although they are not well understood, viruses are known to be spread by a common insect, aphids, as they move from plant to plant. The symptoms can include retarded leaf development, dark green blisters on the leaves, crumbly fruit, and leaves smaller and a darker green than normal and be curled inward and down. The yields can be cut in half and eventually the plant is killed. The best approach to coping with the problem is to buy specimens that are "virus free" (which actually means almost virus free). They are readily available. Commercial growers eradicate any wild brambles within a few hundred feet of a new planting if they suspect the brambles harbor any of the viruses. If you see any infected canes in your plantings, dig them out, roots and all, carry them a distance from the planting, and burn them. Carrying them away is necessary because you do not want any aphids jumping onto new plants as the burn pile heats up. Careful observation is probably the most important way of making sure that viruses do not get ahead of you.

gummosis

growth, which turns black as if it had been burned by fire. An early warning signal is the crooking of the new branch tips. If the infestation is not too bad, only a few branches may be affected; in a bad attack, many will suffer. There are good blight-resistant cultivars of both pears and apples. If you have fire blight nearby, use a preventive spray of streptomycin (which is expensive), a 4 percent chlorine bleach spray, or a mild Bordeaux spray (2-2-20). After blight hits, you can only prune it out. It moves fast, so make your cuts 12″ closer to the trunk than the infected area. Be sure to disinfect your shears with chlorine bleach between cuts. Burn the infected wood and understand that by August the tree won't look any different than any plant that got a good pruning that year. Since both apples and pears bear on older wood, you will still get plenty of fruit.

Bacterial Spot A common and moderately serious problem on peaches and, to a lesser degree, on cherries and plums. As shown, it can affect the leaves, fruit, twigs, and trunk. It is variously called canker and gummosis (on the trunk or branches), bacterial leaf spot (on the leaves), or shothole (on the fruit). The disease winters on old leaves and produces spores in the spring. The spores infect the new leaves most easily during rainy weather. Trees can eventually die from bacterial spot, although even in extreme cases this would take many years. Bordeaux mixture and fixed copper compounds control it to a degree, and a late Fall raking–up of dead leaves is very helpful. Fungicides labelled for control of bacterial leaf spot can be used at petal–fall, but some of the modern antibiotics are better. Products sold under the trade names Bacticin, Agristrep, and Agrimycin are effective.

Apple Scab Another common and moderately serious fungus problem. It attacks both the foliage and the fruit of apples, but it rarely destroys the tree. With a bad infestation, the leaves will wither and fall off. For the tree to die, all or almost all the leaves have to fall off for two or three years in a row—which is highly unlikely. The marks on the fruit look like scabs. Once again, there are disease-resistant varieties; but the apple scab disease is not systemic in the plant. It lives through the winter in the fallen leaves; therefore, if it is possible to rake up the leaves and burn them, scab will not be a problem the next year. Orchard Spray, which is used as a preventive, is effective; and Cyprex and Captan are other good individual controls. Tougher measures are needed once you have an infection, since a secondary one follows a week or two later. Phygon or lime-sulfur sprayed within three days of the first infection will suffice.

Fire Blight A common and serious disease of pears. It also affects plums and apples but to a much lesser degree. It attacks the foliage and young

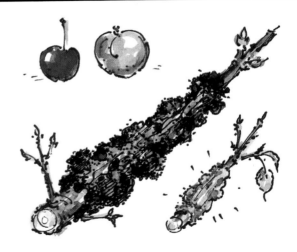

Fruit Rot   A moderately serious fungus problem. It does not kill the plant or even threaten it. Brown rot is one type of fruit rot found on peaches and especially on nectarines. If it gets bad enough, it can infect twigs. Stone fruit rot enters through the bloom, although some can enter through holes made by insects during the growing season. If blossoms brown off and drop prematurely, you can suspect a fruit rot fungus. The spores lie dormant until the sugar content increases as the fruit begins to ripen. The infected fruits will get brown spots and either shrivel up or rot before they ripen. Since the fungus spreads rapidly, removing and destroying any fruits with rot will keep down losses. Be especially alert when the fruits are just beginning to ripen. Pruning off any dead twigs will help for the following year. Orchard Spray, wettable sulfur, or Captan are individual preventives; they can be sprayed as the fruit begins to ripen if it looks as if you are going to have trouble. Some authorities recommend spraying twice during a wet season. Whether you spray or not, if you live in a humid area, brown rot will get its share of your fruit in wet years.

Cedar-Apple Rust   A moderately serious fungus problem of apples. It is probably more common in the literature than in reality but is mentioned here because junipers are common landscape plants. The cedar-apple rust is interesting because it needs two different plants to get through its life cycle: an apple and a juniper (it is called cedar-apple rust because its favorite alternate host is the red cedar, a form of juniper). Removing the alternate host is commonly recommended, but that can be drastic in the home landscape. Disease-resistant cultivars are available and recommended. For nonresistant ones, being aware of any cedar-apple rust in the neighborhood is the first step. If there is some around, be sure to check all junipers carefully each summer for galls. Remove them. Home Orchard and Zineb sprays work.

Black Knot   A moderately severe fungus problem with plums and cherries. It affects twigs and branches and, if let go, can eventually kill the tree. To control it, prune out the growths as you see them, and burn the infected tissue. To stop it, you have to prune out the young olive-green knots that look like swollen bark. The second year the knots turn black. Be alert for reinfection from trees in the area. It spreads slowly, so cutting out 4″ past the knot on good wood is conservative enough. Once again, make sure to use shears disinfected in undiluted chlorine bleach.

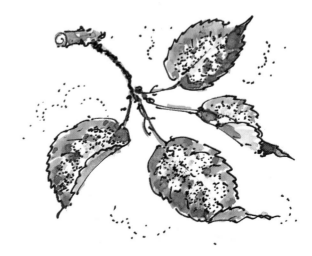

Powdery Mildew   A common but minor fungus problem that can affect just about any plant. It usually appears as a white or gray powdery coating on the leaves. In humid and shady areas—and during rainy spells—it might get bad enough to cause the death of a few leaves and stems or cause blotching on the fruit. There are resistant varieties of apples. Orchard Spray is effective, or you can spray with milk. Prune for better air circulation (which might mean pruning some other plant that is blocking the summer breeze) or spray with Bordeaux or wettable sulfur.

all look much like the drawing, they come in just about every color. Dormant oil works well for control because it kills the overwintering eggs. Regular Orchard Spray will kill the hatched ones, as will the single spray Malathion. Aphids are capable of producing six or more generations a season. If you are doing a regular home spray program, you won't have to worry. Aphids are delicious prospects for lacewing larvae (aphis lions). Knocking them off with water under pressure from a hose works too. If you don't have too many trees, you can dip infested twig ends into Ryania (4 tablespoons to the gallon). To help the aphid predators, band the trees with tanglefoot to keep the ants out; the ants collect the honeydew so they will herd the aphids together on the leaves and protect them from their enemies.

Scale A serious insect problem in zones 8 and 9 and a moderately serious one for the rest of the country. The scale insect gathers on twigs and sometimes on fruit. There are many different types of scale, and they affect most plants to varying degrees. Two of the most serious are the San José scale (shown; they look like miniature barnacles) and oyster shell scale (they resemble miniature oyster shells). The adults all have a hard shell, but the young ones are soft-bodied and crawl along the branches to new locations. The best treatment is dormant oil. If you are too late and they get to the crawling stage, you can wipe them off by hand or spray with Malathion.

Pear Psylla Attacks fruit only and is a relative of the aphid. The pear psylla is the most serious problem in the Northwest, where long-term spraying programs have made the local species resistant to pesticides. Dormant oil is an adequate control for home gardeners and ladybugs provide some control as well. The commonly marketed California ladybug is not effective in the East (they just go home). Orchard Spray works for everybody except the commercial growers in the Northwest. As a single spray, Malathion is effective.

Aphids, or Plant Lice Minor but common insect pests. Occasionally they will get out of hand on apples and sweet cherries. They like to suck the juices from new leaves and twigs. Their excrement is a honeydew that black mold will grow on, causing unsightly spots. Like scale insects, there is a specifically adapted aphid for just about every genus or species of plant. Although they

Apple Maggot, or Railroad Worm A serious pest on apples. It attacks only the fruit. The maggot is a fly larva that eats the apple flesh for food. Unfortunately, it wanders around inside the apple before it emerges, which ruins a lot of the apple. In late May, take Styrofoam balls or croquet balls, paint them red, and cover them with tanglefoot, and hang about six in each tree. (Fishing bobs coated with red or red-and-white tanglefoot also work.) This lures the flies and traps them before they lay their eggs. The maggots hatch out in July, when you can get them with Orchard Spray. Sevin, a single spray, works well.

Leaf Roller A minor to moderately serious pest. The damage is caused by a worm (moth larva) in early spring. The larvae eat the new, emerging leaves and shoots, which they roll up with a web and hide inside to protect themselves from predators. Some have successive generations that will also eat the fruit. Even a relatively serious attack on the emerging growth is not so noticeable once the tree leafs out fully. Hand picking of the curled leaves works (you might also catch some aphids and psyllas in the haul). Home Orchard Spray is effective if you are careful to get it inside the rolled leaves. Sevin is an effective single spray. Some organic growers feel the rollers' "tip pruning" is not bad so long as it doesn't get out of hand.

Coddling Moth A serious pest on apples and can go after pears as well. The worms (moth larvae) only attack the fruit, but they are the worst of the apple fruit pests. Rather than wandering around inside the fruit like the railroad worms, they prefer

to tunnel directly out of the fruit, so not so much of the fruit is ruined. Sex lure traps (the same principle as the Bag-a-Bug traps for Japanese beetles) are somewhat effective. Orchard Spray works, as does Malathion as a single spray. The granulosis virus also helps the organic grower.

Borers A very serious pest on peaches and nectarines. There are many types here, too, although only the peach tree borer (which burrows in at the ground line) is really bad. The less serious peach twig borer does its share of damage but bores in much higher up on twigs and branches and does not threaten the entire tree. The flat-headed borer can be dangerous on many fruit trees in arid areas. The larvae of the oriental fruit moth is damaging to peaches and nectarines in warmer areas. Borers are a serious pest because they can girdle the tree and kill it, since they tunnel along under the bark. The peach tree borer is so damaging because of its large size (1" long), which means it eats a lot. It tunnels in at the ground line, which means that if the trunk is girdled the whole tree will be killed instead of just a branch. This borer is particularly hard on the novice grower. They are so common they can appear quickly and do their damage before you cultivate the habit of watching out for them. New growers also have to learn to make sure they cover *everything* when they spray; it is easy to miss the critical bottom couple of inches of the trunk. Sex lure traps are available for use in the spring. After the adults lay their eggs (in June and July) you should be alert for holes. If they are still shallow, you can kill the borer by poking in a wire; an older, deeper hole will require an eyedropper squirt of Sevin. As a preventive, wood creosote (*not* the plant-damaging, coal-derived type commonly used for a wood preservative) can be used to paint the bottom foot or so of the trunk. You can brew a strong "tea" from wood-stove creosote residue. Home Orchard Spray works, as does Sevin as a single spray.

Rodents and Small Mammals Mice, voles, and moles will chew enough of the bark (especially young bark) at ground line to girdle (and thereby kill) a tree. Hardware cloth (¼″) placed an inch or two below the soil line is the only conservative way to protect the trees. Poison baits work but might harm pets or children. Make sure you loosen the hardware cloth over the years or it too can girdle the tree. Unless you live in an area of the country that's very arid, you will need some kind of enclosure to keep small animals out of your herbaceous plants. If raccoons persist in getting through your fence, put a single-strand electric line on the upper and outer part of it.

Circulio A serious pest that threatens plums and sometimes apples. It affects only the fruit and is worse in warmer climates, where more than one generation can be produced in a single season. Not long after the flower petals fall, the female adult snout beetle (weevil) lays her eggs on the very young fruit. When they hatch out into larvae, they eat so much of the fruit that it falls off the tree. The larva then pupates into a beetle in the soil. Cleaning up fallen fruit at "June drop" time is important. A week or so before and after the flowers bloom, the adults can be shaken out of the tree onto a plastic sheet. They don't run away (they are busy playing dead), giving you enough time to dump them into a can of kerosene. Orchard Spray works, as does Sevin as a single spray.

Birds Taken on balance, birds are a help in the edible landscape due to their value as insect predators. This is not true of those roving bands of blackbirds you see from time to time. Nor is it true for grain eaters like sparrows, who will eat buds in the spring. Generally, however, birds are only a major problem on their favorites: red-colored sweet cherries, blueberries, and strawberries. If birds are getting too much of your crops as the fruit begins to ripen, you can cover your plants with netting. Fasten it securely at the bottom for complete enclosure. Use green or black nets—they are less obtrusive. Ultraviolet-resistant types are more expensive, but they last many times longer. If you know birds are a big problem in your area, use only dwarf or semidwarf cherries that you can easily net. Providing food that the birds like even better—and that ripens at the same time as your crop—works too. For example, birds are extremely fond of mulberries. There are lots of other remedies suggested for bird control, but in fact birds get adjusted to anything after a few days. This includes shiny, waving, and flapping objects and various noises and monsters.

Deer Deer can be very damaging to gardens and can chew fruit and nut tree bark badly in winter. How much they hurt your plants and how easily they are controlled depends on population pressure, that is, how many deer there are in your area relative to the amount of food available for them. If the population pressure is low, they will generally stay away from you, and even a 3′ to 4′ fence will be discouraging to them. You can also hang bags filled with human hair cuttings or creosote-soaked rags on your trees and shrubs. These will work as long as the population pressure is not too great—and as long as the odor is fresh. If the population pressure is high, depending on who you talk to, only a fence 7′ to 9′ high will work—or a five-strand so-called New Zealand electric fence. In most of the populated parts of the country, the deer population is not naturally controlled; state hunting and fishing commissions regulate the hunting season to keep numbers low enough so that the deer do not become ravenous destroyers.

APPENDIX A

Recommended Variety List for

Edible Landscaping with Sources

There are significant differences between the criteria for choosing varieties for commercial use and for home use. Maximum productivity of a variety is clearly important to a commercial grower. So is fruit that ripens all at once so the pickers can move in, pick, and move on. To homeowners, these qualities may mean they are being bombed by fruit rather than having a harvest. Since commercial growers must keep their losses at such small percentages of the crop to make a living, they spray pesticides to both stop problems and to ensure they don't develop any. Because of this they're not concerned if one variety is relatively more or less resistant to pests or diseases than another.

Although it wouldn't be fair to say commercial growers have *no* concern for flavor, it is fair to say they have learned the hard way that the general public buys on the basis of appearance and familiarity, not flavor. Commercial varieties are also chosen for (1) their ability to withstand shipping well; (2) their ability to ripen well off the tree or shrub; (3) their ability to be harvested mechanically; and (4) their ability to hold up well in storage. The last includes such esoteric values as not breaking down or becoming bitter at the core.

The following list for edible landscaping is eclectic. Some varieties have been in home gardens for centuries, others have been out barely a year. Few are well known. The criteria for selection are listed below, and with the exception of flavor and ornamental quality need no further explanation. Each variety is coded with the reasons for

its inclusion in the list and with its sources. The sizes available from a given source are indicated after the source name by "S" for standard, "SD" for semidwarf, and "D" for dwarf.

The reader will find many inclusions with 'F' for flavor behind the name. This is as it should be, as a main criterion for inclusion in our list was flavor. There are thousands of varieties of fruits, nuts, and berries available to the general public. All the inclusions on our list are delicious. If the produce is not tasty in the first place, it is not so wonderful for cooking, canning, juice, or freezing. So varieties marked "F" are the best of the best.

Ornamental quality means the plant of the variety listed is particularly beautiful in the landscape, or it is attractive and fills an important niche in size or shape.

The abbreviations used in the Recommended Variety List stand for the following:

F	Flavor
PDR	Partially Disease Resistant
DR	Disease Resistant
ES	Extended Season
CT	Cold Tolerant
HT	Heat Tolerant
OQ	High Ornamental Quality

The numbers following each variety refer to the Source List at the end of this Appendix. Varieties are listed in order of ripening

Almonds

Nonpareil - OQ, F. Excellent flavor, very popular. Soft shelled. 99, 17, 18, 91, 8, 48.

Halls Hardy - OQ, CT. Large nut, fast growing, beautiful tree. Bears young. Widely available.

Garden Prince - OQ, F. Genetic dwarf tree, soft shelled. Excellent flavor. Beautiful ornamental. Productive. 99.

Price - OQ, F. Soft shelled, very good flavor. Beautiful, semidwarf tree. 99.

All-in-One - OQ, F. Soft shelled, similar to Nonpareil but self-pollinating. Small, attractive, semidwarf size tree. 30.

Apples

Anna - HT. Light green with red blush, semisweet. Popular Southern variety. 48 (SD, D), 99 (S, SD, D), 10 (SD), 102 (SD, D), 38 (SD, D), 54 (SD), 45 (S).

Ein Schmer (Elin Schmer) - HT. Golden yellow, tender, and juicy. Tarter flavor than Anna. Self-pollinating. Bears young. 10 (SD), 102 (S, D), 40 (D), 38 (S, SD), 54 (SD), 48 (SD).

Quinte - ES, F, CT. Crimson with yellow streaks. Keeps well for early type. 51 (SD), 10 (SD, D), 41 (SD, D), 2 (D), (S).

Irish Peach (Early Crofton) - CT, ES, F. Green with faint red stripes. Rich flavor and aroma. 78 (SD, D), 9 (SD), 80 (S).

Duchess (of Oldenberg) - CT, OQ, PDR. Pale yellow with red stripes, yellow flesh. Rich tart flavor. Excellent for pies and sauce. Somewhat resistant to many diseases. Large profuse flowers. 78 (SD, D), 27 (S), 68 (S), 100 (SD), 21 (S), 80 (S).

Anoka - F, PDR, CT. Yellow with red stripes, bears young. Good for cooking as well as fresh eating. Resistant to blight. 28 (S), 68 (S), 35 (S), 10 (SD).

Akane (Tokyo Rose, Prime Red) - F, PDR. Bright red with white flesh, crisp and juicy. Pearmain/Jonathan cross. Resistant to apple scab. 10 (SD), 66 (SD, D), 6 (SD), 58 (STD, D).

Garden Delicious - OQ. Gold, taste similar to Golden Delicious. Genetic dwarf to 6 or 8 ft. height. 30, 38.

Summer Rambo - ES, F. Greenish yellow with red stripes. Tender and juicy. Very old and popular variety. 2 (SD), 78 (SD, D), 10 (SD, D), 62 (SD), 94 (S, D), 100 (S), 54 (SD), 71 (D).

Prima - DR. Yellow with red blush, semisweet, heavy bearer. 99 (SD, D), 10 (STD, D), 96 (STD, D), 103 (STD, D), 41 (SD, D), 50 (SD).

Wealthy - PDR, CT, OQ, F. Red striped, white tinged pink flesh. Excellent for eating and cooking. Long blooming period. Scab and mildew resistant. Widely available.

Novamac - PDR. Red striped medium size. Very good flavor. Spritely sweet. Juicy. Resistant to rust and fireblight. 66 (S, SD, D)

Gala - F, ES, PDR. Yellow with red blush. Rust resistant. 102 (S, SD, D), 41 (Imperial strain, S, SD, D)

Kandil Sinap - OQ. Arguably the most beautiful fruit. Light, creamy yellow blushed with pink, porcelain-like finish, elongated shape. Crisp, juicy, and fine grained. 78 (SD, D).

Priscilla - DR. Yellow with red blush, semisweet. 99 (SD), 10 (STD, D), 102 (STD, D), 41 (SD, D), 50 (SD).

Sinta - F, OQ, PDR. Bright Yellow, this Golden (Yellow) Delicious/Grimes Golden cross is sweeter, jucier, and more aromatic than either parent. Scab resistant. 78 (SD, D).

Macoun - F, CT. Dark red with stripes, white flesh. Juicy and crisp. Loses quality quickly if overripe. Tree shaped similar to Tydeman types. Widely available.

Sweet Sixteen - ECT, PDR. Red Striped, sweet and distinctive flavor. Good for cooking. Keeps well. Resistant to scab and fireblight. 10 (SD), 66 (D), 26 (S, D), 27 (S), 80 (S).

Fameuse (Snow Apple) - CT, F. Crimson red with snow-white flesh that does not brown off as quickly as most in salads. Sweet and fragrant. Particularly fussy about well drained soil. Widely available.

Freedom - DR, F. Red crisp, semisweet, one of the best tasting of the disease resistant types. 66 (SD, D).

Jonafree - F, DR. Red and medium to small, flavor like Jonathan but sweeter. Immune to scab, resistant to fireblight and cedar apple rust, somewhat susceptible to mildew. 41 (S, SD, D).

Liberty - DR, F. Red crisp, semisweet, one of the best tasting of the disease resistant types. KB (SD), 10 (STD, D), 66 (SD, D), 102 (STD), 6 (STD), 40 (D).

Macfree - PDR. Red striped, medium size. Good, somewhat sweet flavor, similar to Macintosh. Ripens best in storage. Keeps well. Resistant to rust and fireblight. 66 (SD).

Cox Orange Pippin - OQ, F. One of the best flavored, red/yellowskin. Shy bearer, fussy about pollination (see Appendix B). Best grown with standard spray program. Keeps well. Small but profuse blooms. 78 (SD, D), 62 (SD), 66 (SD), 100 (SD), 34 (SD), 21 (SD).

Honeygold - ECT. Greenish yellow to yellow, juicy and sweet taste similar to Golden Delicious. 35 (S), 41 (SD, D), 26 (S, D), 27 (S), 50 (S, D), 80 (S).

Red Bouquet Delicious or Pink Pearl - OQ. Pink blooms. Good all around fruits. Pink Pearl has excellent flavor and pink flesh 78 (SD, D), 102 (S, SD).

Rhode Island Greening - OQ. Green with yellow flesh. Juicy, tart flavor. Excellent for sauce and pies. Large, showy flowers. Picturesque broad spreading tree. Keeps well. Widely available.

Ashmeads Kernel - F, PDR. Excellent russeted variety, yellow flesh, crisp. Keeps well for mid-late season. Somewhat resistant to scab. 78 (SD, D), 9 (SD), 80 (S, SD).

Roxbury Russett - F, OQ. Yellow/brown, juicy flesh with high sugar content. Always include some in cider. Stores well. Beautiful broad spreading tree. 78 (SD, D), 10 (SD), 62 (SD), 66 (SD).

Stayman Winesap - F, ES. Large red, very popular. Excellent multipurpose apple. Keeps well. Widely available.

Tompkins King (King) - F. Deep red, sometimes striped with lighter red, with white flesh. Sweet and juicy. Excellent all-around apple. Buy semidwarf or dwarf because of susceptability to collar rot. 78 (SD, D), 30 (S, SD, D), 17 (S, SD, D), 100 (SD), 58 (S, D).

Golden (Yellow) Delicious - F, PDR, OQ. Bright yellow, sweet type, very productive. Tree has three sets of blooms. Keeps well but fruit wrinkles. Susceptible to cedar apple rust, resistant to scab. Included in list because of immense popularity. Should probably be replaced in the home garden with Sinta, a very similar but superior Golden Delicious/Grimes Golden cross. Widely available.

Tolman Sweet - F, CT. Green with light red blush and distinctive striping. Very juicy, arguably the best of the sweet types. Not for storage. 60 (SD, D), 21 (SD), 80 (S), 57 (S, SD).

Regent - ECT, PDR. Red with white flesh, juicy. Excellent all-around apple. Stores well. Resistant to cedar apple rust. 41 (SD, D), 26 (S, D), 27 (S), 80 (S).

Spigold - F, PDR. Large fruit, very juicy and delicious when fresh. Northern Spy, Golden Delicious cross. Resistant to mildew and scab. 78 (S, SD), 62 (SD), 66 (SD, D), 6 (SD, D).

Mutsu (Crispin) - F, PDR. Bright greenish yellow, crisp. Excellent, somewhat spicy flavor for dessert or cooking. Keeps extremely well. Mildew resistant. Widely available

Tydeman's Late Orange - OQ, CT, F. Crimson and orange, with yellow flesh. Richly flavored. Tree shaped like Tea Crabapple. 78 (SD, D), 6 (SD), 21 (SD).

Esopus Spitzenburg - F. Brilliant orange/red with gray spots. Flesh hard and crisp. Semisweet. Thomas Jefferson's favorite. Keeps well. Pyramidal shaped tree. 78 (SD, D), 62 (SD), 66 (SD, D), 91 (D), 100 (SD), 21 (SD), 9 (SD), 57 (S, SD).

Calville Blanc d'Hiver - F. Pale green with light red dots. Fruit lobed like orange segments, pocelain-like skin. Classic French dessert apple. High in Viatmin C. Ripens best in storage (3–4 weeks). 78 (SD, D), 21 (SD), 9 (SD).

Newton Pippin (Albermarle Pippin) - F. Solid green with reddish blush, one of the best flavored. Semisweet, ripens best off the tree. Keeps well. Makes good cider. 41 (SD, D), 30 (SD, D), 18 (SD), 91 (SD), 100 (SD), 58 (STD, D), 10 (SD), 94 (STD).

Granny Smith - F. Pure green, flesh hard and crisp. Distinct flavor. Excellent all around apple. Keeps well. Requires *very* long ripening season. Widely available.

Apricots

Harcot - ES, CT, PDR. Medium sized oblong orange fruit with slight blush. Sweet, very good flavor. Good resistance to canker, bacterial spot, and brown rot. 66, 41.

Goldcot - CT, PDR. Medium sized round yellow-orange fruit. Very good, sprightly flavor. Self-pollinating. Very productive, reduces thinning. Flower buds hardy. Moderate resistance to bacterial spot. Widely available.

Harglow - OQ, CT, PDR. Medium sized bright orange fruit. Very good flavor. Late blooming, dense, full, attractive tree. Productive. Resistant to bacterial canker and brown rot. Moderate resistance to bacterial spot. 66, 41.

Hargrand - CT, PDR. Very large orange fruit with a speckled blush. Very good flavor. Productive. Good resistance to bacterial spot, perennial canker, and brown rot. 66, 41.

Alfred - F, CT. Small, round, bright orange fruit. Sweet, rich, excellent flavor. Productive. Self-pollinating. Early blooming but bud hardy. 78, 66.

Moorpark - F, HT. Large, round, bright orange fruit with brown-red blush. Juicy, excellent flavor, arguably the best flavored of the apricots. Long ripening period. Widely available.

Harlayne - CT, PDR. Medium sized orange fruit with red blush. Very good flavor. Keeps well. Productive. Good resistance to perennial canker and brown rot, moderate resistance to bacterial spot. 66, 41.

Berries

Creeping Blueberry

Wells Delight - OQ, F, DR. Small dark blue fruit on 5–8" height plant. Dense and trailing. Beautiful ground cover. Long ripening period. Wild blueberry flavor. 37.

Bloodstone - OQ, F, DR, ECT. Small dark blue fruit on 6–18" height plant. Beautiful groundcover. Slow growing at first but spreads rapidly once established. 37.

Elderberries

Adams - OQ, DR, CT. 8–20' tall mounded shrub, very dense hedge in 2 years. Good eating, freezing, and baking. Insect & disease free. Widely available.

Kent - OQ, DR, CT. 5–6' tall mounded shrub, very profuse flowering and productive. 28.

Johns - OQ, DR, CT. Improved, similar to Adams. 28.

Nova - F, OQ, DR, CT. Large berries, sweetest variety. 66, 95, 24, 69.

York - F, OQ, DR, CT. Largest berry of all. 10, 66, 95, 61, 40, 24, 69.

Juneberry (Saskatoons) - DR, OQ, ECT. Red to blue, flavor similar to blueberry. Very hardy, very decorative. Giant white blossoms, but short blooming period. High in Vitamin C. 4–6 ft. shrub. 26, 29, 35.

Ligonberry - OQ, F, DR, CT. Small white-tinged, pink clusters of flowers. Small blueberry fruit. 70, 43 (seed only).

Wineberry (Sparkling Gem, Japanese Wineberry) - F, OQ, DR, CT. Glossy red. Full flavor. Good for fences or hedgerows, easy to prune. Partial or full shade. Most disease free of Raspberry/Blackberry family. 15, 29.

Blueberries

Flordablue - OQ, DR, HT. Large light blue fruit on rounded 5–6' shrub. Very good flavor, stores well. Plant is fairly fussy about acidity and fertility of soil. 37.

Avonblue - F, OQ, DR, HT. Large light blue fruit with excellent sub-acid flavor. 4–5′ height, rounded shrub. Profuse bloomer, so much so that light pruning is helpful for large berry size. 37.

Sunshine Blue - OQ, DR, HT. Medium size light blue fruit on 3–4′ ht., rounded shrub. Very good mild flavor. Long ripening period. Profuse blooming, fine textured shrub. Tolerates high pH. 37.

Beckyblue - F, OQ, DR, HT. Very large medium blue fruit on 6–10′ ht., narrowly oval shrub. Excellent sweet, mild flavor. Outstanding cool green foliage in summer with yellowish-blue fall and winter color. Deep red stems. 37.

Choice - OQ, DR, HT. Small medium blue fruit on 8–12′ ht. shrub. Very good flavor. Beautiful ornamental with outstanding winter character and attractive foliage when in leaf. 37.

Spartan - ES, OQ. Large light blue berry on 8′ ht, vase shaped shrub. Very good flavor. Keeps well, 31, 37, 7.

Bluetta - OQ. Medium light blue fruit on a 4′ ht., broad rounded shrub. Attractive ornamental with dense growth. Very good flavor. Stores well. Widely available.

Erliblue - ES. Large light blue fruit on 6–10′, oval shrub. Firm berry, keeps well. Mild, sweet, good flavor. Widely available.

Northland - OQ, ECT. Medium sized, medium blue fruit on 4′ ht., rounded shrub. Good flavor. 96, 61, 50, 37, 5, 63, 7.

Bluecrop - F, CT. Medium/large light blue fruit on 6–8′, oval shrub. Excellent tart flavor. Keeps well. Good for cooking. Drought tolerant. Widely available.

Northblue - OQ, F, ECT. Small dark blue fruit on 2½–3′ ht., broad rounded shrub. Excellent flavor, semi-sweet with character. Beautiful red fall color. 80, 37.

Northsky - OQ, F, ECT. Small dark blue fruit on 2–2½′ ht., broad rounded shrub. Excellent flavor, semisweet with character. Beautiful red fall color. 80, 37.

Ornablue - OQ. Small, dark blue fruit on 3′ ht. by 5′ spread shrub. Very good wild blueberry-like flavor. Very attractive ornamental with beautiful scarlet red fall color. 37.

Patriot - F, ECT. Large medium blue berry on 6′ ht., broad oval shrub. Excellent sweet flavor. Productive. 51, 31, 15, 37, 75, 63, 7.

Top Hat - F, CT, OQ. Medium sized, medium blue fruit on 18″ dense rounded dwarf shrub. Sweet, delicate, excellent flavor. Self-pollinating. 35, 28, 26, 77, 29, 37.

Berkeley - Large pale blue fruit on 8–12′, rounded shrub. Very popular, mild, sweet flavor. Widely available.

Bluehaven - OQ, CT. Large light blue fruit on a 4–5′ ht., oval shrub. Good flavor. Keeps well. Ripens over long period. Productive. 37, 5, 7.

Blueray - CT, F. Large light blue fruit on 5–6′, rounded to broad rounded shrub. Sweet, excellent flavor. Beautiful red fall color. Widely available.

Collins - F, CT. Large light blue fruit on 6–8′, oval to rounded shrub. Excellent sweet flavor. 73, 65, 66, 31, 18, 100, 37, 16, 63, 7, 57.

Evergreen - OQ, F. Small dark blue fruit on 4′ ht., rounded shrub. Very sweet, excellent flavor. Holds leaves all winter in mild climates, hardy to −20° F. 37.

Stanley - F, OQ. Large medium blue fruit with excellent, distinctive (somewhat spicy) flavor. Attractive 6–8′, oval shrub. 12, 96, 7, 80.

November Glow - OQ. Small dark blue fruit on graceful 4′ × 6′ graceful shrub. Very good wild blueberry-like flavor. Holds its leaves late into fall. Exquisite scarlet red fall color. 37.

Herbert - F, ECT. Large dark shiny blue fruit on 4′ ht., broad rounded shrub. Excellent sweet flavor. Productive. 12, 10, 62, 28, 29, 5, 7.

Burlington - F, OQ. Large dark berry on attractive oval 6–8′ shrub. Excellent flavor for late season. 24, 37, 16, 7, 80.

Darrow - F. Large light blue fruit on 5–6′ rounded shrub. Excellent mild/tart flavor. Productive. Long ripening period. 100, 37, 63, 7.

Coville - F, OQ, ES. Large light blue fruit on 8–12′, oval, fairly open shrub. Excellent flavor, tart until dead ripe. Inconsistant bearer. Widely available.

Blackberries

Ebony King - CT, F, PDR. Large sweet fruit. Resistant to rusts. 35, 90, 29.

Evergreen and Evergreen Thornless - F, HT, OQ. Large, firm black fruit on long semi-trailing canes. Very attractive ornamental if trained. 103.

Thornfree Loganberry - F, HT. Medium sized, reddish-purple fruit on long semi-trailing canes. Excellent, sweet/tart flavor. Hardier than most trailing types. 35, 81, 61, 30, 38, 29.

Thornless - DR. Firm medium sized fruit on thornless canes. Very good flavor. Resistant to many diseases. Widely available.

Darrow - CT, F. Large fruit with sweet, excellent flavor. Not truly everbearing, but a long ripening season. Productive. Widely available.

Boysenberry and Thornless Boysenberry - F, HT. Large, deep red fruit on long trailing cane. Excellent, distinctive flavor. Widely available.

Black Raspberries

Jewel - F, DR, CT. Large glossy black fruit. Sweet, excellent flavor. Juicy. Not susceptible to any serious diseases. 51, 62, 66, 24.

Allen - F, PDR, CT. Large glossy black fruit. Very sweet, excellent flavor. Productive. Berries ripen at one time. Tolerant of viruses (Cumberland and Bristol) 3, 62, 66, 95, 50, 69, 53.

Logan - F, PDR. Medium to large black fruit. Very firm. Sweet, excellent flavor. Productive. Drought resistant. Tolerant of viruses and resistant to many diseases. 96, 26, 29.

Black Knight - F. Large fruit, sweet rich flavor. 29.

Dewberries

Thornless Dewberry - F, HT. Similar to blackberry, but milder, larger, and sweeter. Grows on vine. 42, 14, 3, 35, 29.

Lucretia - F, HT, DR. Large, sweet. Disease resistant. Hardy. Low growing on trailing vines. 28, 94, 29.

Thornless Gardenia - F, HT, DR. Deep black, very sweet. Disease free. Ripens 2 weeks earlier than blackberries. 59.

Red Raspberries

Southland - HT, DR. Medium sized light red fruit. Firm. disease resistant. 4, 102, 28, 40, 69.

Canby - F, CT. Large fruit, excellent flavor. Productive. Thornless. 42, 14, 35, 79, 24, 30, 29, 63.

Citadel - F, PDR. Large, firm fruit. Productive. Resistant to leaf spot. 54.

Newburgh - PDR, OQ. Large fruit with very good flavor on 4' to 5' ht. plant. Tolerates heavier soils than most. Tolerant of viruses. 53, 63, 57.

Taylor - F. Large, firm fruit with excellent flavor. Tall plant but doesn't need support. 62, 66, 63.

Latham - CT, PDR, OQ. Large fruit with very good flavor on 4' ht. plant. Productive. Extremely tolerant of viruses. Widely available.

Fall Gold - PDR, CT. Yellow fruit, very good sweet/tart flavor. Tolerant of viruses. Widely available.

Royalty - F, CT, PDR. Large purple fruit, excellent flavor. Sweeter than other purple types. Productive. Resistant to carrier of mosaic viruses. 66.

Heritage - F, CT. Firm fruit with excellent flavor. Light crops in summer, heavy in fall until frost. Widely available.

Bush Cherries

Black Beauty - ECT, DR, O. Small glossy bluish-black fruit on attractive, spreading 4–6' ht. shrub. Trouble free. 28.

Golden Boy - ECT, DR, OQ. Small golden yellow fruit on attractive spreading 4–6' ht. shrub. Trouble free. Mild, good flavor. 28.

Hansen's Bush Cherry (Black Velvet) - ECT, DR, OQ. Small dark purple fruit on attractive 4–6' ht. shrub. Profuse white blooms. Trouble free. Widely available.

Nanking (Scarlet Gem) - ECT, DR, OQ. Small bright red fruit on attractive 4–6' ht., spreading shrub. Profuse white blooms. Trouble free. Widely available.

South Dakota Ruby - ECT, DR, OQ. Medium sized bright red fruit on 6–8', oval shrub. Probably the best bush cherry for size and flavor of fruit. Attractive, trouble free shrub. 28.

Sour Cherries

Early Richmond - F, ECT. Bright red fruit approaching Morello for tartness. Heavy bearer. Widely available.

Montmorency - F. Bright red fruit. Juicy. Standard pie cherry in the United States. Crack resistant. Widely available.

English Morello - F, CT. Dark red fruit. Sharp sour taste, excellent for pies and other cooking. Widely available.

North Star - F, ECT. Small dark red fruit on 10' tree. Distinctive spicy flavor. Widely available.

Meteor - F, ECT. Bright red fruit on 10–15', semidwarf tree. Tart, but not as tart as Morello. Widely available.

Sweet Cherries

Governor Wood - F, ES. Yellow with red blush. Juicy and mild. Sweet, excellent flavor. 78 (SD), 12 (S).

Sam - ES, CT. Large black fruit, very good flavor. Cracking resistant. 35 (D), 41 (S, SD), 17 (S, SD), 91 (S), 100 (S), 60 (S), 58 (S, SD).

Merton Bigarreau - F. Large, dark red fruit. Juicy but firm. Excellent flavor. 78 (SD).

Ranier - F, CT. Yellow fruit with pink blush. Sweet, excellent flavor. Keeps well, resistant to cracking. Broad spreading tree. Widely available.

Bing - F. Dark red fruit with excellent flavor, included on list because of its immense popularity. Cracks easily in humid areas. More subject to bacterial diseases than most. Widely available.

Garden Bing - F, OQ. Dark red fruit, 6' dwarf version of extremely popular variety. Has same problems as standard Bing. 28, 30.

Kirkland's Mary - F. Rosy-pink fruit. Crisp, meaty, bigarreau-type fruit. Excellent flavor. 78 (SD).

Starkrimson Dwarf - OQ. Dark red fruit on compact (to 15') tree. Sweet, very good flavor. 102 (SD).

Stella and Compact Stella - OQ. Dark red fruit. Sweet, juicy, and firm. Very good flavor on 15–25' tree (Stella), or 10–14' tree (Compact Stella). Widely available.

Yellow Glass - F, ECT. Yellow fruit. Sweet and juicy. Excellent flavor for pure yellow type cherry. 65 (S), 44 (S), 15 (S), 59 (S).

Gold - F, ES, ECT. OQ. Clear yellow fruit, small but firm with distinctive flavor. Profuse bloomer and pollinator. 41 (S, SD), 102 (SD), 58 (S, SD).

Yellow Spanish - F, ES. Yellow with red blush. Rich, very sweet, excellent flavor. 78 (SD, D).

Downers Late Red - F, ES. Light to dark red fruit. Sweet, rich, excellent flavor. Pick when fully ripe. 78 (SD).

Cherry-Plums

Compass - CT, OQ, DR. Medium size dark red fruit with yellow flesh. Juicy, tart. Good cooking. Hardy in all zones. Best pollinator for all cherry-plum hybrids. 26, 50.

Delight - CT, OQ, DR. Red to black fruit with very good flavor. Strong and tangy. Good for cooking. 99, 38, 8.

Red Diamond - ECT, OQ, DR. Deep red fruit with red flesh. Freestone. Sweet. Extra hardy. Needs pollinator. 26, 50.

Sapalta - ECT, OQ, DR. Dark purple skin and flesh. Early bearer. Very hardy. 28, 27.

Sapa - CT, OQ, DR. Purple to black fruit with clear flesh. Sweet, small, and bushy. Good cooking. 35, 24.

Oka - CT, OQ, DR. Purplish red fruit with dark red flesh. Juicy, sweet. Good quality. Heavy bearing. 35, 24, 28.

Sprite - CT, OQ, DR. Nearly black fruit with light amber flesh. Distinctive flavor. 99, 38, 8.

Stark Giant Cherry-Plum (Kellog Cultivar) - CT, OQ, DR. Solid red with red flesh. Sweet, spicy, Good, all purpose. 102.

Mistawasis - ECT, OQ, DR. Dark red with red flesh. New, excellent quality, and most hardy. 26.

Currants

Minnesota 71 - F, DR, CT. OQ. Large red fruit on attractive spreading shrub. Productive and trouble free. 66.

Red Lake - F, DR, CT, OQ. Large red fruit on oval shrub. Very productive and trouble free. Widely available.

White Imperial - F, DR, CT, OQ. White fruit on attractive rounded shrub. Sweet, rich flavor. Arguably the best-tasting currant. 78, 66.

Consort - F, DR, CT, OQ. Black fruit on attractive spreading shrub. Fragrant leaves and stems. Delicious sweet flavor. High in Vitamin C. One of very few black currants that are not an alternate host to white pine blister rust. 70.

Figs

Black Mission (Mission) - OQ, HT, DR. Black fruit with pinkish red flesh. Rich flavor. West's most popular. Subtropical. 99 (S), 30 (S), 8 (S).

Brown Turkey (Black Spanish) - OQ, HT, DR. Medium large coppery fruit with white to pink flesh. Good bearer. Small tree. Hardy as far north as Maryland. 95, 61, 30, 94, 38, 8, 69.

Celeste (Celestial, Sugar) - Violet fruit with rosy/white flesh. Sweet. Most widely planted in the Southeast. 62, 102, 40, 94, 38.

Conadria - F, OQ, HT, DR. Greenish yellow fruit with thin skin, flesh pink. Excellent flavor. Resistant to spoilage. Leaf mosaic. Vigorous grower. 99 (S).

Everbearing (Texas Everbearing, Eastern Brown Turkey) -F, OQ, HT, DR. Firm, meaty, straw-colored fruit with very sweet flesh. Excellent eating and cooking. Continuous fruiting through season. 24, 99, 77, 51, 10, 28, 15.

Kadota - OQ, HT. DR. Medium sized green/yellow fruit with tough skin. More winter-hardy than most. 30.

Miscellaneous Fruits

Beach Plum - CT, OQ, DR. Small red to purple fruit on beautiful 6' ht., spreading shrub. Profuse single and double white flowers. Improved varieties available locally in New England. 28, 35, 51, 90.

Chinese Date (Jujube)

Lang - OQ, DR, HT. 1½–2" pear-shaped brown fruit. Tastes like cross between apple and date. Heavy bearer. Weakly self-pollinating. 30, 99, 6.

Li - OQ, DR, HT. 2" pear-shaped brown fruit. Like Lang, but with smaller pit. Also weakly self-pollinating. 30, 99, 6.

Manchurian Bush Plum - ECT, OQ, DR. Red Japanese plum-type fruit on 4–5' ht. shrub. Gets to 10' ht. in warmer zones. Good flavor. 10, 40, 10, 90.

Medlar

Nottingham - OQ, CT, DR. Dark russet brown, ripened flesh light brown, lightly acid. Easy to grow. Good for dessert and cooking. 78.

Mulberry

Black Beauty - OQ, DR. Large, long fruit. Semidwarf, seedless, self-fruitful. Tart/sweet. Excellent all-purpose. 95, 8.

Hardy Russian - OQ, DR. Black. Hardy, fast growing. Good all-purpose, best for wine and jelly. 28, 61.

Wellington (Downing, New American) - F, OQ, DR. Best of mulberries for eating out of hand. 66.

Northern Kiwi - OQ, DR, CT. The following varieties are available: Geneva HH1 & HH2, 74-55, Hood River, Ananasnaja and Issai. Issai is part sun only and somewhat self-fertile. Others require a male pollinator: 74-46, 1971, or Pacific. 37, 104.

Paw-paw (Winter Banana) - OQ, DR. CT. Fruit sweet, banana flavored. Purple blooms. 14, 35, 28, 61, 40, 24, 77, 29, 55, 37.

Pomegranate

Wonderful - OQ, DR. Glossy purple with deep red flesh. Tangy flavor. California's main cultivar, very beautiful ornamental. 99 (S), 95 (GD), 30 (GD), 38 (S), 69 (S).

Raisin Tree - OQ, DR. CT. Red fruit, flesh chewy, and sweet. Heart-shaped leaves, green and white flowers. Very attractive ornamental. 14.

Gooseberries

Hoenigs Earliest - F, DR. Medium golden-yellow fruits European type. Excellent, sweet plum-like flavor. Trouble-free plants. 78.

Poorman - F, CT, DR. Medium sized wine-red fruit. Excellent, rich, sweet flavor. American type. Very productive. Fast growing, trouble-free shrub. 78, 66.

Welcome - ECT, DR. Light green to pink fruit. Arguably the best flavored of tart types. Excellent for cooking. Very productive. 44, 28, 26, 24, 29.

Whitesmith - F, DR, OQ. Large oval pale green fruit. European type. Profuse flowering. Excellent delicate flavor. Attractive trouble-free shrubs. 78.

Captivator - F, DR, ECT. Medium sized, pear-shaped fruit. Very sweet, excellent flavor. Completely thornless, trouble-free shrub. Canadian type (Spinefree-Clark). 78.

Howard's Lancer - F, DR. Large oval pale green fruit with yellow markings. Excellent flavor. English type. No hairs. Trouble-free shrub. 78.

Grapes, Hybrid Wine

Cayuga White - F. Light green fruit. Vigorous, productive, trouble-free vines. Clean, light, neutral. Resembles White Reisling. 66.

Seibel 9110 (Verdelet) - F. Large, grayish-green fruit. Sweet yet neutral. Crisp and meaty. Also good for juice and table grapes. Vines need winter protection in Northern zones. 78, 4.

Seyve-Villard 20-365 - F. Large grayish-yellow fruit in large clusters. Crisp, meaty texture. Excellent, sweet, clear flavor. Also excellent for table grape and juice. Vines need winter protection in colder zones. 78.

Seyve-Villard 18-307 - F. Medium sized red fruit. Mellow, fruity, excellent flavor. Also excellent for table and juice. 66.

Grapes, Muscadine

Dearing - F, HT. Large bronze fruit. Very productive. Self-fertile. Excellent flavor. 93, 38, 11.

Hunt - F, HT, PDR. Large black fruit. Very good flavor, excellent for juice and wine. Trouble-free vines. Needs pollinator. 93, 11, 45.

Magoon - F, HT, PDR. Medium reddish-black fruit. Excellent flavor. Trouble-free vines, self-polinating. 38, 93, 11.

Scuppernong - F, HT. Very large bronze fruit. Excellent sweet flavor and aroma. needs pollinator. 35, 102, 28, 15, 94, 38, 45.

Southland - F, HT. Large purple fruit. Excellent sweet flavor. Self-pollinating. Most heat tolerant of the group. 35, 28, 38, 11, 45.

Grapes, Table

Himrod - F, ES, CT. Seedless, pale greenish-yellow fruits. Excellent sweet delicate flavor. Arguably the best table grape for most grape growing areas. Widely available.

Seneca - F. Golden yellow at maturity. Excellent, sweet, aromatic, distinctive flavor. One of the very best. Hangs well on vine. 78, 66, 62, 77.

Canadice - F, CT, OQ. Seedless red fruit. Very sweet, rich flavor similar to Delaware. Very attractive vine, hangs well. 51, 62, 66.

Ontario - F. Small green fruit. Highly aromatic. Sweet, rich, foxy flavor. Hangs well on vine. 78, 66, 62, 77.

Barry - F. Large black fruit. Delicate sweet flavor. Far superior to Concord. Productive, trouble-free vine. Must be fully matured on vine. 78.

Buffalo - F. Dark, bluish-black fruits. Rich, sweet flavor. Vigorous trouble-free vines requiring almost no care. Superior Concord type. Arguably the best seeded type for homeowners. 78, 66, 62, 28, 77.

Delaware - OQ, F. Pale red, excellent small fruit. The most attractive vine for ornamental use. Richly flavored. Widely available.

Dutchess - F. Pale green speckled fruits. Distinctive, refreshing flavor. Clusters hang beautifully on vine. 78, 66.

Edelwiess - F, CT. Greenish white fruit. Excellent, very sweet flavor. Also used for juice and wine. 35, 26, 27.

New York Muscat - F. Reddish black fruit. Rich, distinctive yet sweet flavor. Extremely delicious. 78, 66.

Suffolk Red. - F. Seedless large red fruit. Spicy, juicy, sweet flavor. Widely available.

Swenson Red - F, CT. Red fruit. Sweet, excellent flavor. Also used for juice and wine. 35, 26, 27.

Golden Muscat - F. Large pale greenish-yellow fruit. Extremely juicy. Excellent, refreshing flavor. Should be fully ripened on vine. Widely available.

Steuben - F, CT. Purplish-black fruit. Spicy, rich, excellent flavor. Superior Concord type. Very productive. Widely available.

Nectarines

Nectarines are not generally recommended for home growing because of brown rot and other bacterial disease problems. The following are the best of the lot and are recommended for the less humid parts of the Midwest and West.

Morton - F, PDR. Small to medium greenish-white with red blush. Excellent, juicy, rich flavor. Resistant to brown rot. 78 (SD, D), 66 (S, SD).

Pocohontas - F, OQ, PDR. Medium-large red fruit. Excellent flavor. Showy flowers. Flower buds hardy. Brown rot resistant. 94 (S), 29 (S, SD), 45 (S).

Hardired - ECT, PDR. Medium sized red fruit. Very good flavor and texture. As hardy as Reliance peach. Important to thin fruits. Resistant to bacterial spot and brown rot. 41 (S), 66 (S, SD), 96 (S), 28 (S), 66 (D).

Harko - CT, PDR. Medium sized fruit. Very good flavor and texture. Slightly hardier than Redhaven peach. Resistant to bacterial spot and brown rot. 41 (S), 66 (S, SD), 17 (S).

Red Chief - OQ, PDR. Medium sized red fruit. Very good flavor. Showy flowers. Important to thin fruits. Resistant to brown rot. 65 (S, SD), 61 (D), 91 (S, SD), 22 (S).

Nuts, Miscellaneous

Chinese Chestnuts

Crane and Nanking - F. Sweet, fast growing, blight resistant. Excellent flavor, good for roasting. 55, 98.

Hazelnuts (Filberts)

Barcelona - F, HT. Excellent flavor, large nut, popular variety. Widely available.

Royal - F, HT. Excellent flavor, even larger nut than Barcelona. Productive. 62, 15, 24, 18, 55.

Hall's Giant - OQ, HT. Late maturing, long blooming period. Very beautiful ornamental. 99.

Jone's Hybrids - OQ. American-European crosses. Hardier than above European types, smaller, but very good, nuts. Very attractive ornamentals. 23, 82, 55.

Hicans

Clarksville - F, OQ, CT. Extends pecan range, excellent flavor, beautiful tree. 40, 55.

Gerardi - F, OQ, CT. Similar to Clarksville and somewhat hardier. 55.

Burton - F, OQ, CT. Excellent flavor, very productive.

Butternuts

Kenworthy - F, OQ, CT. Large, easily cracked nuts on beautiful tree. 55, 34, 98.

Craxezy - OQ, CT. Similar to Kenworthy with very good flavor and even easier cracking. 97, 98, 34.

Hickories, Shellbark - The following recommended improved varieties are available: Missouri Manmouth, 102; Bradley, 98; Kaskaskia, Lindauer and others, 55.

Hickories, Shagbark - The following recommended improved varieties are available: Wilcox, 55, 97, 98; Weschecke, 55, 98; Grover, Harold, and others, 55.

Heartnuts - The following recommended improved varieties are available: Ebert, 55, 34; Fodermaier, 55, 98; Schubert, 55, 34; Wright, 55, 98.

Peaches*

*White cling types are generally far more disease tolerant than the more popular yellow freestone.

Junegold - HT. Yellow with red blush, yellow flesh freestone. Arguably the best flavored of the heat tolerant peaches. Stores and freezes reasonably well. 102 (S), 38 (S), 8 (S, SD), 22 (H, N, L).

Polly - F, CT, PDR. Yellowish white with red blush, white fleshed freestone. Excellent sweet flavor. Productive. Somewhat resistant to fungal and bacterial diseases. 78 (S), 35 (S, SD), 44 (S, SD), 28 (S, SD), 27 (S), 59 (S, SD).

Candor - CT, PDR, ES. Red with yellow blush, freestone, yellow flesh. Flower buds hardy. Freezes well. Resistant to bacterial spot. 41 (S, SD), 10 (S), 66 (S), 22 (S).

Compact Redhaven - OQ, F, PDR. Red and yellow, yellow fleshed freestone. Excellent flavor. Productive. Freezes well. Genetic dwarf to 10 ft. tall. Somewhat resistant to bacterial diseases. 50 (S), 102 (S).

Redhaven - F, PDR. Red and yellow, freestone, yellow flesh. Juicy, excellent flavor. Productive, freezes well. Resistant to bacterial diseases. Widely available.

Reliance - OQ, ECT. Greenish yellow with red blush, freestone, yellow flesh. Heavy cropper, hardiest of peaches for cold areas. Showy flowers. Widely available.

Raritan Rose - OQ, F, PDR. Creamy white with red blush, white fleshed freestone. Rich, aromatic flavor. Juicy melting flesh. Productive. Showy flowers. Somewhat resistant to bacterial diseases. 41 (S), 65 (S), 2 (S), 48 (S, SD).

Bonanza II - OQ. Yellow with red blush, yellow fleshed freestone. Genetic dwarf 4–6 ft. ht. Profuse pink semidouble flowers. Widely available.

Ranger - CT, PDR. Yellow with mottled red, freestone, yellow flesh. Freezes and cans well. Productive. Melting flesh. Resistant to bacterial spot. 99 (S), 65 (S), 96 (S), 65 (S), 22 (S).

Sunapee - ECT. OQ. Yellow with red blush, yellow fleshed freestone. Second only to Reliance in cold tolerance. Good flavor. Showy flowers. 78 (S).

George IV - F, PDR. Greenish white with pink blush, white fleshed freestone. Excellent rich sweet/tart flavor. Juicy, somewhat resistant to fungal and bacterial diseases. 78 (S).

Champion - F, CT, PDR. Creamy white with red blush, white fleshed freestone. Juicy, sweet, delicate flavor. Somewhat resistant to fungal and bacterial diseases. 64 (S), 78 (S), 62 (S, SD), 28 (S), 61 (S), 41 (S, SD).

Loring - F, PDR. Yellow with red blush, yellow fleshed freestone. Sweet and firm but melting. Productive dependable (sets fruit in adverse weather). Somewhat resistant to bacterial diseases. Freezes well. Widely available.

J. M. Mack - PDR, CT, F. Large white with red blush, white fleshed freestone. Excellent, tender, sweet melting flavor. Somewhat resistant to bacterial and fungal diseases. 78.

Madison - CT, F. Yellow/orange with red blush, yellow fleshed freestone. Productive. Freezes well. Hardier than Redhaven, especially buds. Thin, tender skin. Widely available.

Starks Sensation - OQ. Yellow with red blush, yellow fleshed freestone. Good flavor for genetic dwarf. 4–6 ft. ht. 102 (S).

Belle of Georgia - F, OQ. Creamy white with red blush, white flesh. Juicy, excellent flavor. Brilliant red flowers. Widely available.

Biscoe - F, CT, PDR. Yellow with red blush, freestone, yellow flesh. Excellent yellow melting flesh. Flower buds heavy. Resistant to bacterial spot. 41 (S, SD), 22 (S), 2 (S), 48 (S).

Elberta - F, OQ, PDR. Yellow with red blush, freestone, yellow flesh. Arguably the most flavorful yellow freestone. Early types (July, Kim, Gleason) considered tastier by some. Fantastic Elberta has double pink flowers. Productive, cans and freezes well. Brown rot resistant. 99 (S), 102 (S, SD), 18 (S, SD), 17 (S), 91 (S, SD), 58 (S, D), 65 (S, D), 15 (SD), 30 (S, SD), 8 (S, SD).

Honeybabe - OQ, F, ES. Yellow with dark red blush, yellow fleshed freestone. Arguably the best tasting of the 4–6 ft. genetic dwarfs. Flavor rich and tangy. Showy flowers. 30, 99.

Oldmixon Free - F, PDR. White with red blush, white fleshed freestone. Rich juicy flavor. Somewhat resistant to fungal and bacterial diseases. 78 (S).

Sweet Sue - F, ES, OQ. Yellow with red blush, yellow fleshed freestone. Similar to and replacement for Rio-oso-gem. Less susceptible to bacterial spot than Rio-oso-gem. Excellent storage quality for a peach, good freezing. Profuse, large, Light pink blooms. 41 (S, SD).

Late Crawford - F. Yellow and red, yellow flesh freestone. Arguably the best flavored yellow peach. 78 (S).

Peento - DR, F. Greenish white with red blush, flattened appearance, clingstone white flesh. Very juicy and flavorful. Resistant to fungal and bacterial diseases. 48 (S).

Indian Blood Free (Indian Red) - F, PDR. Large red fleshed freestone. Tarter flavor than most peaches. Resistant to leaf curl. 65 (S), 99 (S), 30 (S, SD), 8 (S, SD), 48 (S), 22 (S).

White English - DR, F. Greenish white with red blush, white fleshed clingstone. Somewhat resistant to fungal and bacterial diseases. 93 (S), 48 (S).

Pears

Chapin - F, ES, PDR. Small pyriform shape, russet brown to dark red with specks. Juicy, sweet, excellent flavor. Seedling of Seckel with same small, pyrimidal shaped tree. Good fireblight resistance on old home interstem. 78 (SD, D).

Harrow Delight - ES, PDR, CT. Medium sized pyriform yellow with red blush. Similar to Bartlett but with excellent fireblight resistance. 41 (SD).

Aurora - F. Large pyriform shape, russet yellow. Melting flesh. Juicy and sweet. Keeps well. Susceptible to fireblight. 78 (SD, D), 41 (SD), 60 (S).

Le Conte - HT. Medium sized pyriform with creamy white skin. Good flavor. 19 (S).

Harvest Queen - PDR, CT. Small to medium pyriform green fruit very close to Bartlett in flavor but with excellent fireblight resistance. Excellent for cooking. 41 (SD).

Moonglow - PDR. Medium pyriform yellow fruit. White, juicy, very good flavored flesh. Excellent fireblight resistance. Widely available.

Collete - OQ. Medium pyriform, yellow with pink blush. Rich, spicy, very good flavor. Exceptionally long blooming period. 35 (S), 62 (S, SD), 28 (S), 24 (D).

Starking Delicious (Maxine) - PDR, CT. Medium pyriform. Bright yellow. White soft flesh, juicy and very good flavor. Good fireblight resistance. 78 (SD, D), 35 (S), 102 (S, SD), 65 (S, SD), 28 (S), 27 (S), 38 (S).

Atlantic Queen - F, PDR. Large rounded-pyriform shape fruit, yellowish green with specks. Excellent buttery flavor. Very juicy with good aroma. Tree is adaptable to adverse growing conditions and fireblight resistant. Arguably the best choice for the home landscape. 57 (SD, D).

Buerre Superfin - F. Medium sized round-conical green fruit. Melting flesh. Sweet, juicy. Excellent flavor and aroma. Some fireblight resistance if purchased on old home interstem. 78 (SD).

Michelmas nellis - F, OQ. Large sized pyriform shape. Yellowish green with brown dots. Sweet, juicy, excellent flavor. Extremely beautiful scarlet red fall color. 78 (SD, D).

Belle Lucrative (Fondante D'Automne) - Medium round-conical fruits, greenish yellow skin with specks. Excellent, distinctive flavor and aroma. Very sweet and buttery. 78 (SD, D), 57 (SD, D).

Luscious - F, PDR, CT. Small pyriform bright yellow with red blush. Very juicy and sweet. More intense Bartlett-type flavor. Fireblight resistant. 41 (SD), 26 (S), 27 (S), 50 (S), 68 (S).

Magness - PDR. Medium large pyriform-rounded, russet brown. Juicy and sweet with very good flavor. Very fireblight resistant, also resists insect damage. Grows well. 94 (S), 38 (S), 78 (SD), 99 (S), 12 (S), 19 (S), 2 (S).

Bosc (Buerre Bosc) - F. Medium long-necked pyriform shape, Brown and golden russet. Excellent, rich, somewhat spicy flavor. Juicy, tender. Some fireblight resistance if purchased on old home interstem. Widely available.

Comice (Royal Rivera) - F, ES. Large oval-pyriform shaped fruit with red blush, slightly russet. Excellent buttery flavor. Juicy with good aroma. Erratic cropping. Prefers fertile soil and watering. Somewhat susceptible to fireblight; most feel it's worth the effort. Widely available.

Passe Crassane - ES, F. Large roundish-cylindrical shape fruit, yellowish brown with reddish purple spots. White flesh with juicy, excellent flavor. Famous in Europe. Variable quality. Prefers watering and fertile soils. Keeps well. 78 (SD, D).

Pears, Salad (Asian)

Shinseiki - OQ, DR. Large bright yellow fruit. Sweet, crisp flavor. Self-pollinating. Pick before fully ripe. Long ripening period. 30, 41, 99.

Hosui - F, OQ, DR. Medium large russet greenish brown with orange-red blush when ripe. Sweet, juicy, excellent flavor. 30, 41.

Niji Seiki (Twentieth Century) - OQ, DR. Medium large greenish yellow fruit. Very good, fruity, refreshing flavor. Firm, must be thinned. 36, 41, 99, 78, 17.

Shinko - F, OQ, DR. Medium large golden russet fruit. Sweet, excellent flavor. Very productive. Keeps well. 30, 41.

Pecans

Colby - CT, OQ. Very good flavor. Tree holds foliage late into fall. 65, 28, 15, 94, 77, 55, 98.

Giles - CT, F, PDR. Excellent flavor, not quite as cold hardy as Colby. Scab resistant. 65, 55, 98.

Major - CT, PDR. Large meaty nuts, crack easily. Scab resistant. Widely available.

Desirable - HT, PDR. Sweet, very good flavor. Meaty, very productive. Scab resistant. 38, 22, 19.

Cape Fear - HT, PDR, F. Excellent flavor. Disease resistant. 102.

Schley - HT, OQ. Very good flavor, very thin shell. Productive. Picturesque tree. 102.

American Persimmons

John Rick - F, OQ, CT, DR. Medium sized fruit. Excellent flavor. 32, 47.

Early Golden - OQ, CT, DR. Large yellow fruit. Very good flavor. Seeded. 32, 47.

Golden Supreme - OQ, CT, DR. Very large yellow fruit. Very good flavor. Seeded. 32.

Meader - F, OQ, CT, DR. Medium sized fruits. Excellent flavor. Will bear seedless fruit if not pollinated by male plant. 32, 47.

Oriental Persimmons

Eureka - F, OQ, DR. Red-orange, Excellent flavor. Relatively hardy. Attractive, thick foliage. 61, 94, 19.

Fuyu (Fuyugaki) - OQ, DR. Shiny red with light orange flesh. Firm, crunchy, and sweet. Heavy bearer. Good ornamental. 99, 10, 95, 40, 30, 38, 8, 45.

Hachiyai - F, OQ, DR. Very large, deep red with red flesh. Rich flavor. Vigorous. Good cooking. Ornamental. 99, 30, 8.

Tamopan - OQ, DR. Very large red-orange with light orange flesh. Tender, juicy, sweet, non-astringent. Fairly hardy. 10, 61, 30.

Tane-nashi - OQ, DR. Very large light yellow to red seedless. Weeping growth. 15, 30, 94, 38, 45.

European Plums

Erliblue - ES. Dark bluish purple with greenish-yellow flesh. Similar to Stanley but softer flesh. Good flavor. 102 (S), 41 (S).

California Blue - CT, OQ. Large, nearly freestone blue fruit. Slightly tart flavor. Narrowest of vase-shaped plums. 41 (S).

Mowhawk - CT, OQ. Large blue with yellowish green flesh, productive. Good flavor. Keeps relatively well. Broad, rounded tree. 66 (S).

Mount Royal - ECT. Medium size dark blue with greenish-yellow flesh. Productive, juicy, good flavor. 15 (S), 41 (S), 26 (S), 27 (S), 50 (D).

American Mirabelle - F. Small bright yellow with yellow flesh. Very sweet and delicious. 66 (S).

Stanley - OQ, PDR. Medium to large, dark bluish purple with greenish yellow flesh. Freestone juicy and sweet. Included because of wide popularity. Somewhat resistant to brown rot. Keeps relatively well. Seneca (66) and Iroquois (66) are similar. Widely available.

Italian (German, Fellenburg) - OQ. Large purple with greenish yellow flesh. Freestone. Very productive. Good, somewhat tart flavor. Extremely popular variety, long ripening period. Widely available.

Jefferson - F. Medium large yellow with pinkish-red blush, orange flesh. Juicy, richly flavored. 78 (SD, D).

Shropshire Damson - CT, PDR, F. Small blue fruit. Arguably the best of the Damson types. Excellent for cooking and preserves. Curculio resistant, bacterial spot resistant. 10 (S), 61 (S), 15 (S), 41 (S), 24 (S), 39 (S).

Green Gage (Reine Claude) - PDR, F, CT. Small to medium yellowish green fruit with yellow flesh. Very sweet. Juicy, rich flavor. Does not keep well. Somewhat resistant to brown rot and bacterial spot. Widely available.

Pearl - F. Medium to small yellow with red specks, yellow flesh. Melting flesh, very sweet. Arguably the best flavored of all European plums. Luther Burbank introduction. 78 (SD, D).

Imperial Epineuse - F, ES. Large mottled reddish and purplish with greenish yellow flesh. Excellent sweet, rich flavor. 78 (SD, D), 30 (S, SD), 57 (S, SD).

Prune D'Agen (French Prune, Agen, Petite) - F. Dark bluish purple with greenish yellow flesh. Very sweet. Excellent flavor. 78 (SD, D).

Yellow Transparent Gage (Reine Claude Diaphne) - PDR, F, CT. Similar to but larger than Green Gage. Also very sweet and delicious. Richer aroma. Somewhat resistant to brown rot and bacterial spot resistant. Does not keep well. 78 (SD, D).

Count Althann's Gage (Reine Claude Conducta) - F, PDR, CT. Large, dark reddish-purple with yellow flesh. Sweet, juicy, delicious. Somewhat resistant to brown rot and bacterial spot resistant. Does not keep well. 78 (SD, D), 102 (SD).

Japanese Plums

Methley - ES, HT. Small to medium reddish-purple fruit with red flesh. Sweet, juicy, very good flavor. Susceptible to circulio but some resistance to black knot. Long ripening period. Widely available.

Shiro - ES, PDR, HT. Medium sized golden yellow fruit with yellow flesh. Flavor suffers more than most commercial varieties when picked early, but excellent when allowed to fully ripen on tree. Productive. Resistant to black knot. Widely available.

Allred - OQ, CT. Medium sized freestone red fruit. Vase-shaped tree with red foliage and red flowers. Excellent accent plant. 28 (S), 19 (S), 44 (S).

Formosa - OQ, PDR. Large greenish yellow fruit with red blush. Flesh is creamy yellow. Juicy but firm. Very good flavor. Broad, vase-shaped tree. Alternate bearer. Resistant to black knot. Holds leaves late into fall. 66 (S), 60 (S), 2 (S).

Ozark Premier - OQ, PDR. Large red fruit with yellow flesh. Good flavor. Juicy but firm. Beautiful mounded shaped tree. Bacterial spot resistant. Some resistance to brown rot and canker. Widely available.

Weeping Santa Rosa - OQ. Medium reddish purple fruit with light specks, flesh yellow. Slightly tart; very good flavor. Weeping tree form more attractive and later blooming than standard commercial form. Shy bearer in east. Susceptible to bacterial spot in humid climates.

Frontier - OQ. Medium sized very dark blue fruit with red flesh. Very good, distinctive flavor. Very productive. 22 (S), 29 (S, D), 48 (S).

Burbank (Grand Prize) - PDR, HT, F. Large, reddish-purple with yellow flesh. Firm fruit. Very flavorful. Very productive. Wide climatic range. Circulio resistant. Widely available.

Laroda - F. Large very dark red fruit with light specks, yellow flesh. Sweet, rich, excellent flavor. 78 (SD, S), 30 (S, SD), 91 (S).

Cocheco - OQ, CT. Small red fruit, white flowers with reddish purple foliage. Excellent accent plant. 10 (S).

Superior - OQ, ECT. Large yellow to deep red with yellow flesh. Actually an American-Japanese cross. Sweet, rich, very good flavor. Very productive. Profuse bloomer. Widely available.

Mariposa - F. Large light purple fruit with dark red flesh. Very sweet. Excellent flavor and aroma. 78 (D), 99 (S).

Elephant Heart - F. Large reddish green to dark purple fruit with reddish purple flesh. Extremely juicy, with excellent flavor. Long ripening period. 78 (SD, D), 96 (S), 102 (S), 41 (S), 30 (S, SD), 17 (S, SD), 91 (S).

Plumcots

Fowler Plumcot - CT, OQ, DR. Yellow fruit with golden flesh. Tree has plum characteristics. 30.

Kaga - CT, OQ, DR. Native wild plum-apricot cross. Heavy bearer. 35.

Mesch-Mesch-Amrah - CT, OQ, DR. Red fruit with yellow flesh. Sweet to tart. 78.

Plum Parfait (Zaiger) - CT, OQ, DR. Pinkish orange fruit with marbled reddish amber flesh. Freestone. 99.

Quinces

Orange Quince - OQ, DR. Golden yellow, firm. Excellent cooking. 51 (D), 62 (D), 96 (S), 102 (S), 61 (D), 24 (SD), 30 (S).

Pineapple Quince - OQ, DR. Pale yellow fruit with white flesh. Slight pineapple flavor. Excellent for cooking and wine. 99 (S), 96 (S), 30 (S), 17 (D), 8 (S).

Smyrna - F, OQ, DR. Extra large light yellow fruit with yellow flesh. Heavy bearer. Good for preserves. Dense, attractive foliage on tree. Arguably the best for home growing. 30 (S), 8 (S), 78 (SD).

Black Walnuts

Thomas - ECT. Larger nuts than natives, more easily cracked. Widely available.

The following recommended improved varieties are available: Elmer Myers, 32, 97, 34, 98; Emma Kay, 32, 34, 98; Ohio, 32, 34, 97.

Persian Walnuts

Carpathian - F, CT. Large nuts, thin shelled, rapid growing. Widely available.

Clark's Jumbo #1 - F, CT. Largest nuts. 34.

Hartley - F. Popular, thin shelled, bears young. Excellent flavor. 99, 30.

Stark Kwik-Krop (Boellner) - Very good flavor, bears 2 years after planting. 102.

Source List

NURSERY	NUMBER

Abundant Life Seed Foundation — 1
P. O. Box 772
Port Townsend, Wash. 98368

Adams County Nursery — 2
Aspers, Penn. 17304

Ahrens Strawberry Nursery — 3
R.R. 1
Huntingburg, Ind. 47542

W. F. Allen Co. — 4
Salisbury, Md. 21801

Alexander's Nurseries—Blueberries — 5
Wareham St.
Middleboro, Mass. 12346

Amberg's Nursery, Inc. — 6
3164 Whitney Rd.
Stanley, N.Y. 14561

A. G. Ammon — 7
Box 488, Barnegat Rd.
Chatsworth, N.J. 08019

Armstrong Nurseries, Inc. — 8
P. O. Box 4060
Ontario, Calif. 91761

Baum's Nursery — 9
RD 2
New Fairfield, Conn. 06810

Bountiful Ridge Nurseries — 10
Princess Anne, Md. 21853

Bryants Nursery — 11
Box 422
Helena, Ga. 31037

Bunting's Nurseries, Inc. — 12
Selbyville, Del. 19975

Bruck Filbert Nursery — 13
29665 SW 3529
Wilsonville, Ore. 97070

Burgess Seed and Plant — 14
905 Four Seasons Road
Bloomington, Ill. 61701

W. Atlee Burpee Co. — 15
Warminster, Penn. 18974

Calkin's Blueberry Farm — 16
Bradford Rd.
Newport, N.H. 03773

Carlton Nursery Co. — 17
Rte. 1, Box 214
Dayton, Ore. 97114

C. and O. Nursery — 18
1700 N. Wenatchee Ave.
Wenatchee, Wash. 98801

Cockrells Riverside Nursery — 19
Rte. 2
Goldthwaite, Tex. 76844

Columbia Basin Nursery — 20
P. O. Box 458
Quincy, Wash. 98848

Converse Nursery — 21
Amherst, N.H. 03031

Cumberland Valley Nurseries — 22
Box 430
McMinnville, Tenn. 37110

Thomas Dicoff — 23
Rte. 1, Box 225
Zionsville, Ind. 46077

Emlong Nurseries — 24
Stevensville, Mich. 49127

Epicure Seeds — 25
Box 23568
Rochester, N.Y. 14692

Farmer Seed and Nursery — 26
Faribault, Minn. 55021

Ferris Nursery — 27
811 4th St., NE
Hampton, Iowa 50441

Henry Field Seed and Nursery Co. — 28
Shenandoah, Iowa 51602

Dean Foster Nurseries — 29
Hartford, Mich. 49057

Fowler Nurseries — 30
525 Fowler Rd.
Newcastle, Calif. 95658

Galetta Bros. and Sons — 31
Hammonton, N.J. 08037

Louis Gerardi Nursery — 32
R.R. 1
O'Fallon, Ill. 62269

Glecklers — 33
Metamora, Ohio 43540

Grimo Nut Nursery — 34
R.R. 3, Lakeshore Rd.
Niagara-on-the-Lake,
Ontario, Canada

NURSERY	NUMBER
Gurney Seed and Nursery Co. Yankton, S.D. 57079	35
Joseph Harris Moretow Farm Rochester, N.Y. 14624	36
Hartmann's Plantation Rte. 1 Grand Junction, Mich. 49056	37
Hastings 434 Marietta St., NW Atlanta, Ga. 30302	38
Herberle Nursery Co. 478 Browncroft Blvd. Rochester, N.Y. 14610	39
High Yield Gardening 401 Market Ave. N Canton, Ohio 44750	40
Hilltop Orchards and Nurseries, Inc. Rte. 2 Hartford, Mich. 49057	41
House of Wesley 2200 E. Oakland Bloomington, Ill. 61701	42
J. L. Hudson P. O. Box 1058 Redwood City, Calif. 94064	43
Inter-State Nurseries Hamburg, Iowa 51644	44
Ison's Nursery and Vineyards Brooks, Ga. 30205	45
Jackson and Perkins Medford, Ore. 97501	46
Jersey Chestnut Farm 58 Van Duyne Ave. Wanye, N.J. 07470	47
Johnson Orchard and Nursery Rte. 5 Ellijay, Ga. 30540	48
Jonny's Selected Seeds Albion, Maine 04910	49
J. W. Jung Seed Co. Randolph, Wisc. 53956	50
Kelly Bros. Dansville, N.Y. 14437	51
Kitazawa Seed Co. 356 W. Taylor St. San Jose, Calif. 95110	52
Krider Nurseries, Inc. Box 29 Middlebury, Ind. 46540	53
Lawson's Nursery Rte. 1, Box 294 Ball Ground, Ga. 30107	54
Le Jardin Du Gourmet West Danville, Vt. 05873	55
Le Marche P. O. Box 566 Dixon, Calif. 95620	56
Henry Leuthardt Nursery Box 666, Montauk Highway East Moriches, N.Y. 11940	57
May Nursery Co. P. O. Box 1312 Yakima, Wash. 98907	58
Earl May Seed and Nursery Co. Shenandoah, Iowa 51603	59
Mayo Nurseries 8393 Klippel Rd. Lyons, N.Y. 14489	60
Mellinger's 2310 W. South Range N. Lima, Ohio 44452	61
J. E. Miller Nurseries Canandaigua, N.Y. 14424	62
Walter K. Morss and Son RFD 3 Bradford, Mass. 01830	63
National Arbor Day Foundation Arbor Lodge 100 Nebraska City, Neb. 68410	64
Neosho Nurseries Neosho, Missouri 64850	65
New York State Fruit Testing Co-op Assoc., Inc. Geneva, N.Y. 14456	66
Nichols Garden Nursery 1190 N. Pacific Highway Albany, Ore. 97321	67
L. L. Olds Seed Co. 2901 Packers Ave. Madison, Wisc. 53707	68
George W. Park Seed Co., Inc. S.C. Highway 254 N. Greenwood S.C. 29647	69
Plumtree Country Garden 387 Springtown Road New Paltz, N.Y. 12561	70

NURSERY	NUMBER
Preservation Apple Tree Co. First and Birch Street Mt. Gretna, Penn. 17064	71
Progressive Gardening Institute P. O. Box 500 Morrison, Tenn. 37357	72
Rayner Bros. Inc. P. O. Box 1617 Salisbury, Md. 21801	73
Redwood City Seed Co. P. O. Box 361 Redwood City, Calif. 94064	74
Roaring Brook Nurseries Rte. 1, Box 728 Monmouth, Maine 04259	75
Rodakowski Farms 45317 Mckenzie Vida, Ore. 97488	76
R. H. Shumway's Rockford, Ill. 61105	77
Southmeadow Fruit Gardens Birmingham, Mich. 48012	78
Spring Hill Nurseries 6523 N. Galena Rd. Peoria, Ill. 61632	79
St. Lawrence Nursery RD 2, Star RT 56 A Potsdam, N.Y. 13676	80
Stanek's Garden Center E. 2929 27th Ave. Spokane, Wash. 99203	81
Steep Nursery R. R. 6, Box 79 Greenwood, Ind. 46142	82
Stokes Seeds 737 Main St. Buffalo, N.Y. 14240	83
Stribling Nursery 1620 W 16th St. Merced, Calif. 95340	84
Talbot Nursery R. R. 3, Box 212 Linton, Ind. 47441	85
Tennessee Nursery Tennessee Nursery Rd. Cleveland, Tenn. 37311	86
Thompson and Morgan P. O. Box 100 Farmingdale, N.J. 07727	87
Tsang and Wa 1306 Old Country Rd. Bellmont, Calif. 94002	88
Upper Bank Nursery P. O. Box 486 Media, Penn. 19063	89
Van Bourgondian 24G Farmingdale Rd. Babylon, N.Y. 11702	90
Van Well Nursery P. O. Box 1339 Wenatchee, Wash. 98801	91
Vermont Bean Seed Co. Garden Lane Bomoseen, Vt. 05732	92
Warren County Nursery, Inc. Rte. 2 McMinnville, Tenn. 37110	93
Waynesboro Nurseries Wayside Gardens Waynesboro, Va. 22980	94
Wayside Gardens Hodges, S.C. 29695	95
Weston Nurseries E. Main St., Rte. 135 Hopkinton, Mass. 01748	96
Wileys Nut Grove Nursery (Formerly Pataky's) 1116 Hickory Lane Mansfield, Ohio 44905	97
Leslie H. Wilmoth Nursery Rte. 2, Box 469 Elizabethtown, Ky.	98
Dave Wilson Nursery Box 4G Hughson, Calif. 95326	99
M. Worley Nursery Rte. 1 York Springs, Penn. 17372	100
Zilke Bros. Nursery Baroda, Mo. 49101	101
Stark Brothers Louisiana, Mo. 66353	102
Patrick Vineyard Orchard, Nursery Pomegranate Blvd. Tyty, Ga. 31795	103
Pacific Tree Farm 4301 Linwood Dr. Chula Vista, Galif.	104

APPENDIX B

Pollination

Requirements

Almonds Needs cross-pollination from another almond variety.

Apples Baldwin and Yellow Transparent are self-fertile. The following varieties are weakly self-fertile and in a good year would set good crops. They are never planted commercially without cross-pollination from another apple variety and if possible the homeowner should also provide for cross-pollination: Duchess of Oldenburg, Golden Delicious, Grimes Golden, Jonathan, Newtown Pippin, Ein Schemer Rome, Tropical Beauty, York. The rest of the apple varieties require cross-pollination.

Some apple varieties provide pollen of such a poor quality for cross-pollination that it is advisable to have a third variety included in the planting. These include: Arkansas Black, Baldwin, Bramleys Seedling, Canada Reinette, Gravenstein, Jonagold, Mutsu, Paragon, Rhode Island Greening, Ribston Pippin, Staymen, Staymen-Winesap, Summer Rambo, Tompkins King, Spigold, Winesap.

A few varieties seem to be fussy about what pollinates them. Varieties that pollinate Cox Orange particularly well are Golden Delicious, IdaRed, Spartan; Bramleys Seedling is well pollinated by Cox Orange and IdaRed; Mutsu by Cox Orange and Worcester Pearmain; IdaRed by Worcester Pearmain; Jonagold by Jonathan and Spartan; Spartan by Cox Orange and Golden Delicious; Worcester Pearmain by Golden Delicious and Spartan.

Some apples are cross-unfertile with closely related varieties. These include Cortland and Early Macintosh; Delicious and their color sports Golden Delicious and Mutsu; Jonathan and Northern Spy. Grimes Golden will not pollinate Arkansas Black.

Apricot Self-fertile.

Blackberries (Black Caps) Included are Thornless, Boysenberries, Youngberries, and Olalli. Self-fertile.

Blueberries Some cultivars of both Rabbit Eye and Highbush are weakly self-fertile or better than weakly self-fertile. However, better fruit set will be obtained on the cultivars that are self-fertile if cross-pollination is provided. Many of the Rabbit Eye/Highbush and Highbush/Lowbush hybrids are self-unfertile. Good practice for the homeowner would be to provide cross-pollination from two or three varieties. Rabbit Eye and Highbush types cannot pollinate each other.

Butternuts Self-fertile. Plant two or more for best crops.

Cherry, Bush   Nanking is self-fertile. Hansens is self-fertile but will benefit from planting two or more for better pollination. Black Beauty, Goldenboy, South Dakota Ruby (also Sioux and Brooks if you can find them) must be cross-pollinated.

Cherry Plums   All require cross-pollination from another plumcot (plum crossed with apricot), cherry plum, or Japanese plum.

Cherry, Sweet   All require cross-pollination from another sweet cherry variety except Stella, Garden Bing, and Starkrimson, which are self-fertile. Some groups of sweet cherry are cross-infertile within the individual group. However, members within a group have no trouble pollinating any sweet cherry outside the group. These groups are: 1) Black Tartarian, Early Rivers; 2) Van, Venus, Windsor; 3) Bing, Emperor Francis, Lambert, Napoleon; 4) Gold, Victor, Viva, Vogue; 5) Hedelfingen, Vic; 6) Hudson, Giant, Schmidts; 7) Sebeca, Vega.

Cherry, Tart (Pie, Sour)   Self-fertile. Tart cherries cannot pollinate sweet cherries.

Chestnut, Chinese   Self-fertile.

Currant   Self-fertile.

Elderberry   Must be cross-pollinated with another elderberry variety.

Fig   Self-fertile.

Gooseberry   Self-fertile.

Grape, Northern   Self-fertile.

Grape, Muscadine   Some Muscadines are self-fertile; others produce only female flowers and require pollination from another self-fertile muscadine. One self-fertile for four females will ensure pollination. These varieties are self-fertile: Albermarle, Bountiful, Carlos, Chief, Chowan, Dearing, Dixie, Dixieland, Dixie Red, Magnolia, Magoon, Noble, Redgate, Regale (Reigel), Roanoke, Southland, Sterling, Triumph, Welder. These varieties are female: Fry, Georgia Red, Higgins, Hunt, Jumbo, Lucida, Pride, Scuppernong, Sterling, Sugargate, Summit, Topsail, Watergate, Yuga.

Hazelnut (Filbert)   Weakly self-fertile; plant two or more for best crops. Cross-pollination from different varieties is best.

Heartnut   Self-fertile. Plant two or more for best crops.

Hican   Self-fertile. Plant two or more for best crops. Cross-pollination from a different variety is best.

Hickorys   Self-fertile. Plant two or more for best crops. Cross-pollination from a different variety is best.

Juneberry (Saskatoon)   Self-fertile.

Lingonberry   Self-fertile.

Medlar   Self-fertile.

Mulberry   Self-fertile.

Nectarine   Self-fertile.

Oriental Date (Jujube, Chinese Date) Self-fertile.

Pawpaw (Northern Banana) Weakly self-fertile. Plant two or more for best crops.

Peach   Self-fertile except J. H. Hale, which needs a pollinator.

Pear, European   Very weakly self-fertile. Must be cross-pollinated with another pear variety. European and oriental pears can pollinate each other, although orientals are somewhat earlier blooming. Seckel and Bartlett won't pollinate each other. Magness has sterile pollen; plant with two other varieties. Early bloomers like Duchess and Kieffer are not good pollenizers for later bloomers (like Bartlett). Very late bloomers like Winter Nellis are not good pollenizers for earlier varieties. The bearing age of pear varieties varies by two to three years, so cross-pollination will not necessarily take place until they're both mature. Cuttings in bloom from a neighbor can be brought in. Poor pollination of pears is possible if there is no highly active bee population.

Pear, Oriental (Salad Pear, Asian Pear)   Includes both Japanese and Chinese pear. Weakly self-fertile; should be cross-pollinated with another Asian or early to mid-season-blooming European pear. Exception is Shinseiki, which will set fruit well without a pollenizer.

Pecan   Pecans have separate male and female flowers which can mature at different times. If they mature together, they are self-fertile. If they don't, they fall into one of two types and require cross-pollination from a pecan variety of the opposite type. Barton, Missouri Hardy, Princess, Success, Western Schley, and Tejas are self-fruitful, although planting two or more for best crops is advisable. The following varieties are Type I and must be pollinated with self-pollinators or Type II's: Cape Fear, Cheyenne, Desirable, Jackson, Major, Peruque, San Saba, Shawnee, Starking Hardy Giant. The following are Type II's and must be pollinated with self-pollinators or with Type I's: Apache, Chickasaw, Chocktaw,

Colby, Comanchee, Green River, Hastings, Kiowa, Mahan, Mohawk, Stuart, Shoshone, Sioux, Sumner, Stark Surecrop, Schley, Wichita.

Persimmon, American   The sexes are primarily separate with the persimmons; they are almost always either male or female plants. Improved varieties bought from nurseries are female plants. When nurseries say "needs a pollenizer" they mean a male plant, which they will offer for pollination but which will not normally set fruit itself. One variety, Meader, will set good crops of fruit without pollination (they'll be seedless).

Persimmon, Oriental   Like the American persimmon, the sexes are separate; however, pollination is not necessary for good fruit set with the oriental persimmons. The fruit from unpollenized trees is seedless. Some horticulturists feel pollenized persimmons are sweeter.

Plums, Japanese   Japanese plums are mostly not self-fertile. Even the few that are weakly self-fertile benefit from cross-pollination from another Japanese plum. Japanese/American hybrids and Japanese plums can cross-pollinate each other as can plumcots and cherry plums. European and Japanese plums, with a few exceptions, will not cross-pollinate. A few Japanese plum varieties are considered to be poor pollenizers, so a third variety should be included if good fruit set is desired. These include Eldorado, Formosa, Frontier, Gaviota, Kelsey, Mariposa, Red Ace. The Japanese/American crosses that are poor pollenizers include La Crescent and Underwood. Burbank will not pollinate Shiro although the reverse is okay.

Plums, European   Some European plums are self-fertile, while others require cross-pollination from another European plum variety. The self-fertile varieties include: Agen (including Double X French), Big Blue, Blufre, California Blue, Damson, Italian, Mount Royal, Ouillins, Sannois (Sannoir), Stanley, Sugar, Victoria. Green Gage and Yellow Egg are variable and probably should have a pollinator. California Blue, Imperial Epineuse, Italian, and Yellow Egg may bloom too late to provide cross-pollination in some seasons and some localities for early bloomers like Green Gage.

Plumcot   Needs cross-pollination from another plumcot variety. Cherry plums and Japanese plums can also provide pollination.

Pomegranate   Self-fertile.

Quince   Self-fertile.

Raisin Tree   Self-fertile.

Raspberry, Black   Self-fertile.

Raspberry, Red   Self-fertile.

Walnut, Black   Self-fertile, but benefits from planting two or more trees. Will not pollinate Carpathian types.

Walnut, Persian (English)   Generally weakly self-fruitful. Requires cross-pollination from another English Walnut.

APPENDIX C

Blooming Time

Corrections

Spring blooming dates can vary about two weeks or so depending on the weather. Although the order of bloom will be consistent, warm spells and cold spells can advance or retard the bloom of individual species. The following list provides a general geographical correction to the Boston bloom dates given on the ornamental information sheets.*

Great Falls, Mont.; Madison, Wisc.	4–6 weeks later
Bismark, N.D.; Billings, Mont.	3–4 weeks later
Bangor, Maine; Souix Falls, S.D.	2–3 weeks later
Chicago, Ill.; Ames, Iowa	2–3 weeks later
Pittsburg, Penn.; Seattle, Wash.	1–2 weeks later
Kansas City, Kan.; Cincinnati, Ohio	1–2 weeks later
Boston, Mass.	—
New York City; Amarillo, Tex.	1–2 weeks earlier

St. Louis, Mo.; Philadelphia, Pa.	1–2 weeks earlier
Washington D.C.; Bowling Green, Ky.	3–4 weeks earlier
Richmond, Va.; Knoxville, Ky.	4–5 weeks earlier
Greenville, S.C.; Pine Bluff, Ark.	5–6 weeks earlier
Atlanta, Ga.; Birmingham, Ala.	6–7 weeks earlier
Augusta, Ga.; Montgomery, Ala.	7–8 weeks earlier
Jackson, Miss.; Mobile, Ala.	7–8 weeks earlier
Daytona, Fla.; Tampa, Fla.	8–9 weeks earlier

* Elevation changes and the "lake effect" of large bodies of water in California and both western Oregon and western Washington State create a complex spring bloom picture. Local knowledge should be relied upon particularly in the form of cooperative extension service pamphlets and the cultivar evaluation sheets published by Dave Wilson Nursery. (See source list.)

APPENDIX D

Quality

Root Stocks

Apple Root Stocks

M9 Produces a dwarf tree, slightly smaller than M26. Does best in a fertile soil. Homegrowers with poor soil should make a special point of annual fertilizer spikes. It also does best with adequate moisture; trees should be watered in dry periods. The trees are not well enough anchored to stand alone and should be tied to an inconspicuously placed stake. M9 is resistant to collar rot.

M26 Produces a dwarf tree slightly larger than M9. It provides better anchorage but permanent staking is still recommended especially in shallower soils. The root stock does not do well in poorly drained soils. In such cases, M9 would be a better choice. The root stock is more susceptible to fire blight, and also sucker growth, and calls for vigilant removal of suckers. It is also susceptible to woolly aphids, but is virus free and somewhat hardier than M9.

M9/MM106 Produces a dwarf tree about the same size as M26. These are combinations of a larger, more profuse root stock with a trunk section (interstem) of M9, which creates most of the dwarfing. The combinations have the anchorage and soil adaptability benefits from MM106 or MM111 roots and the resistance to collar rot of M9. Interstem (or topworked) trees should be planted so the ground line is about the middle of the stem piece, where collar rot might normally occur. Staking is beneficial for young trees. M9/M111 interstems are probably the best dwarf choice for most homegrowers.

M7 and M7A Produces a semidwarf tree. M7A is the virus-free, more modern version of M7 and is preferred where available. The trees should be staked when young but are well anchored after a few years, particularly if they are high grafted. Does well in heavy clay soils. Should definitely have supplemental watering in dry periods in light, sandy or droughty soils. Not good in soils with poor subdrainage.

MM106 Produces a semidwarf that is generally slightly larger than M7. It is better anchored than M7 but can still benefit from staking when young. It is tolerant of high temperatures and drought. Although it is hardy it continues growth late into the fall, creating hardening off and consequently winter freeze problems in colder zones. MM106 is highly productive and wooly-aphid resistant. Does not tolerate waterlogging; susceptible to collar rot.

MM111 Produces a semidwarf that is generally slightly larger than MM106. Best anchoring of the dwarf root stocks, and best for heavy soils and poorly drained soils. It is drought resistant and tolerant of high soil temperatures. MM111 is resistant to wooly aphids and collar rot. It does not sucker.

Apricot Root Stocks

Peach Root stocks. The same root stocks recommended for peaches have the same advantages and disadvantages for apricots (see "Peach and Nectarine Root stocks" below). The respective root stocks produce trees that have about the same size-controlling effect on apricots as they do on peaches, except all are somewhat larger as the standard apricot is larger than the standard peach.

p. Besseyi Produces a dwarf-size tree. Seems to be a better dwarfing root stock for apricots than for plums. Does sucker and shorten the life of the grafted variety. Very hardy.

Manchurian and Siberian Apricot These bush-type apricots produce a dwarf-size tree. They are very hardy and adaptable to varying soil conditions. Will not tolerate wet soil well. Probably superior to Besseyi for dwarfing.

Cherry Root Stocks

Mazzard Produces a standard-size sweet cherry that is large semidwarf or small shade tree size and is sometimes used for tart cherries in heavier soils. It produces a standard tart cherry that is a semidwarf size. It is more tolerant of wet soils, and hardy, but not quite as hardy as Mahaleb. It is longer lived than other cherry root stocks and very well anchored.

Mahaleb Produces a standard-size tart cherry which is semidwarf in size. Tolerant of droughty and sandy soils, less tolerant of wet soils. Hardier than Mazzard (as are the respective scions). Well anchored and adaptable to various soil types. Used for some sweet cherry varieties where it produces a semidwarf-size tree. The sizes of these are determined to a degree by the length of the stem piece, 30″ being the most dwarfing.

Montmorency Used on some sweet cherries to produce a semidwarf-size tree. Similiar to Mahaleb.

North Star Produces trees in the large dwarf to small semidwarf size range. Similar to Mahaleb.

Peach and Nectarine Root Stocks

Siberian C Produces a standard peach that is semidwarf size and makes scion variety more cold hardy. It causes slightly earlier and consistent bearing. Although it produces a tree that is somewhat smaller than standard, it's not considered a dwarfing root stock.

Halford Standard root stock. Produces a standard peach that is semidwarf size and very adaptable to different soil and growing conditions.

Lovell The other standard root stock. Produces a standard peach that is semidwarf size. Provides potentially longer tree life and a higher degree of disease resistance.

Nemagard A nematode-resistant root stock for areas where nematodes are a serious problem. Not cold hardy. Generally available.

Prunus Tomentosa Only satisfactory dwarf root stock on peaches. Produces a tree of dwarf size. Suckers freely and shortens the life of the grafted variety. Not suitable for all varieties.

Pear Root Stocks

Provence Quince Produces a large dwarf to small semidwarf tree, depending on the variety. Is probably the superior dwarfing root stock. It is more drought- and disease-resistant and more tolerant of alkaline soils than Angers A. Provence bears larger and showier flowers.

Angers Quince (Quince A) Produces a large dwarf to small semidwarf size tree, depending on the variety. Trees on Quince A should probably be permanently staked because of weakness at the graft union.

Angers Quince/Old Home Interstem Produces a large dwarf to small semidwarf size tree. The Old Home variety trunk piece (interstem) imparts disease resistance and creates a more compatible union between the variety and the roots. Makes a superior dwarf than Angers A alone and worth the nominal extra cost.

Plum Root Stocks

Myrobalan Produces a standard plum that is semidwarf in size. It is the standard root stock for both European and Japanese plums and is very adaptable to varying soil conditions. It is tolerant of heavier and more poorly aerated soils as well as dry soils.

Nemaguard Produces a standard plum that is semidwarf in size. It is a peach root stock and recommended for those areas where nematodes are a serious problem. Not cold hardy.

P. americana Produces a semidwarf plum that is small semidwarf or large dwarf in size. It is particularly recommended in colder plum-growing areas. The scion can outgrow the root stock, and permanent staking may be advisable if planted in windy locations.

St. Julien A Produces a semidwarf plum that is small semidwarf or large dwarf in size. Superior to common plum root stock for semidwarfing. Widely used in Europe.

St. Julien K Produces a small dwarf-size tree. Satisfactory but not commonly available commercially. Care should be taken to thin the fruits or support the branches that bear heavily so as not to snap the tree at the graft union. Permanent staking should be considered.

P. besseyi Produces a small dwarf-size tree, bushlike in character. Apparently more successful than p. Pumila for extreme dwarfing. A satisfactory root stock but one that suckers and shortens the life of the grafted variety. Care should be taken to thin the fruit or support the branches that are heavily fruited so as not to snap the graft union. Permanent staking should be considered. Not suitable for all varieties.

APPENDIX E

Wet Area

Correction Techniques

The most basic approach to wet areas, if they're not too serious, is to just plant high, either in gentle mounds or raised beds. Railroad ties make nice raised bed containers. If you do mounding or raised bed planting, always thoroughly rototill the area to be covered before you add soil. Remember that dwarf or semidwarf tree roots can penetrate to a depth of about 3'.

Water will not drain off a perfectly flat surface. About a 2' vertical drop is needed for every hundred feet for draining. If you are planting in a low area surrounded by higher ground all around, or too flat a lot, a swale is an effective way of providing surface drainage. Swales are better than drainage ditches because they are not unsightly and are less dangerous; people can accidentally step into ditches and hurt themselves. You'll need to hire a backhoe or small bulldozer to put it in, but they usually have half-day rates. If the machine operator doesn't have a level, it would probably be a good idea for you to rent one to check and make sure you have that 2'/100' drop (½ bubble on a 4' level). Reading grade changes is very tricky to do by eye. It's easier than you would imagine to create a swale that's level or going uphill when you think it's going downhill. A swale sized and shaped like the drawing will do the trick very neatly. Only a trained eye would even notice it's there. Make sure it goes toward the street or to a natural drainage structure, like a stream. It's not legal to drain onto your neighbor's property in most areas.

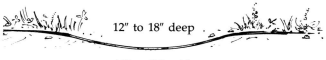

12" to 18" deep

10' to 15' wide

If you have particularly heavy (clayey) soil or if the water table is high, which can happen if you're close to a body of water, you may have to take more serious measures: you'll need to have a backhoe dig a trench and put perforated ADS (soil conservation service) pipe in it as shown, again making sure you have enough pitch and are not draining it toward a neighbor. Pour some concrete mix or pile some rocks around the lower end outlet to keep it from collapsing. Plug the upper end shut with a big rock or concrete; you want water to filter up from the bottom so the pipe won't get clogged.

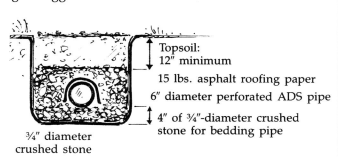

Topsoil:
12" minimum

15 lbs. asphalt roofing paper

6" diameter perforated ADS pipe

4" of ¾"-diameter crushed stone for bedding pipe

¾" diameter crushed stone

APPENDIX F

Vegetable Varieties Well Suited to Container or Intensive Growing

Beans, Bush Greencrop, Greensleeves, Tendercrop, Tenderpod

Beets Crosby Egyptian, Early Wonder, Little Egypt

Cabbage Baby Head, Dwarf Morden, Little Leaguer

Cantaloupe Bushwopper, Short and Sweet

Carrot Baby Fingers Nantes, Little Finger, Round Paris Market, Tiny Sweet

Chinese Cabbage Michili, Pak-Choy, Wong-Bok

Cucumber Bush Champion, Bush Wopper, New Novelty, Patio Pick, Pot Luck, Spacemaster

Eggplant All varieties

Herbs Any small variety, for example, chives, mint, thyme

Honeydew Olivers Pearl

Lettuce, Bibb Bibb, Buttercrunch, Ruby, Tom Thumb

Lettuce, Loose Four Seasons, Marvel, Green Ice, Royal Oak Leaf, Simpson Black Seeded, Slobolt Salad Bowl

Parsley All varieties

Peas Sugar Bon

Peppers All varieties

Pumpkin Cheyenne, Cinderella, Spirit Hybrid

Radicchio Rouge de Verone

Radishes All varieties

Squash, Summer Baby Crookneck, Baby Straightneck, St. Patties Scallop, Scallopini

Squash, Winter Butterbush, Butternut, Golden Nugget, Table Ace

Tomato Better Boy, Big Girl, Patio, Pixie, Presto, Small Fry, Sugar Lump, Tiny Tim

Watermelon Kengarden, Little Midget

Zucchini Aristocrat, Burpee Hybrid, Elite

APPENDIX G

Evergreen

Edging Plants

Dwarf needlelike-leaved evergreens tend to be extremely slow growing and prohibitively expensive for edging or border use, although most would be attractive. The following is a list of appropriate broad-leaved evergreens. They all take shearing well and can be grown in a vertical-sided or more mounded form.

Barberry, Dwarf Magellan (*Berberis buxifolia nana*): Zone 5, flowers and fruits inconspicuous, one of the hardiest barberries, gets to 1½' if unsheared.

Barberry, Paleleaf (*Berberis candidula*): Zone 5, has bright yellow flowers in May and purple berries in fall. Fairly large-leaved (1½" long), gets to 2' if unsheared.

Boxwood, Dwarf Littleleaf (*Buxus microphylla* Compacta): Zone 5, gets 1' tall if unsheared. A similar form, Green Pillow has somewhat larger leaves.

Boxwood, Edging (*Buxus sempervirens* Suffruticosa): Zone 5, the true edging boxwood, one of oldest known. Gets to 2½' if unsheared. Leaves ¾" long. Very dense and slow growing. Leaves fragrant. Winter damage susceptible.

Boxwood, Korean (*Buxus microphyla koreana*): Zone 5+, the hardiest little-leaf boxwood. Gets to 2' if left unsheared. Turns brown in winter but two forms keep their green color: Tidewater and Wintergreen; Wintergreen is the hardier.

Boxwood, Vadar Valley (*Buxus sempervirens* Vader Valley): Zone 4, hardiest of boxwoods. Grows to 2' if left unsheared. Dense, flat-topped habit.

Germander (*Teucrium chamaedrys*): Zone 5, gets small purple or rose flower spikes in summer. Gets 1' high, and has ¾" toothed leaves. Neat compact form without shearing.

Japanese Holly (*Ilex crenata*): Zone 6, with exception of two culivars, has small black berries in fall and attractive lustrous dark green foliage. Only a few of the cultivars are dwarf enough for edging use. Green Island and *I. crenata* Convexa or Hetzi are hardy in Zone 5. Helleri is naturally mounded in form and Kingsville Green Cushion is extremely dwarf (less than 1').

APPENDIX H

Espalier Forms

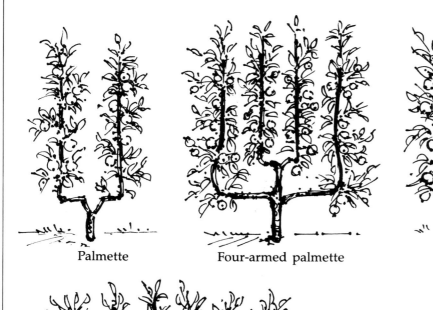

Palmette

Four-armed palmette

Six-armed palmette

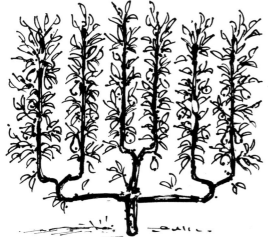

Triple "U"

Double horizontal cordon

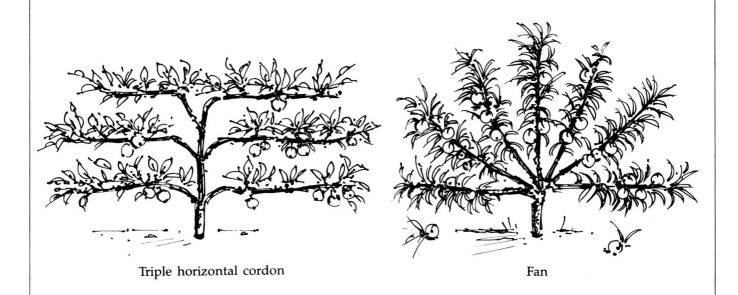

Triple horizontal cordon

Fan

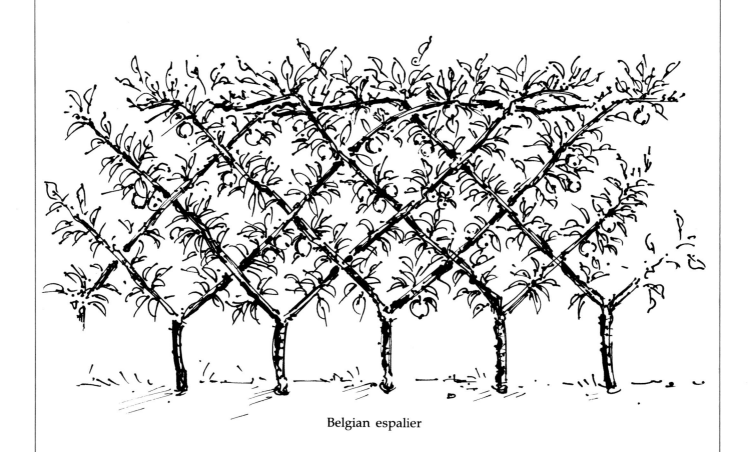

Belgian espalier

APPENDIX I

Shade-Tolerant

Food Plants

I. **Shade Loving** (will produce good crops in medium shade):
  Currants
  Gooseberries
  Wineberries

II. **Shade Tolerant** (will produce crops in medium shade but will not be as productive as in full sun. Plants will be healthy and attractive):
  Blueberries
  Bramble Fruits
  Cherries
  Elderberries
  Juneberry
  Some herbs (including angelica, chervil, chives, coriander [not for seed], dill, fennel, garlic, garlic chives, parsley, sorrel, sweet woodruff)
  Some strawberries (including Alpine, Baron Solemacher, Frais de Bois, Paris Spectacular, Reugen, Reugen Improved, Snow King)

APPENDIX J

Water Volume Calculations

The objective of watering is to provide an inch of water at a given watering, meaning one surface inch of water over the area to be watered. One surface inch of water translates to wetting the soil to a depth of six or seven inches. If it's a planting bed, the whole area is included in the calculations. For a tree it's the area under the branches. To figure the volume of water required, multiply the length times the width to be watered (you can approximate for odd-shaped areas). Then take that area times .08 (1" depth expressed in feet). This will give you the volume of water needed in cubic feet.

Next, go to your outlet and fill a bucket using the attachment (hose, sprinkler, and so forth) you'll use to water. Note how long it takes to fill the bucket. Bucket sizes are expressed in gallons, with the two-gallon size being the most common. But check the size of the bucket you are using. Next convert the cubic feet of water required to gallons by multiplying by 7.5. By multiplying the time it took to put one gallon of water in the bucket by the number of gallons required, you'll know how long you have to water. You'll be shocked. Most people who have read horticultural books know you need an inch of water every week to ten days overall, but don't realize just how long it takes to provide it by hand. Consequently, they vastly underwater new plantings in their establishment period.

APPENDIX K

Additional Sources

of Information

United States Agricultural Extension Services

The U.S. Department of Agriculture, in conjunction with the state land grant colleges, provides a tremendous amount of information on agriculturally related matters. Just about every county has its own extension agent, whose office is normally located in the county seat. These offices either stock or provide access to a wealth of useful pamphlets and booklets. The county agents devote most of their efforts to commercial growers and farmers, but they are also available to answer questions from the general public.

Associations and Organizations

The following organizations are associations of professional and sometimes interested, knowledgeable amateurs who share information in the areas of their interest:

American Pomological Society
103 Tyson Building
University Park, Penn. 16802

California Rare Fruit Growers, Inc.
Fullerton Arboretum
California State University, Fullerton
Fullerton, Calif. 92634

Herb Society of America
300 Massachusetts Avenue
Boston, Mass. 02115

Home Orchard Society
2511 S. W. Miles St.
Portland, Ore. 97219

International Tree Crops Institute
Rte. 1
Gravel Switch, Ky. 40328

New York State Fruit Testing Co-operative
Geneva, N.Y. 14456

North American Fruit Explorers
10 South Madison St.
Hinsdale, Ill. 60521

Northern Nut Growers
4518 Holston Hills Rd.
Knoxville, Tenn. 37914

General Publications

American Horticulturist (bimonthly)
Journal of American Horticultural Society
East Boulevard Drive
Alexandria, Va. 22308

The Avant Gardner (monthly)
P. O. Box 489
New York, N.Y. 10028

Flower and Garden (bimonthly)
4251 Pennsylvania Ave.
Kansas City, Mo. 64111

Gardens For All Newsletter (monthly)
180 Flynn Ave.
Burlington, Vt. 05401

Horticulture (monthly)
300 Massachusetts Ave.
Boston, Mass. 02115

Organic Gardening (monthly)
33 East Minor St.
Emmaus, Pa. 18049

Trade Journals

American Fruit Grower
37841 Euclid Avenue
Willoughby, Ohio 44094

American Vegetable Grower
37841 Euclid Avenue
Willoughby, Ohio 44094

Compact Fruit Tree
International Dwarf Fruit Tree Association
Room 301-B, Horticulture
Michigan State University
East Lansing, Mich. 48824

Fruit Varieties Journal
c/o Business Manager
American Pomological Society
103 Tyson Building
University Park, Penn. 16802

Horticulture Science
American Society of Horticulture Science
701 North St. Asaph
Alexandria, Va. 22314

Plants and Gardens
Brooklyn Botanical Garden
1000 Washington Avenue
Brooklyn, N. Y. 11225

Pome News
Home Orchard Society
3526 S. E. Johnson Creek Blvd.
Portland, Ore. 97222

SELECTED BIBLIOGRAPHY

General Gardening and Landscape Design

Better Homes and Gardens New Garden Book. Des Moines, Iowa: Meredith, 1961.

Bubel, Nancy. *The Seed Starters Handbook.* Emmaus, Pa.: Rodale, 1978.

Bush-Brown, James, and Bush-Brown, Louise. *America's Garden Book.* rev. ed. New York: Scribner, 1980.

Carpenter, Philip, et al. *Plants in the Landscape.* San Francisco: W. H. Freeman, 1976.

Eckbow, Garrett. *The Art of Home Landscaping.* New York: McGraw-Hill, 1962.

Garland, Madge. *The Small Garden in the City.* New York: Braziller, 1974.

Hebb, Bob. *Low Maintenance Perennials.* Cambridge, Mass.: Harvard University Press, 1983.

Hubbard, Henry, and Kimball, Theodora. *Landscape Design.* Cambridge, Mass.: Harvard University Press, 1959.

King, Ronald. *The Quest for Paradise: A History of the World's Gardens.* New York: Mayflower Books, 1972.

Lees-Milne, Alvilde, and Verey, Rosemary. *The Englishwoman's Garden.* Toronto: Clark, Irwin, 1980.

Logsdon, Gene. *A Gardener's Guide to Better Soil.* Emmaus, Pa.: Rodale, 1978.

Reader's Digest Practical Guide to Home Landscaping. Pleasantville, N.Y.: Reader's Digest, 1977.

Simonds, John O. *Landscape Architecture: The Shaping of Man's Natural Environment.* New York: McGraw-Hill, 1961.

Sunset magazine. *Gardening in Containers.* Menlo Park, Calif.: Sunset-Lane Publishing, 1968.

Edible Plants

Angier, Bradford. *Free for the Eating.* Harrisburg, Pa.: Stockpole Books, 1966.

Brooklyn Botanic Garden Handbooks: #67 Fruit Trees and Shrubs; #28 Culinary Herbs; #68 Herbs and Their Ornamental Uses. Brooklyn, N.Y.: Brooklyn Botanic Garden, various dates.

Bryan, John E., and Castle, Coralie. *The Edible Ornamental Garden.* San Francisco: 101 Productions, 1974.

Chevron Chemical Company. *All About Growing Fruits and Berries.* San Francisco: Ortho Books, 1976.

Childers, Norman F. *Modern Fruit Science.* New Brunswick, N.J.: Rutgers University Press, 1978.

Creasy, Rosalind. *The Complete Book of Edible Landscaping.* San Francisco: Sierra Club Books, 1986.

Crockett, James W. *Crockett's Victory Garden.* Boston: Little, Brown, 1977.

Flanagan, Ted. *Growing Food and Flowers in Containers.* Pownal, Vt.: Garden Way.

Foster, Gertrude B. *Herbs for Every Garden.* New York: Dutton, 1966.

Gibbons, Euell. *Stalking the Wild Asparagus.* New York: McKay, 1962.

Gilmore, Grand, and Gilmore, Holly. *Growing Midget Vegetables at Home.* New York: Lancer, 1973.

Hill, Lewis. *Fruits and Berries for the Home Garden.* New York: Knopf, 1977.

Harrington, Geri. *Grow Your Own Chinese Vegetables.* New York: Macmillan, 1978.

Harris, Ben Charles. *Eat the Weeds.* New York: Barre, 1968.

Hyland, Robert. *Food Gardening.* Kennett Square, Pa.: Longwood Gardens Press, 1982.

Jaynes, Richard A. *Nut Tree Culture in North America.* Hamden, Conn.: Northern Nut Growers Association, 1979.

Jeavons, John. *How to Grow More Vegetables in Less Space Than You Ever Imagined.* Palo Alto, Calif.: Ecology Action of the Mid-Peninsula, 1974.

Logsdon, Gene. *Organic Orcharding.* Emmaus, Pa.: Rodale, 1978.

———. *Successful Berry Growing.* Emmaus, Pa.: Rodale, 1974.

New York State Fruit Testing Cooperative. *New and Noteworthy Fruits.* Geneva, N.Y.: New York State Fruit Testing Cooperative, 1987.

O'Connor, Audrey H. *An Herb Companion.* Ithaca, N.Y.: Cornell University Press, 1984.

Organic Gardening magazine. *Encyclopedia of Organic Gardening.* Emmaus, Pa.: Rodale, 1978.

Ourecky, Donald K. *Bulletin 11: Minor Fruits in New York State.* Ithaca, N.Y.: Cornell University College of Agriculture and Life Sciences, 1977.

Saunders, Charles Francis. *Edible and Useful Wild Plants.* New York: Dover, 1948.

Simmons, Alan. *Growing Unusual Fruit.* New York: Walker, 1972.

Tompkins, John P., and Oberly, Gene. *Bulletin 156: Home Fruit Planting.* Ithaca, N.Y.: Cornell Extension Publishers, 1979.

Tukey, Harold Bradford. *Dwarfed Fruit Trees.* Ithaca, N.Y.: Cornell University Press, 1974.

Pest Control

Brooklyn Botanic Garden. *Handbook on Biological Control of Plant Pests.* Brooklyn, N.Y.: Brooklyn Botanic Garden, 1979.

Cornell University College of Life Sciences. *Small Fruits Pest Control and Culture Guides.* Ithaca, N.Y.: Cornell University Extension Service, 1985.

Garden Way Publishing Company. *Scat: Pest Proofing Your Garden.* Pownal, Vt.: Garden Way, 1977.

Goldstein, Jerome, ed. *The Least Is Best Pesticide Strategy: A Guide to Putting Integrated Pest Management Into Action.* San Francisco: J. G. Press, 1978.

Kramer, Jack. *The Natural Way to Pest-Free Gardening.* New York: Scribner, 1972.

Philbrick, John, and Philbrick, Helen. *The Bug Book: Harmless Insect Controls.* Pownal, Vt.: Garden Way, 1974.

Pirone, Pascal P. *Diseases and Pests of Ornamental Plants.* New York: Wiley, 1978.

Sill, Webster H. *Plant Protection: An Integrated Interdisciplinary Approach.* Ames, Iowa: Iowa State University Press, 1982.

Ware, George W. *The Pesticide Book.* San Francisco: W. H. Freeman, 1978.

Wescott, Cynthia. *The Gardener's Bug Book.* Garden City, N.Y.: 1973.

Cooking and Food Preservation

Ballister, Barry. *Barry Ballister's Fruit and Vegetable Stand.* Woodstock, N.Y.: Overlook, 1987.

Chandonnet, Ann. *The Complete Fruit Cookbook.* San Francisco: 101 Productions, 1972.

Chevron Chemical Company. *When the Good Cook Gardens.* San Francisco: Ortho Books, 1974.

Crowhurst, Adrienne. *The Flower Cookbook.* New York: Lancer, 1973.

Hawkes, Alex D. *A World of Vegetable Cookery.* New York: Simon & Schuster, 1968.

Hertzberg, Ruth, et al. *Putting Food By.* Brattleboro, Vt.: Stephen Greene Press, 1974.

MacNicol, Mary. *Flower Cookery: The Art of Cooking with Flowers.* New York: Fleet, 1979.

McKinney, John. *The Willow Farm Pickle Book.* Santa Fe, N.M.: Lightning Tree, 1973.

Schuler, Stanley, and Schuler, Elizabeth M. *Preserving the Fruits of the Earth.* New York: Dial, 1973.

Tillona, Francesca, and Stowbridge, Cynthia. *A Feast of Flowers.* New York: Funk & Wagnalls, 1969.

Pruning and Espaliering

Brooklyn Botanic Garden. *Handbook #17: Trained and Sculptured Plants.* Brooklyn, N.Y.: Brooklyn Botanic Garden, 1982.

Hill, Lewis. *Pruning Simplified.* Emmaus, Pa.: Rodale, 1965.

Leuthardt, Henry. *Espaliered Fruit Trees.* East Moriches, N.Y.: Leuthardt Nurseries, 1959.

Sunset magazine. *Pruning Handbook.* Menlo Park, Calif.: Sunset-Lane Publishing, 1968.

Index